Embodied Playwriting

Embodied Playwriting: Improv and Acting Exercises for Writing and Devising is the first book to compile new and adapted exercises for teaching playwriting in the classroom, workshop, or studio through the lens of acting and improvisation.

The book provides access to the innovative practices developed by seasoned playwriting teachers from around the world who are also actors, improv performers, and theatre directors. Borrowing from the embodied art of acting and the inventive practice of improvisation, the exercises in this book will engage readers in performance-based methods that lead to the creation of fully imagined characters, dynamic relationships, and vivid drama. Step-by-step guidelines for exercises, as well as application and coaching advice, will support successful lesson planning and classroom implementation for playwriting students at all levels, as well as individual study. Readers will also benefit from curation by editors who have experience with high-impact educational practices and are advocates for the use of varied teaching strategies to increase accessibility, inclusion, skill-building, and student success.

Embodied Playwriting offers a wealth of material for teachers and students of playwriting courses, as well as playwrights who look forward to experimenting with dynamic, embodied writing practices.

Hillary Haft Bucs is a Professor of Theatre at Western New England University, where she teaches Playwriting, Acting, and Improvisational Comedy. With Valerie Clayman Pye, she co-edited *Objectives, Obstacles, and Tactics in Practice: Perspectives on Activating the Actor* (Routledge 2020).

Charissa Menefee is a playwright and poet, the Artistic Director of The EcoTheatre Lab, and a Professor of English and Theatre at Iowa State University, where she co-directs the MFA Program in Creative Writing & Environment.

Embodied Playwriting
Improv and Acting Exercises
for Writing and Devising

Edited by
Hillary Haft Bucs
and Charissa Menefee

NEW YORK AND LONDON

Designed cover image: Shutterstock

First published 2023
by Routledge
605 Third Avenue, New York, NY 10158

and by Routledge
4 Park Square, Milton Park, Abingdon, Oxon, OX14 4RN

Routledge is an imprint of the Taylor & Francis Group, an informa business

© 2023 selection and editorial matter, Hillary Haft Bucs and Charissa Menefee; individual chapters, the contributors

The right of Hillary Haft Bucs and Charissa Menefee to be identified as the authors of the editorial material, and of the authors for their individual chapters, has been asserted in accordance with sections 77 and 78 of the Copyright, Designs and Patents Act 1988.

All rights reserved. No part of this book may be reprinted or reproduced or utilised in any form or by any electronic, mechanical, or other means, now known or hereafter invented, including photocopying and recording, or in any information storage or retrieval system, without permission in writing from the publishers.

Trademark notice: Product or corporate names may be trademarks or registered trademarks, and are used only for identification and explanation without intent to infringe.

Library of Congress Cataloging-in-Publication Data
Names: Bucs, Hillary Haft, editor. | Menefee, Charissa, editor.
Title: Embodied playwriting : improv and acting exercises for writing and devising / edited by Hillary Haft Bucs and Charissa Menefee.
Description: New York, NY : Routledge, 2023. |
Includes bibliographical references and index.
Identifiers: LCCN 2022061029 (print) | LCCN 2022061030 (ebook) |
ISBN 9781032152059 (hardback) | ISBN 9781032152042 (paperback) |
ISBN 9781003243014 (ebook)
Subjects: LCSH: Playwriting—Study and teaching. |
Improvisation (Acting)—Study and teaching.
Classification: LCC PN1661 .E63 2023 (print) | LCC PN1661 (ebook) |
DDC 808.2071—dc23/eng/20230405
LC record available at https://lccn.loc.gov/2022061029
LC ebook record available at https://lccn.loc.gov/2022061030

ISBN: 978-1-032-15205-9 (hbk)
ISBN: 978-1-032-15204-2 (pbk)
ISBN: 978-1-003-24301-4 (ebk)

DOI: 10.4324/9781003243014

Typeset in Bembo
by codeMantra

Contents

Contributors ix
Introduction: Embodied Playwriting xxi
HILLARY HAFT BUCS AND CHARISSA MENEFEE

PART I
Creating Characters 1

1 The Meet and Greet: Creating Opportunities
  for Surprise and Discovery 3
  CHARISSA MENEFEE

2 Improvising Between the Lines: Enhancing the
  Script by Embodying Subtext 11
  AMY SEHAM

3 Using Improv to Create Original Plays:
  Respectfully Writing Diverse Characters 27
  STEPHANIE RAE

4 Character's *Search for Authenticity*:
  Improvisation for the Revision Process 39
  MUNEEB UR REHMAN

PART II
Body and Mind 63

5 The Picture Project: Originating Story
  through Movement 65
  SARAH KOZINN

6 Physical Expressions in Devised Playwriting   79
   LUANE DAVIS HAGGERTY AND AARON KELSTONE

7 Active Group Playwriting: Psychodrama
   Techniques Adapted for Theatre-making   91
   DAVID KAYE

PART III
Playing Games   105

8 Building the World of the Play Through
   Collaborative Performance   107
   MIKE POBLETE

9 It's All About Play: Locating the Game
   in Embodied Playwriting   121
   JOHN P. BRAY

10 Folkgames as Creative Stimulus for Devising:
   The Case of *Chaskele*   131
   SOLOMON Y. DARTEY

PART IV
Changemaking   141

11 "Laughter that Shatters": Improv Techniques
   for Social Justice Comedy Playwriting   143
   ELSPETH TILLEY

12 Writing for Change: Guiding Activist
   Playwrights in Classrooms and Communities   160
   DANA EDELL

13 Community-Based Play Creation   175
   HOPE McINTYRE

14 Writing Climate Justice: Personal Storytelling and
   Source Material Devising as Embodied Methodology 190
   JOAN LIPKIN AND KASEY LYNCH

PART V
Curated Exercises 203

15 Embodied Playwriting Exercises for Classroom, Workshop, and Studio: Skill-Building and Content Generation 205
HILLARY HAFT BUCS AND CHARISSA MENEFEE

The Ceiling Fan Speaks! 205
ALEXIS LYGOUMENOS AND GABRIELLE SINCLAIR COMPTON

Letters to Self: An Improvisational Exercise for Playwriting and Personal Writing 209
RAMÓN ESQUIVEL

Find the Event in the Tale of the Inanimate Object 213
JEANNE LEEP

Many Characters, Many Objects 218
WESLEY BROULIK

Collaborative Drafting 226
RACHEL LYNETT

Activating a Character 228
DENNIS SCHEBETTA

Sharing the Story: A Playwriting Train 233
STEVE KALISKI

Word Choice: Working in Space 237
MEREDITH MELVILLE

Uncovering Character through Mask Exploration 241
ELIZABETH HESS

Writing Inside the (Rasa) Box 249
TIFFANY ANTONE

16 Embodied Playwriting Exercises for Classroom, Workshop, and Studio: The Revision Process 255
HILLARY HAFT BUCS AND CHARISSA MENEFEE

Half-Life as a Tool for Revision 255
MATT FOTIS

Acting Tactics for Writers: An Improvisational Exercise for Revising Dialogue 259
RAMÓN ESQUIVEL

Spectator Storyboarding 262
SAGE TOKACH

Diagnosing the (Rasa) Box 266
TIFFANY ANTONE

Acknowledgments	273
Index	275

Contributors

Tiffany Antone, Assistant Teaching Professor of Theatre at Iowa State University, is an actor, theatre-maker, and teaching artist who has produced and directed several nationwide new play festivals and theatre actions through her companies Little Black Dress INK and Protest Plays Project. Her newest project, PlagueWrites, facilitates collaboratively written, pandemic-proof plays. PlagueWrites' first script, *Alice in Quarantine: A Drive-Thru Adventure*, was produced in 2021. Tiffany has presented at conferences held by the Dramatists Guild, Association for Theatre in Higher Education, University of Iceland, and the Society for Arts Entrepreneurship Education, and has published essays with HowlRound.com and other digital platforms. Tiffany is a member of the Dramatists Guild and has had plays read and/or performed across the country, including in Los Angeles, New York, DC, and Minneapolis. She is a proud alum of the American Academy of Dramatic Arts and UCLA, where she earned her MFA in Playwriting. Tiffany is grateful to have had some truly fabulous teachers and mentors along her journey, including Hanay Geiogamah, Edit Villarreal, Gary Gardner, and Jose Luis Valenzuela.

John P. Bray is a playwright, new play dramaturg, scholar, anthology editor, and screenwriter. His plays are published with Next Stage Press, Original Works Publishing, and in several anthologies and journals. He has edited *The Best American Short Plays 2018–2019* and the forthcoming *Stage It and Stream It: Plays for Virtual Theatre* for Applause Theatre and Cinema Books. He has an MFA in Playwriting from the Actors Studio Drama School at The New School and a PhD in Theatre from Louisiana State University. He serves as Graduate Coordinator and the Head of the Undergraduate Dramatic Writing Concentration in the Department of Theatre and Film Studies at the University of Georgia. He is grateful to all his teachers, especially those who have shaped his writing: Ken Greenman, Elyse Scott, Bob Dederick, Larry Carr, Mike Weida, Steven Press, Jim Ryan, Jeffrey Sweet, Jack Gelber, Andreas Manolikakis, Gary Vena, Leslie A. Wade, Mari Kornhauser, Angela Hall (a great colleague and friend), Femi Euba, and Neal Bell.

Wesley Broulik is a theatre-maker, educator, and Assistant Professor at Central Connecticut State University. Wesley serves as Producing Artistic Director of *Time's Fool Company*, a not-for-profit 501(c)(3) professional theatre that serves Connecticut's Greater-Hartford-Area, and believes that art is a human right. His work has been seen off-Broadway and regionally, in commercials, feature films, and television, and at Shakespeare theatres around the world. Wesley holds an MFA in Acting from Rutgers University, is a certified teacher of the Michael Chekhov Technique, completed his teacher training under Aretha Sills, and is an alum of the directing studio at Shakespeare's Globe/Globe Education. He is a member of Actors' Equity Association, SAG-AFTRA, Dramatists Guild, and an associate member of the Stage Directors and Choreographers Society. He is forever grateful to his teachers William Esper, Moisés Kaufman, Lenard Petit, Wil Kilroy, Lisa Dalton, Theresa Robbins Dudeck, Carol MacVey, William Forsythe, Nilo Cruz, Mary Gallagher, Joseph Hart, Deborah Hedwall, and, most of all, Aretha Sills, who opened up the work of Viola Spolin in a way that continues to transform him as an artist and teacher.

Hillary Haft Bucs is a Professor of Theatre at Western New England University, where she won the 2021 Teaching Excellence Award. With Valerie Clayman Pye, she coedited *Objectives, Obstacles, and Tactics in Practice: Perspectives on Activating the Actor*, published by Routledge. Hillary's improv training and performance work began in Chicago where she graduated from the Second City Training Center, trained and performed with I.O. (Improv Olympics) and Annoyance Theatre, and was an improv actor with Michael Gellman's *TheatreWorks*. Hillary is presently part of *The Silver Lining* improv troupe and Zodiac Roundtable, the *Happier Valley Comedy* Long Form House Team in Hadley, MA. Her TYA musical, *It's Good to Be an Ant*, has been performed at the John Anson Ford Theatre (CA), Eric Carle Museum (MA), and Gretna Theatre (PA), and toured throughout Los Angeles County. Hillary received her BS from Northwestern University and her MFA from the University of Pittsburgh. Hillary owes great gratitude to her many amazing teachers over the decades including Sarah Barker,

Scott Braidman, W. Stephen Coleman, Martin Demaat, Theresa Dudeck, Meghan Gray, Kiki Gounaridou, Louis Kornfeld, Will Luera, Mick Napier, Michael J. Gellman, and Pam Victor.

Gabrielle Sinclair Compton is a PhD candidate in Theatre and Performance Studies at the University of Georgia and an award-winning playwright and deviser. Her plays include her immersive work *Showing* (Ingram New Works Lab, Nashville Rep); *The Resolute: All Hands In* (premiered at the Hewitt School, NYC), *The Resolute* (finalist for the Jane Chambers playwriting award, Wyoming Theatre Festival), and *The Bride Project* (Love Me Gender Festival, Vienna). She earned her MFA in Playwriting from the Actors Studio Drama School and is currently playwright-in-residence for Hidden Well Theatre in New York City. She is forever grateful for and indebted to her transformative teachers and mentors, among them Edward Allan Baker, Elizabeth Kemp, George Singleton, Mick Napier, Marla Carlson, and the theatre-artists at The Celebration Barn (namely Karen Montanaro and Davis Robinson).

Solomon Y. Dartey is Artistic Director and Performing Arts Facilitator at Association International School (AIS) in Accra-Ghana. He holds a PhD in Arts and Culture, with his research focused on how to use devised theatre and folklore to promote the Sustainable Development Goals in Ghana. He also holds an MFA in Directing and BFA in Radio, Film, & Video Production. He is a certified International Baccalaureate (IB) and International General Certificate of Secondary Education (IGCSE) Educator and a member of International Schools Theatre Association (ISTA). His directing repertoire includes The Africa Institute: *Song of a Pharaoh* Book Launch (2022); Heritage Theatre Series: *Wogbe Jeke* (2022); *Chaskele* (2020); Al-Rayan International School: *Mamma Mia* (2021); *The Greatest Showman* (2019); *Sarafina* (2018); Disney's *Moana* (2017); MIS: *Esther* (2018); *Misago* (2017); and *Pregnancy Tales* (2017). He also directed a film adaptation of Mohammed Ben Abdallah's *Land of a Million Magicians* (2012) and a documentary film about youth unemployment, *I Have a Dream* (2009). Thanks to his theatre trailblazers on the educational front, for their contribution is what has inspired him to reach this far.

Dana Edell, an activist-scholar-artist-educator, is the author of *Girls, Performance, and Activism: Demanding to Be Heard* (Routledge, 2022) and the co-director of SPARK Movement, an antiracist, arts-driven, feminist youth activist organization. She has co-directed and produced more than seventy-five original, activist theatre productions written and performed by teenage girls and nonbinary youth, and she consults with organizations and schools throughout the US and abroad about gender justice, civic engagement, youth activism, feminist Jewish education, and arts integration. She has an MFA from Columbia and a PhD from NYU. She is currently an Assistant Professor at Emerson College where she teaches Applied Theatre and Theatre & Social Justice. Dana sends deep gratitude to her teachers/mentors, including Anne Bogart, Augusto Boal, and Jan Cohen-Cruz.

Ramón Esquivel is a playwright, director, dramaturg, and educator. His published plays include *The Hero Twins: Blood Race*, *Luna*, *Nasty*, and *Nocturnal*, and his work is featured in the anthologies, *Palabras del Cielo: An Exploration of Latino/a Theatre for Young Audiences, Volumes 1–2*; *New Visions/New Voices: 25 Years/25 Plays*; and *I Have a Story: Plays from an Extraordinary Year* (Dramatic Publishing). He holds an MA in Educational Theatre from New York University and an MFA in Creative Writing from the University of British Columbia, Vancouver. Ramón is currently Assistant Professor of Theatre, Playwriting at California Polytechnic State University, San Luis Obispo. He has learned from writers, formally and informally, such as Laurie Brooks, Bryan Wade, Alison Acheson, Mark O'Donnell, and Jose Cruz Gonzalez.

Matt Fotis is Chair of the Theatre Department and Director of Undergraduate Research at Albright College, where he teaches writing for performance, improvisation, and comedy studies. His plays have been presented or developed at such places as The Lark, The Playwrights' Center, The Kennedy Center, The Great Plains Theatre Conference, City Theatre, and many others. His plays have received numerous awards, including The Mark Twain Prize for Comic Playwriting. As an improvisor, he's performed and taught from coast-to-coast and currently is a member of The Boscov Improv Players and Joan McNeil. His work has been published in *Theatre Journal*, *Theatre Topics*, *Theatre/Practice*, *The Journal of American Drama & Theatre*, *The Academic Minute*, *The Encyclopedia of Humor Studies*, *The Encyclopedia of American Studies*, *McSweeney's*, and *MLB.com*. He is the author of *Satire & The State: Sketch Comedy and the Presidency*; *Long Form Improvisation and American Comedy: The Harold*; and co-author of *The Comedy Improv Handbook*. He is grateful for Jeanette's daily reminders to stay present and make discoveries.

Luane Davis Haggerty is co-founder of the Interborough Repertory Theatre (IRT), a non-profit AEA Off-Off Broadway Company dedicated to inclusion and outreach to women, the disabled, and other minorities. She is a Principal Lecturer in the National Technical Institute for the Deaf (NTID) Department for Performing Arts at Rochester Institute of Technology. She is the creator of the Del-Sign acting technique and Artistic Director of the Del-Sign Project in NYC. She has directed several of NTID's most popular productions in this technique, garnering a feature article in *The Chronicle of Higher Education*, RIT's Four Presidents Distinguished Public Service Award, and an Off-Off Broadway Review Award. Her production of *The Tempest* with Rochester Shakespeare Players, performed with Deaf and hearing actors, won the CITY "Best Local Theatrical Production" award. Her recent production of *Fences* won a Kennedy Center Award for Excellence in Ensemble Performance. She has a PhD from Antioch University and is a member of the Dramatists Guild. Many thanks to the teachers who pulled her along: Grandmother Ida Wheeler, Ruth Davis, Peter Haggerty, Dr. Robert Panara, and all my Dangerous Signs performers.

Elizabeth Hess is a playwright, arts educator, actor, director, and artistic director of The Hess Collective (THC). She has performed extensively in New York City, regional theatre, TV, and indie film. Her award-winning solo work, including *Birth Rite* and *Dust to Dust*, has travelled the globe. Her company's work has premiered at La MaMa, including *Love Trade* and *Spoiled: The Film Project*. Her book, *Acting & Being: Explorations in Embodied Performance*, published by Palgrave Macmillan, is based on her hybrid approach culled from teaching performance and playwriting principally at New York University (NYU), as well as international workshops in Armenia, Chile, Italy, Kosovo, and Britain, including the Royal Academy of Dramatic Art (RADA), her alma mater. Ms. Hess is grateful to her New York-based colleagues and international collaborators who inspired her explorations in mask work, including Per Brahe (Sacred Mask); Dawn Saito (Butoh); Penny Kreizer (Extended Voice); and the Huli Wigmen (Sing Sing Dance).

Stephen Kaliski is a playwright, director, and actor. He is currently a Visiting Assistant Professor of Theatre and Writing Studies at Davidson College. Playwriting includes *The Refugees* (A.R.T./New York and Davidson); *Gluten!* (59E59 Theatres); and *West Lethargy* (Fringe NYC/Edinburgh), and directing includes *Charlie and the Chocolate Factory* on Broadway (Resident Director); *Three Sisters* at CSC (Assistant Director); and lead credits at 59E59, the Yale Dramat, and A.R.T./New York. He is the Artistic Director of the award-winning company Adjusted Realists, and he is also a founding member of Charlotte Conservatory Theatre in North Carolina, where he recently acted in Jen Silverman's *Witch* and will soon be directing Selina Fillinger's *POTUS*. He would like to thank his Brooklyn College MFA mentors, specifically Rose Bonczek, Mary Robinson, and Tom Bullard, and all of his Adjusted Realists partners.

David Kaye has served on the faculty of the University of New Hampshire Department of Theatre and Dance since 1996. His major focus is Acting and Directing, and he also specializes in Applied Theatre. He is a published and produced playwright and has been author or co-author of several articles and book chapters. A Fulbright Scholar (2012), he is the recipient of several awards including the New England Theatre Conference Educator of the Year (2009); UNH Outstanding Associate Professor (2012); UNH COLA Teaching Excellence Award (2009); and Spotlight on the Arts Awards for Best Director (2008), Best Supporting Actor (2012), and Best New Play (2014). He is greatly indebted to so many teachers, mentors, and collaborators who have shaped his approach to creating scripts and theatre, including Herb Propper, Norma Bowles, Nate Aldrich, Jeffery Steiger, and Eberhard Scheiffele.

Aaron Kelstone retired from teaching after twenty-two years as a Principal Lecturer in the Departments of Performing Arts and Cultural and Creative Studies at the National Technical Institute for the Deaf (NTID) at the Rochester Institute of Technology. His teaching areas included Deaf Studies and Performing Arts. Prior to his work at NTID, Dr. Kelstone was actively involved in performing arts as an actor, director, playwright, and artistic director with Cleveland Signstage Theatre, the National Theatre of the Deaf, and various community theatres in the Southwest.

Sarah Kozinn is a Theatre and Performance Studies scholar, director, and performer. She is an Associate Professor and Chair of the Theatre and Performance Studies Department at Occidental College in Los Angeles. She received her MA and PhD in Performance Studies from NYU, and she is the author of *Justice Performed: Courtroom TV Shows and the Theatres of Popular Law* (Methuen Drama). She recently wrote and directed the play *Statute 21.06: Homosexual Conduct*, based on events surrounding the 2003 Supreme Court case *Lawrence v. Texas*. She is a 2020 recipient of the Graves Award in the Humanities. She would like to acknowledge Richard Schechner, Anna Deavere Smith, Faye Simpson, and M. Graham Smith for their influence on her own practice.

Contributors   xv

Jeanne Leep is the producer and Chair of Edgewood College Theatre in Madison, Wisconsin. She received her PhD in directing from Wayne State University, her MA from the University of Michigan in Theatre Studies, and has also studied at the Moscow Art Theatre and the Royal Shakespeare Company. She is the author of *Theatrical Improvisation: Short Form, Long Form, and Sketch-Based Improv*, and the co-founder of River City Improv, a performance improvisational troupe based in Michigan. Former Chair for the ATHE Acting Focus Group, Dr. Leep is a longtime member of the Association for Theatre in Higher Education. Jeanne would like to thank all the many teachers, mentors, and colleagues who have helped her along the way, including James Korf, Patricia VandenBurg, Peter Ferran, Lavinia Hart, Cynthia Blaise, Gilliam Eaton, and everyone who has ever been a part of River City Improv. She also owes a great debt to her family and her husband Chris for their patience and support.

Joan Lipkin is a multi-disciplinary artist and activist who works at the intersection of performance and civic engagement nationally and in Europe. Recipient of Visionary, Arts Innovator of the Year, Leadership in Community-Based Theatre and Civic Engagement awards and more, her work is published by Routledge, Applause, Smith & Kraus, No Passport Press, and others. She is known for her work in short plays, rapid response theatre, and devising. She founded numerous projects as artistic director of That Uppity Theatre Company including the DisAbility Project, Women Centerstage, AC/DC Series, the Louies, As American as Apple Pie, We Love Immigrants, Dance the Vote, and Climate Change Theatre Action St Louis. Her play, *About that Chocolate Bar*, commissioned by Climate Change Theatre Action and published by The Arctic Cycle in *Lighting the Way*, has had fifty productions throughout the US and internationally. She created a prototype for students to study climate change and create theatrical responses online or in person and has worked as a dramaturg for work about environmental racism.

Alexis Lygoumenos is a Theatre and Performance Studies PhD student at the University of Georgia where she has taught a variety of performance-based classes. She received her MFA in Acting from the New York Film Academy, trained at the Yale Summer Actors Conservatory, the New York Conservatory for Dramatic Arts, and the University of Oxford's Light Entertainment Society. Under the stage name Alexis Nichols, she is an award-winning actor, writer, director, and voiceover artist. She is most noted for appearing as Lucille Ball in *Becoming Lucy*, a film she co-wrote, which premiered at the Festival de Cannes Court Metráge and for voicing three characters in the Netflix Original Series English Dub of *Little Witch Academia*. Alexis is forever grateful for the mentorship of a bevy of scholars and artists, particularly Dr. Marla Carlson, Valorie Hubbard, and Debi Derryberry.

Kasey Lynch is a PhD student in Theatre and Performance Studies at the University of Missouri where she also received her MA in Theatre. She previously received her BA in Communication from Villanova University. Her research interests lie in the intersections of performance, health, and gender, and she has been published in *Theatre Topics*. In addition to her research, Kasey is a writer, performer, teacher, and director. When she is not performing on MU's stages, she can be found directing such performances as *Charlotte's Web* (2020), *The Cat in the Hat* (2022), and *The Wolves* (2023). She has also served as the Managing Director of MU Theatre's Life and Literature Series, notably managing Mizzou's Climate Change Theatre Action performances in 2021. Kasey is endlessly grateful for her many incredible mentors, especially Heidi Rose, Claire Syler, and M. Heather Carver.

Rachel Lynett is a queer Afro-Latine playwright, producer, and teaching artist. Their plays have been featured at San Diego Rep, Magic Theatre, Mirrorbox Theatre, Laboratory Theatre of Florida, Barrington Stage Company, Theatre Lab, Theatre Prometheus, Florida Studio Theatre, Laughing Pig Theatre Company, Capital Repertory Theatre, Teatro Espejo, the Kennedy Center Page to Stage Festival, Theatresquared, Equity Library Theatre, Talk Back Theatre, American Stage Theatre Company, Indiana University at Bloomington, Edgewood College, and Orlando Shakespeare Theatre. Their plays, *Last Night* and *He Did It* made the 2020 Kilroys List. Lynett is also the 2021 recipient of the Yale Drama Prize for *Apologies to Lorraine Hansberry (You Too August Wilson)*, and the 2021 recipient of the National Latinx Playwriting award for *Black Mexican*. They have previously taught at the University of Arkansas, Fayetteville, the University of Wisconsin, Madison, and Alfred University. Lynett is incredibly thankful to the theatre educators who have helped navigate the American theatrical landscape throughout the years, with special thanks to Kevin Dreyer, Siiri Scott, Anne García-Romero, Les Wade, and Morgan Hicks.

Hope McIntyre is an award-winning playwright, director, and Assistant Professor at the University of Winnipeg (Treaty One Territory).

McIntyre's training includes a BFA in performance (University of Saskatchewan) and an MFA in directing (University of Victoria). She was the founding Artistic Director of Sarasvàti Productions, a company dedicated to social change that she helmed for twenty-two years. During this tenure, she developed community-based play creation methods. She has received the YWCA Women of Distinction, the Bra D'Or, the Mahatma Gandhi Community Service, and Women Helping Women awards. She is a former president of the Playwrights Guild of Canada. She is indebted to many teachers and mentors starting with her high school drama teacher, Blaine Hart, and her undergrad acting teachers, Pamela Haig Bartley and Henry Woolf, in addition to colleagues too numerous to list.

Meredith Melville is a full-time professor at Texas A&M University—Corpus Christi, teaching Directing and Improvisation. She spent ten years in Chicago working in improv and sketch with Infinite Sundaes, the Second City Training Center Musical Improv House Team, the Cupid Players as an understudy, and the Alliance Sketch Group as the artistic director. She is a founding member and still performs with Recapitulation Musical Improv. Meredith completed an MFA at University of Memphis in Directing. Meredith would like to thank her mentors/teachers/influencers, but especially Tina Landau, Kok Heng Leun, and David Diamond.

Charissa Menefee is the founder and artistic director of The EcoTheatre Lab. She is a Professor of English and Theatre at Iowa State University, where she also co-directs the MFA Program in Creative Writing & Environment. Her research focuses on the intersection and interplay of writing and performance, new play development, and theatre that engages with environmental and social justice issues. She recently directed a touring production of *Climate Change Theatre Action*, as well as readings for the New Play Lab at the William Inge Theatre Festival. She has been a Tennessee Williams Scholar at the Sewanee Writers' Conference, an EST/Sloan Project commission recipient, and a writer-in-residence at the Fairhope Center for the Writing Arts and the Utah Shakespeare Festival's New American Playwrights Project. She is grateful for many incredible mentors who embody the concepts of generosity, creativity, and collaboration, but especially Larry Menefee and Christian Moe, as well as her Gig St. improv pals, because they figured it out together and taught each other.

Mike Poblete is originally from Brooklyn, NY. He is a playwright, educator, and academic who has written seven full-length plays and numerous one-acts which have been performed in six countries. As an improviser, he has performed with the Mānoa Improv Players sporadically since 2019. He has a Playwriting MFA from Trinity College Dublin and a PhD in Theatre from the University of Hawai'i at Mānoa, where he teaches theatre history and playwriting. His scholarly research investigates the role of student agency in drama education. His academic work has appeared in publications such as *Theatre Topics* and *Arts Praxis*. Many thanks to Dr. Markus Wessendorf, Dr. Haili'ōpua Baker, Thomas Conway, and Kat Rothman for all of their guidance and support.

Stephanie Rae is a full-time applied improv practitioner who has been studying the form for twelve years. She's directed a Boyz II Men themed show for Upright Citizens Brigade's Del Close Marathon, guest played with everyone from ComedySportz to the Groundlings, and taught classes and workshops for improvisers from Louisiana to Liverpool. As founder and president of the Black Improv Alliance, she's created scholarships and free programming for hundreds of improvisers of color, and as a facilitator for FLS+, she's taught the science of play alongside members of Broadway's Freestyle Love Supreme. Stephanie is passionate about amplifying diverse voices and seeing more melanin onstage. She also has a law degree from Georgetown, but mostly uses it to win arguments online. She is incredibly grateful for the support of mentors and collaborators including (but not limited to) her parents Rick & Phyllis, Felicia Renae, Lola Bakare, Nina Harrison, Kellie Williams, Tezz Yancey, Rochelle McConico, Alsa Bruno, John Gebretatose, the CTC, SWAG writers' group, and the amazing folks of FLS+.

Muneeb ur Rehman is an applied drama practitioner from Pakistan working with the credo "performance-for-all" for the last six years. He has explored dramatic and improvisation frameworks in schools, teacher trainings, NGOs, youth programs, corporate events, play cafes, community events, design classes, actor training, and script devising in Pakistan and Nepal. He is a regular presenter at international forums like *Performing the World* in New York, *SDEA* in Singapore, *Play, Perform, Learn & Grow* in Greece, and *Drama for Life Festival* in South Africa. His theatre forebears include educational drama pioneers Dorothy Heathcote and Jonathan Neelands, expressionist Brecht, Image Theatre progenitor Augusto Boal, and improvisation mentor Adal Rifai.

Dennis Schebetta is an actor, director, and writer in film and theatre as well as Assistant Professor at Skidmore College. He is also the co-author of *Building a Performance: An Actor's Guide to Rehearsal* (with John Basil), published by Rowman & Littlefield. He has worked off-Broadway and regionally in works ranging from Shakespeare to devising to new play development at such organizations as Ensemble Studio Theatre, 13th Street Rep, 29th Street Rep, Vital Theatre, Bricolage Production Company, City Theatre, Saratoga Shakespeare Company, and the NY Fringe Festival. His plays *Hipsters in Love* and *Half Full* were included in the *Bricolage Urban Sprawl Anthology of 10 Minute Plays*, and his play *Dog Park or Sexual Perversity in Magnuson* is published in *Ten 10-Minute Plays*. A proud member of the Dramatists Guild and AEA, he is a graduate of the William Esper Studio and received his MFA from Virginia Commonwealth University. He owes a great debt to the many teachers and mentors who inspired him as a theatre artist including William Esper, Davey Marlin-Jones, Julie Jensen, Dr. Noreen Barnes, Gary Garrison, and John Basil.

Amy Seham is a director, playwright, and scholar/performer of improv. Her publications include the book, *Whose Improv Is It, Anyway? Beyond Second City* (2001), a ground-breaking study of race, gender, and power in Chicago improv comedy, and "Performing Gender, Race, and Power in Improv Comedy" in *The Oxford Handbook of Critical Improvisation Studies* (2013). Her current project, *Improv for the 21st Century*, analyzes the impact of social movements and the pandemic on the improv community and shares innovative exercises and teaching techniques. Seham has taught improv workshops in China, India, England, and across the United States. Productions of her original plays have received positive reviews in New York, New Haven, and Minneapolis, where she also taught *Improv for Playwrights* at the Playwrights' Center. After twenty-five years, Seham has retired from her position as Professor of Theatre and Dance at Gustavus Adolphus College. Her wonderful daughter, Miranda, is currently a sophomore at USC. Enormous gratitude to her playwriting mentor, Linda Jenkins, and her supportive improv team, Beep Sebastian, mentored by master teacher, Liz Allen.

Elspeth Tilley is Associate Professor of Expressive Arts at Massey University in Aotearoa New Zealand. She is the only three-time winner of the British Theatre Challenge international playwriting competition (with social justice comedies about climate change, public health, and animal rights) and a three-time official playwright for Climate Change Theatre Action. Her plays have won prizes in the USA, UK, and New Zealand, been published in the USA, UK, New Zealand, and Canada, and produced in Paris, Rome, Shanghai,

New York, London, Manila, Dubai, Sydney, and more. Elspeth received the 2018 Playwrights' Association of New Zealand Outstanding Achievement Award. She is deeply grateful to the mentors, collaborators, and teachers who, whether they realized it or not, have stimulated and sustained her lifelong love of theatre, including Susan Williams, Shirley Burchelle, Susan Richer, Vanessa Kessler, and Joanne Tompkins, and thankful for her students who inspire her every single day.

Sage Tokach is a theatre artist and educator currently working as the Director of Education at the New London Barn Playhouse in New London, New Hampshire. She received her MFA in Theatre for Young Audiences at the University of Central Florida where she also worked as the Artistic Associate for the School of Theatre. She has also held teaching and directing positions at Orlando Repertory Theatre, Maples Repertory Theatre, Great Plains Theatre, and the Florida State Parks. Sage's research interests include youth agency in theatre, ecofeminism, and youth dramaturgy. Many thanks to the mentors who have guided her through her career, particularly Julia Listengarten, Vandy Wood, and Ralph Krumins, as well as the students she learns from every day.

Introduction

Embodied Playwriting

Hillary Haft Bucs and Charissa Menefee

Although theatre is a collaborative art, writing for the stage can be, strangely, a solitary act, when a playwright stares at the blank page, wondering how to get fingers moving, how to coax ideas into the white space, how to commit to an idea and develop it. Student playwrights often say they are at a loss as to how to begin to create a character or design a plot, even when they've gone through a series of writing exercises to get them started. And they may give writer's block an even greater foothold as they anticipate the vulnerability that will be demanded from them when another group of artists attempts to breathe life into what winds up on those pages.

But what about bringing it to life *while* it's being written, while it's in process? How can the writer use performance techniques to create stronger scripts before they are handed over to a creative team for collaboration and interpretation? Specifically, how can a writer tap into the essential generative energy of improvisation to make work that is fully realized and urgent on the page?

Many writers default to traditional in-progress developmental readings, in writing groups or in front of audiences, as a way to bring performance into the process, but these usually come toward the end of a play's initial drafting or follow a series of written revisions. While readings are a critical step in the process of developing a play, and hearing the dialogue can yield insights that lead to effective rewrites, embracing embodied methods earlier in the process—during the generation of ideas, brainstorming, pre-writing, outlining, character development, and even revision—can lead to more three-dimensional, compelling characters, focused action, and exciting structures. For example, companies such as Second City have successfully used improvisation to create scripted sketch comedy for many years, and the New York Writers' Bloc applied Second City techniques to the development of new plays.

What do we mean by "embodied" playwriting methods? This is not just a playwright reading aloud. This is not listening to actors read aloud. This is about writers engaging in the emotional and physical worlds of their plays during the composition process itself, as a vital part of planning, creating, drafting, and revising. This is about writing as performance, not just *for* performance, with playwrights actively borrowing from performance techniques, tools, and practice to create more vibrant written work. Writing in an embodied way requires a full understanding and embrace of theatre as a three-dimensional art that has to be literally translated through bodies moving in physical space, bringing the voices and actions of characters to life in real time.

While a novelist or short story writer may explore characters by using the tools of interiority, revealing their thoughts and motivations, characters in drama are not in their heads. They are in action, they are moving, they are doing, they are provoking, they are making things happen—to themselves, for themselves, to and for others. They change their reality constantly, in real time and space. This requires playwrights to have a different skill set for problem-solving and understanding characters. Characters on stage, generally, are not seen thinking through what action to take—they take it—and the thinking-through to which fiction would give us unfolding access happens invisibly in characters' minds, just as it does in real life.

The stage doesn't allow for the massaging and tweaking and slowing of time the way prose and poetry do. Even when a character has a monologue, it happens in real time and space, in the present for the audience. The audience cannot flip back a page if they miss something. They can't pause and rewind. They have to listen and pay attention. And all that backstory, all that interior thought, all that subtext is going on right now when a play is underway, provoking and creating the action onstage. The page is not the same for a playwright as it is for a novelist; for example, scripts are discussed in terms of duration, rather than length of manuscript. Script formats are designed to correlate to time, with the usual ideal being a minute per page, and forward momentum is critical. In a play manuscript, the dialogue reaches from margin to margin, revealing the primacy of speech in drama, focused on dialogue's powerful ability to provoke and shape action.

We often tell students that we are *building* plays. Building requires hard work and skilled labor, as well as planning, proper materials, construction, and craft. But it is also a creative process that can benefit from the kind of "play" and experimentation that happens in an improvisational performance space. A willingness to engage with the building blocks of a script off the page, as well as on, centers discovery, specificity, and authenticity. Including embodied exercises and techniques as part of a writing practice can help the playwright resist tendencies for generalization, stereotyping, plot holes, and meaningless dialogue and can lead to more complex, distinct, and compelling characters who interact in a richly imagined environment.

Teachers and students who engage in more traditional writing exercises and explorations may ask how improvisation-based embodied techniques are different. In our own classes, we employ an eclectic mix of exercises, some of which are only worked out on the page. However, techniques that invite the playwright to go beyond the page and inhabit the world of the play in a physical way change the relationship to the text, bringing it into focus as a three-dimensional, living-and-breathing piece of art. At a minimum, improvisation requires tapping into imagination, thinking on your feet, staying in the present moment, engaging with other actors and/or audience members. More advanced tenets of the art form of improvisational comedy require active listening, relationship-building, agreement and augmentation, and constructing environments. The art form also emphasizes giving and accepting gifts of information that establish key elements of scenes; these provide foundational material for further story and character development. And improv asks a performer to make decisions quickly and commit to them, doubling down to justify them when necessary, making sense of characters and scenes while creating them, trusting that any path will lead somewhere interesting. Borrowing from this approach to discovery can be incredibly valuable to writers during the drafting of a play.

What happens when the playwright takes on a character, imagining ways into the psyche, physicality, mundane tasks and routines, unscripted conversations and dialogue? This is different from workshopping with actors, where the playwright is observer and listener, making notes from a safe distance. Approaching writing like an improvisational actor can prompt the writer to bring a character to life in ways that watching someone else do it cannot. The imagination is fueled and spurred as the playwright problem-solves in real time, answering questions posed to a character, committing in the moment to ideas and impulses, trusting—as in improv—that these ideas and impulses will make sense, even if the only reason they make sense is that they've been spoken aloud. Embodied techniques can illuminate both what the writer knows and doesn't know, while encouraging commitment to the kind of specific details that enrich the portrayals of dramatic characters and their world.

★★★★

Embodied Playwriting: Improv and Acting Exercises for Writing and Devising compiles new and adapted exercises for teaching playwriting in the classroom, workshop, or studio through the lens of acting and improvisation. This edited book offers teachers, students, and other writers access to the innovative practices developed by seasoned teachers of playwriting who are also actors, improv performers, and theatre directors. Borrowing from the embodied art of acting and the inventive practice of improvisation, the exercises in this book will engage writing students in performance-based methods that lead to the creation of fully imagined characters, dynamic relationships, and vivid drama. Step-by-step guidelines for exercises, as well as application and coaching advice, will support successful lesson planning and classroom implementation for playwriting students at all levels, as well as individual study. Readers will benefit, too, from curation by editors who have experience with high-impact educational practices and are advocates for the use of varied teaching strategies to increase accessibility, inclusion, skill-building, and student success.

Playwriting students often begin as actors; they fall in love with theatre and want to create dialogue, as well as interpret it. This book provides playwriting instructors with tools to build on students' prior experience with performance, rather than default to traditional creative writing pedagogy and workshop methods. Some instructors called upon to teach playwriting may themselves have a performance background, but may not know how to translate that experience into active classroom strategies that allow them to build on their expertise. At its core, this book recognizes the interdisciplinary nature of theatre and its practitioners, resisting artificial boundaries between acting, playwriting, devising, and directing in the creation of performance texts. Of course, Maria Irene Fornés, Keith Johnstone, and other influential playwrights and teachers have incorporated embodied exercises into their own writing processes and shared these explorations with their students. The contributors to this book build on the legacy of innovative writing teachers, while also bringing rich and diverse improvisation, performance, and devising experience to their development of new methods for creating both single-authored and collaboratively-written plays.

We are thrilled to have contributors from around the globe; each author brings a unique background, perspective, and approach to this exciting work at the intersection of performance-based exploration and the development of playwriting skills and new work for the stage. The exercises in the book are organized into five sections: *Creating Characters, Body and Mind, Playing Games, Changemaking, and Curated Exercises.* The first four sections contain contributed chapters that explore, in depth, specific exercises or series of exercises. *Creating Characters* includes chapters from Amy Seham, who explores the importance of subtext; Stephanie Rae, who guides writers in their development of diverse characters; Muneeb ur Rehman, who focuses on authenticity in the revision process; and Charissa Menefee, who spotlights surprise and discovery in character-building. In *Body and Mind*, Sarah Kozinn highlights an exercise that enlists photographs as vital prompts, Luane Davis Haggerty and Aaron Kelstone share their innovative work in performing arts at the National Technical Institute for the Deaf, and David Kaye applies psychodramatic techniques to writing. *Playing Games* includes explorations of worldbuilding by Mike Poblete, using games to problem-solve writing challenges by John P. Bray; and folkgames as a creative catalyst by Solomon Y. Dartey. The fourth section, *Changemaking*, explores embodied playwriting's role in applied theatre and theatre for/as social change. Elspeth Tilley discusses comedy as a social justice tool, Dana Edell and Hope McIntyre share approaches to creating plays with communities, and Joan Lipkin and Kasey Lynch focus on writing for climate justice.

The fifth section is a curated collection of exercises, by a variety of practitioners, that can be implemented in classrooms or workshops on their own or in combination with other activities. These exercises focus on skill-building, content generation, and revision strategies. Contributors include Alexis Lygoumenos, Gabrielle Sinclair Compton, Ramón Esquivel, Jeanne Leep, Wesley Broulik, Rachel Lynett, Dennis Schebetta, Steve Kaliski, Meredith Melville, Elizabeth Hess, Tiffany Antone, Matt Fotis, and Sage Tokach. We hope this book will provide a wealth of material for teachers, students, and playwrights who look forward to experimenting with dynamic, embodied writing practices in their own classrooms, workshops, and studios.

Part I
Creating Characters

1 The Meet and Greet

Creating Opportunities for Surprise and Discovery

Charissa Menefee

Introduction

I use one of my favorite embodied writing exercises early in the play development process, as we are working on characters. The exercise arose from my frustration with the kinds of two-dimensional characters I kept seeing in student (and sometimes professional) plays. My students would provide a cursory description for a character—the usual age, gender, occupation, relationship to other characters—as they'd seen in plays they read. But the development seemed to stop there. As the dialogue in the play began, it would become clear that the writer knew nothing specific about the character. This would happen even when we had worked on generating character biographies. All the information they knew about the character, had created for the character, was abstract, and had no real bearing on how the character spoke, carried on a conversation, pursued an objective in the play. It was if the character had no life outside the scene s/he was in. Because my classes were fairly large, I needed exercises that would move us quickly, and as a group, toward greater specificity in character development as a foundation for higher quality writing. I began developing and adapting exercises to build characters.

While I was influenced by the character biography work used by many playwrights and playwriting teachers, watching my own students not fully translate this pre-writing into their plays led me to draw from my background performing and teaching improvisational comedy, as well as my background teaching courses in writing as performance. I designed an exercise that would require the writers to move back and forth between writing and performing, using discovery in both modes, to develop exciting, specific characters. The exercise challenges students to think in terms of live performance, character voice, deep history, motivation, and objectives; this is sometimes easier for students who also study acting, but not always, as the text is incomplete—and it

DOI: 10.4324/9781003243014-2

can be new territory for creative writing students used to working in silence on the page. After participating in this exercise, the writers tend to see their characters as more complex, three-dimensional, and capable of agency and surprise.

The Meet and Greet

An Exercise in Character Discovery

What we need

Notebooks and writing utensils

Where we work

Open space with room to move

What we want

Discoveries about characters

How we get there

In this exercise, students begin with their notebooks. Ask them to write a character's name at the top of a fresh page. This may be the central character of the play currently being written—or, in a workshop setting, a brand new character being developed on the spot. Then ask a series of five or six questions.

Experiment with different questions; most successful are questions that writers have likely not already answered in basic character sketches and biographies, questions that force them to make something up on the spot. And it's helpful to mix what seem like trivial questions, such as "What is your character's favorite food?", with more challenging questions, such as "What does your character regret not saying to someone?" Move through some questions so fast that they can write only brief answers. For others, encourage not only an answer, but a brief explanation of why or how. Some examples:

- What did your character want to be while growing up?
- Who was your character's most influential teacher?

- Where would your character like to travel, if money were no obstacle?
- What is your character's favorite food?
- What book does your character recommend to anyone who asks?
- What is your character afraid of?
- When does your character naturally wake up in the morning?
- What does your character regret not saying to someone?
- What would make your character drop everything to go back to school?
- Who is the person your character most admires?
- Where does your character feel most safe?
- Who is the person your character would call in a time of crisis?

Give the writers a few moments, after they have answered the questions, to read back through their notes before putting their notebooks away. Then invite them into the common space in the classroom or workshop, where they will engage in an improvised party or reception where they have to introduce themselves and carry on conversations with each other *as their characters*.

Set a few rules, of course. They must talk about their characters in first person, not third, whether asking or answering questions. When they don't know an answer, they can't say, "I don't know," but have to make something up, which then becomes part of the character and will inform their next conversation.

This is, of course, playing with a basic "yes, and" improv premise, as they answer a question or reveal information in a conversation with another writer's character. Accepting the new information as a discovery and gift, the writer can then commit to it, justify it, and build on it in the next conversation. Encourage movement in the group, so that writers interact with a series of other participants. Actively intercede to discourage the formation of small groups, so that focused dialogue in pairs continues to be the mainstay of the exercise.

After five or ten minutes, pause the conversations and send the writers back to their notebooks to record and reflect on their discoveries. As they write, provide additional verbal prompts, such as:

- What did you learn about your character?
- What surprised you?

- How do these discoveries affect other aspects of your character?
- What did you learn about your character's past?
- What did you learn about your character's present circumstances?

Don't let them write too long before inviting them back onto the floor for a second round of conversations, followed by another session of recording their discoveries. Depending on time and the energy in the room, it can be helpful to add a third round. If writers commit fully to the exercise, they get excited about asking each other questions and engaging in the improvisational setting; that gift of interest in each other leads to more discoveries for everyone.

After the second or third round, have the writers go back to their notebooks and write a scene that is part of their play, based on the surprises and discoveries they made during the exercise. What is a scene that has to happen in the play, given the new knowledge gleaned about the character? Having experienced their characters in conversation, on their feet, using their own voices, can move the writers toward more realistic portrayals, rather than characters who seem like random collections of facts.

Coaching the Exercise

Side coaching can help students get started. They may need to be provided questions or prompts for the "party" part of the exercise. For instance, they may need a goal for their character to pursue, such as finding out things they have in common with other characters at the party. This gets them talking and asking questions, just as it does when I use it as an introductory exercise in other classes, where I often ask students to find, through conversations on their feet, three things they have in common with every other student. It's a game with a definite goal and time frame, but can lead to in-depth dialogues and intriguing revelations. Using this kind of prompt requires the characters to begin with small talk about hobbies, jobs, families, likes, dislikes, etc., but can lead to discoveries about unique characteristics and qualities as they search for commonalities with others.

If you have a group that doesn't need a prompt, that can be even better, as the conversations will be more free-flowing and influenced by how the writers view their characters. They can incorporate individual goals and objectives they think their characters would pursue at the gathering. This kind of agency may even lead to the creation of intriguing conflicts or alliances, as character personalities develop and manifest in their behaviors toward each other.

Sometimes students want to use the answers to the initial questions as conversation starters in the exercise. I try to discourage this, as it will probably ring false. For instance, if I ask them to write down their favorite food, the hope is that it tells them something about the character—not that they go into the conversation announcing it, unless it's particularly pertinent. But something so simple as a character's favorite food invites the writer to construct backstory that informs subtext and motivation. For instance, if a writer is in conversation as the character of Isabel, a high-powered attorney whose favorite food is peach pie, the reason for that choice can be illuminating. Is it because Isabel and her grandmother stopped by roadside stands for fresh peaches during her childhood summers, and she helped make the pies and watched through the window of the oven door as they baked, so that they would have perfect crusts? Or is it because her mother worked in a diner and brought leftover pie home to share on her one night off? Or is it something she discovered at an expensive bakery near the offices of her law firm?

If a character's favorite food is Froot Loops, what does that tell the writer about the character and how the character will interact with others? If all other things are essentially the same about two characters, but one sneaks Froot Loops late at night and the other sneaks cold bologna, there is a differentiation that might lead to other assumptions. Why does the first character hide the fact that he loves a children's sugared cereal? Why does the second hide the fact that she is eating processed lunch meat? Both characters could be, ostensibly, vegetarian, but only because they're doing it for someone else or aren't fully committed. After eating vegetarian meals with his fiancée, Robert may sneak Froot Loops that are hidden in his car trunk, a private rebellion against being healthy. How might that give insight into the way he communicates with her about other things? If he's not committed to being vegetarian, but pretends to be, is he also not committed to the relationship, even though he pretends to be? Or is he committed to his fiancée, but not to being healthy? Does this lead to conflict? And Judy eats bologna late at night, fishing it out of the back of the refrigerator, where she keeps it in an opaque container labelled "anchovies" so no one will open it. Why? Maybe it comforts her, reminds her of late-night snacks with her brother, but she knows this habit is inconsistent with her image as an enlightened, farmers' market and organic foods devotee—she posts photos of all that "good" food on social media and can't bear to think about being exposed. It may be a crucial part of this play that Judy's carefully built image is beginning to show cracks.

Why are people who they are? How did they get that way? Which forks in the road, when taken, shaped ideas, likes and dislikes, career paths, life choices? This kind of imaginative trail-following can open up incredible opportunities for character development for writers who tend to rely on stereotypes like they see on television or who say they feel stymied by advice to create characters who are real. Helping them to find specific details that bring the characters to life for the writer can lead to further discoveries, assumptions, and analysis that bring the characters to life in the script. Dialogue should be action-oriented, provoking response of some kind from other characters or from the character saying the lines. Words have power. Once said, they can't be taken back. This is a critical element of the exercise. Once a playwright is not only answering questions on the page, but answering aloud in conversation, the words become real, they convey meaning, and the character begins to manifest as a result. Who the character is becomes distinct, becomes true.

Writers may get caught up in the fun of the improvisational character conversations, but it's essential that they are interrupted and sent back to their notebooks to write their discoveries. (Of course, they can use laptops, if needed, but it's best if the physicality of the exercise continues into writing with pencil or pen on paper. Reserve laptop usage for students who need that as an accommodation, rather than a convenience.) The back and forth, committing to the discoveries while embodying the characters and then recommitting to them on paper, allows the writers to say "yes, and." They are making discoveries, agreeing to them, and then justifying and building on them. The objective is to have all these discovery notes and then to take those fresh ideas into an unrelated scene that is actually part of the writer's play. The subtext that has been developed allows the writer to create dialogue that is more true to the character, because the writer knows the character so much better than before. The writer's sensibility has explored the character's sensibility—in action, in interaction, in dialogue and conversation—so that, hopefully, that character comes to life on the page in a complex way, one that lends itself to an intricate three-dimensional performance by an actor who will bring intensive analysis and interpretive skill to the text and further build the portrayal.

With a more experienced group of writers, you can add disruption to this exercise, asking them, each time they return to the "party," to change something significant about the character and to explore that reality. For inexperienced writers, this can be problematic, because they may not keep building the character, merely change the character.

However, experienced writers, like experienced improvisational actors, will be able to change one characteristic without shifting others, and that will allow them to explore different possibilities. Keeping these changes to the less dramatic (or melodramatic) will yield better results because, while the build will be disrupted, it won't be stopped or completely altered. And it may allow the writer to find more psychologically sound reasons for the choices being made instinctively, whether those reasons have to do with the character's past history or present circumstances or future aspirations.

Welcome Back to the Page

It's important to remember that improv is not precious. I do not allow the writers to carry notebooks around while engaged in the exercise. They have to commit to and be present for the conversations. Whatever they remember, they can put down on paper afterward, and they won't capture everything; in fact, they may get frustrated about how much they do or don't remember, but they'll have to let go of recording everything. Sometimes, the writers literally run to their seats when I interrupt a round. They rush to their notebooks, barely able to contain their need to write! No fear of the blank page, as the need to get it on paper erases all hesitance.

This impulse is also evident in an exercise I use in a Poetry as Performance class, where poets have to compose poems on their feet, walking around. They're not allowed notebooks or anything to write with. They have to play with the new poem in their heads, in their voices, work on it without paper, without the easy recording of the first draft, roll it around in their minds till it sticks. In this case, too, the poets can hardly wait to get to their notebooks, to take what has been careening around in their brains and commit it to the page in some form, though it may be altered or half-there. The eagerness to get it down on paper is the opposite of staring at the blank page, not knowing where to start, facing down writer's block. Instead, it's a mad dash to feel the pencil in hand and write as fast as they can, so as to retain as much as possible before it fades. The blank page welcomes and invites. While initially frustrating for some poets, most find this exercise challenging yet fun, embracing the disruption of usual habits. As in **The Meet and Greet** exercise, the relationship to words is changed by playing with them aloud, holding onto them in an ephemeral and changeable form until they can be solid on the page. Like invisible ink that needs to be exposed to light or water or something else mysterious to create the alchemical reaction that brings the words back to life.

Some playwrights are resistant to this kind of work. They may say that they are not actors. It's true that not all writers are comfortable taking on the role of an interpretive artist, when they are used to creating on the page and handing it over. However, there may also be a bit of fear keeping them from fully participating in this kind of exercise. Giving a character your voice, embodying and inhabiting that character, not only imagining physical form and sound, but stepping into it, can be scary. The character is no longer a jumble of words on a page. The character is part of you, and you are part of the character. That feels risky, as you bring the character into resonance, rumbling through the body, a kind of channeling that writers may only be comfortable with when it's through fingers typing on a keyboard. A writer doesn't have to be an actor to sense the inauthentic, the lack of the genuine, when speaking a character's lines out loud and waiting for a response. The truth is created as the playwright commits to it. It becomes the reality of the character, the reality of the play.

While there may be changes made during the ongoing drafting and revision process, the playwright will do well to continue building on what felt authentic and beware of what felt inauthentic. Did the playwright feel, in the body, that the answer to a question felt wrong, not the truth for the character? Did the playwright answer something that didn't make sense, given everything else they know about the character, or did that thing that didn't seem to make sense actually illuminate something fundamental and surprising?

An example. Let's say the playwright has noted that a character has been married and divorced three times. Simple. But, in the embodied conversation with other writers playing their characters, the playwright finds herself claiming, as the character, that divorce was never her idea. Suddenly, we're aware that the character sees herself as a victim of circumstances, which is entirely different from the way she might see herself if she claimed that she tired of each of her husbands and needed her own space. The playwright suddenly knows something essential about the way this character approaches the world, other people, her reality. We often assign characteristics, life experiences, and biographical details to characters without thinking about the way the character would talk about these things with others and what stories s/he has told her/himself.

Of course, this is not to say that the playwright should continue to play that character or all the characters in the play! The later addition of actors into the process is an essential step in the development of the script, and talented, innovative actors will likely provide new information and inspiration about the characters, through the performance choices they make, that will lead to targeted, perhaps even substantial, revisions. Embodied exercises, such as the one shared in this chapter, can create evocative, rich explorations for playwrights that lead to written characters that both resonate on the page and reward actors for weeks and months of investment in bringing them to life on stage.

2 Improvising Between the Lines
Enhancing the Script by Embodying Subtext

Amy Seham

Introduction

In his review of a 1928 production of Chekhov's *The Cherry Orchard*, Brooks Atkinson commented on the challenges and rewards of realism in the theatre:

> Nothing is more difficult to act on the stage than Chekhovian drama ... As playgoers we hear and see only the exterior impulses. In consequence the essence of the characters, the essence of the story, lie between the lines or rise above the performance as overtones.[1]

To achieve his goal of depicting "life as it is," Anton Chekhov pioneered a dramatic form that would reflect the way real people behave in real life. This new form of theatrical realism was drastically different from the melodrama and farce that dominated western theatre at the turn of the 20th century.

Raymond Williams explains: "What Chekhov has done, in effect, is to invent a dramatic form which contradicts most of the available conventions of dramatic production."[2] Actors skilled in virtuosic displays of poetic passion were unprepared to play nuanced characters filled with emotions and desires they dared not express. To traditional actors—and to many early audiences—the dialogue in plays such as *The Seagull* and *The Cherry Orchard* seemed trivial or even random. The performers were ill-equipped to portray the multiple levels of suppressed emotion common to everyday social interaction.

After several failed productions of Chekhov's plays, Moscow Art Theatre director Konstantin Stanislavsky developed a new "system" of techniques that trained actors to discover and communicate the *subtext* of a realistic scene. Rejecting the prevailing style of theatre as a formal, polished presentation of language and gesture, he chose improvisation as a core technique for cultivating actors' spontaneity and imagination, as well as for developing the non-verbal communication skills required for expressing *subtext*.

In "Stanislavsky's System: Pathways for the Actor," Sharon Carnicke explains:

> Hidden beneath the words is *subtext*, a term that describes anything a character thinks or feels but does not, or cannot, put into words ... Actors communicate subtext through non-verbal means (body language, the cast of the eyes, intonation and pauses).[3]

Physical posture, facial expression, focus, movement, gesture, activity, silence, engagement with the space or with a prop, all clue the audience into the character's status, attitude, and inner struggle. These elements are often seen as the actor's responsibility—but the playwright can make a point of providing stage directions, crosstalk, pauses, and specific business that offer rich opportunities for actors to reveal unspoken meaning. This ongoing collaboration between text and performance keeps a play current and alive.

In *The Blunt Playwright*, Clem Martini notes that, "Many contemporary writers employ improvisational devices as a catalyst to generate dialogue and character. Writing can, in and of itself, be viewed as a kind of improvisational exercise."[4] Improvisation, however, can also be used to inspire and support playwrights with more than the simple generation of material.

By honing the crucial skills of listening and heightening, improvisers can infer and assert subtextual information from subtle indications that emerge, intentionally or not, from a scene partner's behavior. The challenge for many players is in finding a balance between the need to establish specific elements of the scene swiftly and clearly, and the desire to create believable dialogue in which information is revealed less directly and much more slowly. Playwrights striving to achieve a similar balance must make good use of subtext.

According to Downs and Russin in *Naked Playwriting*, subtext has more significance than a simple analysis of the script can reveal:

> Good dialogue is an iceberg – only part of the meaning appears above the waterline. Writing from the perspective of subtext is also known as "writing between the lines" because what is not said is often more important than what is.[5]

I encourage playwrights to explore the space "between the lines" through improvisation and embodied playwriting. In the following pages, I provide a series of original and adapted improv exercises designed to help playwrights experience and support the variety of ways actors and directors make meaning through, under, and between the words on the page.

Guessing Games

In *Writing for the Stage: A Practical Playwriting Guide*, playwright and educator Leroy Clark explains, "Audiences go to the theatre because of the subtext – the deeper meaning – because they want mystery, suspense and surprise."[6]

A number of popular improv guessing games challenge one player to decipher clues to the secret identity, quirk, or agenda that has been given to each of the other players. Players are not to reveal the secret directly but must provide clues based on the way the secret affects their interactions with the others.

Secrets

Four players leave the stage (or the room) while the audience (or the rest of the class) is asked to suggest four embarrassing *secrets*. These could range from "Alex has a secret crush on Chris" to "Dana can't stop passing gas" or "Jamie has stinky feet." Players are told their secrets privately, so they do not know what the other three have been given.

Four chairs are arranged to represent a car, and the four must collectively improvise a discussion of their destination, their relationships, and their ongoing road trip while simultaneously trying to protect their secrets. The audience enjoys this game most when the players set up risky situations to draw attention to their predicaments. If other inhabitants of the car begin to sniff something unpleasant, Dana might say, for example, "Oh, I hate when we drive through this area—you can always smell the cow manure." This line will get a laugh because the audience knows what Dana is up to. Spectators love being "in the know" as they watch players desperately struggling to escape discovery. At the end of the scene, the players try to identify one another's secrets until everything has been revealed.[7]

Endowing and Inferring Subtext

Improvisers use the dialogue to create a shared reality as it unfolds. Players often ascribe qualities to one another through a process of "endowment." You may start a scene assuming one subtext only to have your scene partner endow you with a different motivation. This can be challenging in improv but it helps to demonstrate that subtext is not real on stage until it is expressed in a readable way. In *The Dramatic Writer's Companion*, playwright Will Dunne warns:

> To have dramatic value, the subtext must be knowable to some degree. If the subtext is so buried that it can't be detected, we have no way to realize that something more is going on.[8]

Emotional Subtext

In a two-person scene, make assumptions based on your partner's otherwise neutral lines to drastically heighten your emotions. Make your partner's slightest contributions matter. For example, Player A may say simply, "The full moon is so beautiful tonight" and B could reply, "I told you I didn't want children right away. Sorry if you think that's selfish."

B is making a huge assumption about why A is mentioning the full moon, and thereby is actually *creating* the subtext for A. Improv rules of "agreement" dictate that Player A will not reject or correct this endowment of their character's underlying motivation, but will accept their partner's gift fully. Going forward, the desire to have children and resentment that their partner is unwilling to start a family will now be a defining subtext for A. Character A might then make a huge assumption about the meaning behind B's reply by saying, "I'm not trying to sabotage your career. It's fine that you earn more money than I do."

The subtext assignments can continue for some time in the scene or can be kept to one exchange. But these subtexts will influence the remainder of the scene.

Written Exercise

Free-write a scene between two characters from the world of the play you are working on. Have each character over-interpret the simplest statements from the other, inferring hidden meanings that have increasing significance. Have fun with the absurdity of their assumptions. Read the scene aloud and consider that people do often read meaning into seemingly innocuous statements. Moreover, many statements that seem mundane do mask an attitude toward another person.

Engaging dialogue includes subtle innuendo, subtext, or attitude that will be grasped by the audience. Experiment with levels of intention and awareness. For example, Character A may compliment Character B with just a hint of sarcasm. Character B takes the statement at face value, but the audience recognizes the subtext of disdain under the surface of A's words. Audiences delight in "dramatic irony"—the engaging condition created when they know more about the truth of a situation than the character on stage knows. Free-write another scene between the characters that makes use of readable subtext to create dramatic irony.

Silent Subtext

In most canonical Western dramatic literature, playwrights did not concern themselves with the inner life of secondary characters such as servants, peasants, or women. In realism, the energy onstage often comes from the tension between characters' individual desires and the strictly enforced performances of gender, class, and status their society requires them to maintain. Playwright Timothy Daly notes, "You learn a lot about the social position, nature, influence and status of the characters in a social realist world."[9]

With the advent of realism and "the problem play" of the 19th century, playwright Henrik Ibsen sought to address social issues on the stage including the rights of women. He wrote lines for female characters, such as Nora Helmer in *A Doll's House*, that demonstrated her need to play a girlish part for her husband while her inner thoughts were more complex. August Strindberg's depiction of Miss Julie, however, leaves little evidence of her inner thoughts or subtext, displaying the playwright's ignorance of and disdain for women. Subtext, however, is not completely within a playwright's control. In the collaborative world of theatre, actors and directors co-create the production of a script.

Quite a few classic plays have been successfully revived in recent decades with a tweak or even radical change to the *subtext* of the lines. Some productions of Ibsen's *A Doll's House*, for example, have allowed actors to bring their own sensibilities to the role of the naïve Nora, resulting in vastly different interpretations of the character. The malleability of the subtext keeps Nora alive and able to adjust to changing insights about women's hearts and minds.

Playwrights may choose to indicate subtext more explicitly or they may choose to allow a wide scope for collaboration and interpretation. In *Naked Playwriting*, Downs and Russin insist that every line in a script carries multiple messages:

> All powerful dialogue is a dance of interpretation and misinterpretation. If your characters' conversations are merely conveying literal information, they aren't carrying the essential freight of theme and characterization.[10]

For playwrights who want to create work that challenges the status quo, subtext must carry the issues, wants, and needs of characters who are not free to voice what they really mean or want to say. Some writers introduce alcohol, drugs, or extreme situations that lower the characters' inhibitions, enabling them to speak more freely, but these devices may not draw the desired attention to the social, political, economic, and physical restraints experienced by subordinated people. Some playwrights have experimented with alternative structures, non-realism, and non-traditional staging in their efforts to bring attention to long-silenced subtexts.

Feminist playwright Bryony Lavery believes that conventional language can no longer express the truth of women's experience. Lavery invents words for her women characters or has them utter a collection of sounds:

> There's something about the characters trying to find the language to express that anger or that hurt or that love, and they need new words for it.[11]

Writing Exercise: Add Subtext

Choose a recognized play with a fairly large and varied cast. Plays written at least fifty years ago work best. Look through the script to identify: 1) characters who appear, but don't speak; 2) servants who are not comic leads; and 3) women whose roles serve the male protagonist's plot. Write monologues for several of these characters in which they speak to the audience, giving their true thoughts and ideas about the main plot, their own status in life, their aspirations. Assume that anything they say in the script is designed to mollify those in power and does not necessarily represent their secret thoughts.

How could this material be included in a realistic play? If your preferred style is realism, might you consider modifying the structure of your play to incorporate non-realistic elements? Note that many critically-acclaimed plays, including Caryl Churchill's *Cloud 9* and Branden Jacobs-Jenkins' *An Octoroon*, mix realism with non-realistic elements that provide opportunities for dissent and commentary.

A number of the improv exercises that follow, including **Asides**, **Hot-seating**, and **One Word Scenes** will provide additional opportunities to explore the secret thoughts of characters who might not otherwise articulate their thoughts.

Inside Information

In *The 90-Day Play*, playwriting professor Linda Jenkins notes, "Often a person's first impression masks something very different within. Give your characters opportunities to shed masks and surprise with what they reveal."[12]

With **Asides**, the player volunteers information drawn from a character's inner monologue, or subtext, at a given moment in the scene. In **Hot-seating**, other participants quiz or even interrogate the character, actively seeking to find the truth behind the mask. **Hot-seating** helps actors flesh out a character's backstory or may inspire a playwright to add detail and dimension to a character.[13]

For the playwright, improv games and scenes can embody the way subtext may be masked but still be visible to the audience. Experiencing this type of game provides insight on the stress of maintaining a public persona while hiding a private passion.

Asides

Improv Exercise

Establish a scene with two or more players where the characters know one another. After the first few moments, any player can stop the scene by shouting "Freeze!" The other performers must freeze the action while Player A (who shouted "Freeze!) steps out of the scene. Staying in character, Player A reveals what the character was really thinking at that moment in the scene. Player A steps back into the frozen tableau, and the scene continues as if there had been no interruption. The previously frozen characters have *not* heard Player A's in-character confession to the audience, but the *players* have heard it, and the information may affect the scene. The secret becomes a significant part of the character's subtext.

Other players may also shout, "Freeze!" and add their characters' personal confessions to the subtext of the scene. Note how the establishment of a secret subtext may change the whole demeanor of the character in that scene.

If your play is realistic, take time to consider what each character is *not* saying and include some of the behaviors revealed through the improv in your stage directions. Good actors with a good director will find many of these moments on their own, but a good playwright will provide specific moments where the audience has the pleasure of noticing something unspoken.

Written Exercise

Write a realistic scene between two characters who have a complex history together. Set the scene at a formal occasion in which both characters have stakes. For example, divorced parents at their daughter's wedding. (You may also choose a scene from the play you are currently writing in which the characters cannot speak freely.) Write the scene with realistic dialogue. Then go back and add "asides" in which the characters speak to the audience to express their unspoken feelings. Read that version aloud. Go back and remove the asides, but think carefully about what additional clues, pauses, actions, or nuances you might add to bring out the subtext revealed by the asides.

Hot-seating

Improv Exercise

This exercise is usually done with actors who have established a character in a scene or play and have a pretty good handle on the public face, or mask, of that character. A chair is placed in the center of the rehearsal space, and the designated player must sit there alone. The other participants ask questions, as if they are reporters at a press conference. This may be done with the whole class or cast. Alternatively, the playwright or director may serve as the primary questioner. This exchange may resemble a lawyer cross-examining a witness, a detective grilling a suspect, or a therapist analyzing a client.

In the hot-seat, characters will be asked about their history and quizzed about their actions, motivations, and emotions. The character may resist at first and may struggle to maintain a mask, but ultimately must tell the truth as far as the player knows it. If the details are unknown, the player is free to invent a story which may later be adopted as the "real" one. After hot-seating, the player returns to the scene in progress with new insights on the character's subtext and motivation that should come through in performance.

Written Exercise

Free-write an imaginary scene in which one of your important characters is interrogated. The questioner wants to know not only *what* this character has done, but *why* they did it and how they *feel* about it. Give the interrogator the ability to make this character crack a bit, revealing a truth they might not even have fully realized. Read the scene aloud. Consider how you might find ways for this truth to be revealed to the audience within the reality your play has established. Perhaps there will only be hints or clues of this in the dialogue, but the script will be richer for that layer of subtext.

Exploring the Non-Verbal

While words are the playwright's primary stock in trade, award-winning Australian playwright, Timothy Daly, warns against "over-writing," or "the putting into language of feelings, emotions, thoughts, actions, and ideas that *can be expressed in other ways*."[14] An effective script is built on a deeper level of thought, emotion, and desire that must be communicated and understood obliquely. This exercise points out the potential for using fewer words and how important it can be to "show" rather than "tell."

One Word Scenes

Create a scene between two characters who know each other, where each player's lines consist of a single word. Character A begins with a one-word line and may not speak again until after Character B has responded with one word. The lines should feel natural at one word, and players should not try to telegraph the rest of a sentence or speak as if they were interrupted. Players should, however, take full advantage of the open space and silences to express their characters in non-verbal ways. The same exercise can be repeated with scenes limited to lines of two, three, or other designated number of words per line. Or each player may be assigned a different word limit. An improvised conversation between a character who speaks in ten-word sentences and one who responds with three words at a time demonstrates the way speech rhythms define and distinguish different personalities.

Written Exercise

Free-write a dialogue between two characters with specific word limits. Generate additional sketches to explore other habits of speech, including vocabulary, catch-phrases, and idiosyncratic imagery, then craft a scene between the two characters with the most distinctive voices.

Pausing for Reflection

Director, performer, and legendary experimental playwright Jean-Claude van Itallie advised playwrights not to rush through silent moments on stage:

> 'Listen' to characters even when they're not speaking. Characters don't need to be constantly talking. Meaning can make itself felt in silence ... 'Listen' not only to the music of your characters' voices, but for the tone of 'where they're at.' If you respect and listen to your characters, so will the audience.[15]

The Playwright's Process author Buzz McLaughlin discusses the particular importance of pauses and silence for the depiction of realism:

> [I]t's during pauses that the most profound glimpses into subtext can occur. Often the most important moment in a scene is during

the silence that ensues after a poignant line, the moment when a profound decision or realization is made. The audience witnesses this happening during the silence.[16]

The choice to pause in the midst of a scene or speech has traditionally been part of an actor's arsenal of style. Most dramatic texts before the advent of realism did not feature a separate subtext. Instead, characters in classical theatre and melodrama speak their thoughts aloud in articulate soliloquies. Notice how redundant it becomes when an actor playing Hamlet, for example, pauses to "think" before saying "To be or not to be"—since the very lines themselves *are* his thought process.

Harold Pinter and Samuel Beckett famously pioneered the stylized use of pauses in absurdist texts. But dramatic realism depends on the tension between public face and private thought. Playwrights from Anton Chekhov to Annie Baker have included strategic pauses in their scripts, while other playwrights have devised new terms for specific periods of silence that speak volumes. Suzan-Lori Parks inserts the stage direction (*Rest.*) and Lynn Nottage writes (*A moment.*) to provide those "glimpse[s] into subtext" that connect so powerfully with the audience.

The following is an adaptation of an exercise by Improv Teacher and Applied Improv Consultant, Kat Koppett.

Pause Button

Improvisers create a scene in which each player pauses (as if someone had pushed a "pause button") for at least ten seconds between every line of dialogue. The character is not frozen during each pause, but remains engaged and open to thoughts, feelings, and impulses that come to mind. The character may have a new insight, decide to explore the surrounding space, struggle with what to say next, or simply space out – any choice will add dimension both to the character and to the scene.

Written Exercise

Experiment with a scene in a play you are currently working on or free-write any scene between two characters. Add the stage direction [*pause*] at the end of each line of dialogue. Add stage directions that happen during some of the pauses. For example,

Irina slowly walks across the room and stares out the window or *With shaking hands, Masha lights a cigarette and takes a slow drag.* Adding the stage direction [*silence*] usually implies a longer pause that engages all characters on stage. A [*silence*] is rarely accompanied by other stage business. For example, *Stanley opens a beer with his teeth and drinks the whole bottle. [Silence] They stare at one another.* Consider what subtext is going on for each character during silent moments. Write your scene with characters responding to each other's [silence] as if they could hear the subtext. Consider the impact and meaning of the silences as they affect the dialogue.

Variation: Pause Button Ding

While two players improvise a scene, another player may ding a bell (or say the word "ding") every time they want the improvisers to insert a pause. Players must *justify* each pause before continuing.

Written Exercise Two

Note the way each [*pause*] affects meaning. Take the scene you used for the first version of the exercise and experiment with different placements of pauses. You might insert a [*pause*] whenever there is a beat shift in the dialogue. Read this version aloud and consider how it differs from the one with a pause at the end of each line. Go back to the scene again, and this time add a [*pause*]—or a longer [*silence*] at random points in the dialogue without considering the smooth development of subtext. Read the text aloud. Does the unexpected open space point to new interpretations that enrich the scene?

Many actors and directors will find meaningful pauses in the dialogue on their own, though others may not. Think carefully about the use of stage-directed pauses and include them only when the pause or silence is essential to your vision of the scene.

Indirect Communication

Whenever the communication between characters is indirect, a variety of actors' tools come into play to keep the audience connected. Someone washing dishes may speak in cheerful tones about a housemate. But the audience will note the angry way they handle the dishes, soap, and towel. Writing dialogue for characters sharing an intimate scene can be especially challenging for the playwright. Playwright Jean-Claude van Itallie points out a common mistake:

> Exchanges between intimates are rarely about intimacy. People who know each other will often use few words ... An exchange about a mundane matter may be full of feeling. People may talk about a broken refrigerator while their tone, rhythm, and pitch may reveal lust, love, contempt, or fury.[17]

Using improv, playwrights can experiment with ways that the actor's body and actions can communicate one thing, even as the words and tone profess something very different.

Relationship/Activity

This classic exercise can be done with a pair of players. Player A begins a scene by establishing a *sustainable* activity to maintain throughout the scene. This can be a complex activity, such as cooking dinner or gardening, but should not be so arduous (i.e., push-ups) as to interfere with conversation.

Version One

Player B initiates a scene entirely focused on the two characters' relationship. Player B may watch or even participate in the activity but must *not* talk it. The scene is *not about the activity*.

Player A interacts with Player B but *must continue* the activity throughout. There will be a temptation to drop the activity in order to interact more intimately, but that impulse must be resisted. This is not the only way such a scene could unfold, but it serves to illustrate the meanings expressed through action rather than words. How does Player A begin to express emotion through the activity? Does Player A use the activity to resist Player B's personal approach?

Version Two

The same pair should repeat the same activity and relationship. But in this version, both players will *only* talk about the activity without directly mentioning the relationship issues. At the same time, those issues should remain as *subtext* for the scene. Explore ways that a conversation about gardening, for example, can reveal the dynamics of a relationship and even the specifics of a conflict.

Writing Exercise

Free-write several quick sketches in which two characters are engaged in a shared chore or other mundane project. Write dialogue with subtext that deliberately provides future actors with juicy opportunities for comical, seductive, or threatening innuendo. Designate pauses that call for silent reaction and realization for the characters.

A Few Last Thoughts

Theatre is a collaborative art in which actors, directors, designers, crew, and audience all contribute to "that rich stew of intellectual and emotional 'stuff' always just under the surface" that Buzz McLaughlin calls "subtext." He urges playwrights to invite their audiences to participate:

> Forced to engage actively with the play to get the whole story, the audience makes their own connections between the surface and what lies underneath."[18]

The improvisational approach outlined in this chapter is designed to assist playwrights, performers, and directors in discovering, understanding, and embodying a complex collection of intersecting subtexts that illuminate and deepen a script in production.

In *Playwriting: Structure, Character, How and What to Write*, influential British playwright Stephen Jeffreys encourages writers to explore subtext through free-writing "the way an actor might discover [subtext] through improvisation."[19] As a playwright, you can discover techniques for communicating subtext by playing some of the improv games listed here. You might play them yourself or have the actors play them in character at a reading or rehearsal of your play.

Plays that provide a strong but flexible framework for the exploration and discovery of subtextual meaning are the texts that last—even as that "meaning" shifts and transforms over time. The play's the thing—the time and the place—where we can explore, discover, and improvise together.

Notes

1 Quoted in Worthen, p. 80.
2 Quoted in Borny, p. 89.
3 Carnicke, p. 20.
4 Martini, p. 196.
5 Downs and Russin, p. 146.
6 Clark, p. 76.
7 Similar guessing games that play with subtext include Party Quirks and the Dating Game (see the Encyclopedia of Improv Games http://improvencyclopedia.org)
8 Dunne, p. 183
9 Daly, p. 188.
10 P. 145.
11 Quoted in Stephenson, p. 110.
12 Jenkins, p. 39.
13 The term *hot-seating* came out of the drama in education literature. An early mention of this title appears in Jonathan Neelands and Tony Goode's book *Structuring Drama Work*.
14 Daly, p. 156.
15 Van Itallie, p. 116–117.
16 McLaughlin, p. 180.
17 Van Itallie, p. 113.
18 McLaughlin, p. 169.
19 Jeffreys, p. 184.

References

Borny, Geoffrey. *Interpreting Chekhov*. ANU Press, 2006.
Carnicke, Sharon Marie. "Stanislavsky's System: Pathways for the Actor" in *Twentieth Century Actor Training*, Alison Hodge, Ed. Routledge: New York, 2000.
Clark, Leroy. *Writing for the Stage: A Practical Playwriting Guide*. Pearson Education Inc.: New York, 2006.
Daly, Timothy. *21st Century Playwriting: A Manual of Contemporary Techniques*. Smith and Kraus: Hanover, NH, 2019.
Downs, William Missouri and Robin U. Russin. *Naked Playwriting: The Art, the Craft and the Life Laid Bare*. Silman James Press: Beverly Hills, CA, 2004.
Dunne, Will. *The Dramatic Writer's Companion*. U Chicago P: Chicago, 2009.
Encyclopedia of Improv Games. http://improvencyclopedia.org
Improv Does Best. https://improvdoesbest.com/2013/02/21/emotional-subtext-exercises/

Jeffreys, Stephen. *Playwriting: Structure, Character, How and What to Write.* Theatre Communications Group: New York, 2009.

Jenkins, Linda. *The 90-Day Play.* L.A. Writers' Lab. Los Angeles: 90-Day Novel Press, 2017.

Johnstone, Keith. *Impro for Storytellers.* Routledge: New York, 1999.

Koppett, Kat. *Training to Imagine.* Stylus Publishing: Sterling, VA, 2012.

Martini, Clem. *The Blunt Playwright.* Playwrights Canada Press: Toronto, 2019.

McLaughlin, Buzz. *The Playwright's Process: Learning the Craft from Today's Leading Dramatists.* Back Stage Books, New York, 1997.

Smiley, Sam. *Playwriting: The Structure of Action.* Prentice-Hall: Englewood Cliffs, New Jersey, 1971.

Stephenson, Heidi. *Rage and Reason: Women Playwrights on Playwriting.* Methuen Drama: London, 2014.

Van Itallie, Jean-Claude. *The Playwright's Workbook.* Applause: New York, 1997.

Worthen, W.B. *Modern Drama and the Rhetoric of Theatre.* University of California Press: Berkeley, 1992.

3 Using Improv to Create Original Plays
Respectfully Writing Diverse Characters

Stephanie Rae

Introduction

As a Black woman who has been performing, teaching, and directing improvisational theatre for more than ten years, I have felt both the positive impact of seeing and playing diverse characters onstage and the painful realization that people like me are not always considered a part of the worlds being created around me. As the founder of an arts organization called the Black Improv Alliance, I have regularly participated in creating new improv theatre games or adjusting existing ones to reflect my perspective as a Black improviser. And as a long-time educator and former college professor, I have frequently used applied improvisation to help students think creatively in the classroom. In this chapter, I will provide applied-improv based exercises which can be used in playwriting to start the brainstorming process, write diverse characters with authentic voices, and check for cultural competence in the revision process—with a particular focus on race.

Diverse cultural representation (or a piece's lack thereof) is an essential factor to consider when creating a play. Culture can be drawn from race, gender, age, religion—or other elements which contribute to a person's life experiences and worldview—and will be either reflected or repressed onstage. While white characters are regularly written with diverse interests and personalities, characters of the global majority (also called POC or BIPOC) have frequently been written as stereotypical caricatures. Significant progress has been made in recent years, but it's still essential for student playwrights to be educated in the importance of respectfully writing diverse characters. Because culture is not a monolith and stereotypes are not "character development," all playwrights and theatre makers must challenge themselves to create non-white characters with diverse interests and worldviews.

DOI: 10.4324/9781003243014-4

Brainstorming to Begin the Writing Process

You Know That Thing?

(two to twenty people)

Origin of the Exercise

- This game was created by the author, inspired by an unnamed warm-up from Kat Kenny of Kat Kenny Improv and Actor's Rep Theatre. In the warm-up, participants were broken into small groups, given the name of a nonexistent short-form improv game, and instructed to create the rules of and play the game in the moment.

Objective

- This exercise gets writers out of their overthinking, pre-editing brains and into a place of letting ideas flow freely without judgment.

What We Need

- This works best when players stand in a circle, facing one another.
- For this exercise, it's great to have an upbeat song playing in the background.

How We Get There

- This is a two-part exercise which involves movement and spontaneous brainstorming.
  Part One, *You Know That Dance?*, requires players to take on the role of choreographers, creating dance moves off the tops of their heads. Person A calls on another person by name and suggests the name of a made-up dance. Person B accepts the offer by teaching the dance to the group.
- Part Two, *You Know That Play?*, requires players to provide a short summary of a non-existent play based on a fictitious title. Person A calls on another person by name and suggests the name of a fictitious play. Person B accepts the offer by providing a brief plot description.

The scripts go as follows:

Part One—You Know That Dance?

- Person A: Hey, _____, you know that dance, the _____?
  The key is for no one to overthink. Rather than trying to be clever, Person A should quickly come up with a name, any name, for a fictional dance. It can be "The potato" or the "I don't know what to say!"
- Person B: Of course, I know the _____. It goes like this.
  Person B should enthusiastically accept and affirm the offer, create a simple and repetitive dance move, and teach it to the group. All other players should dance along.
- After the group does the dance move together, a new round starts with Person B becoming Person A and calling on someone else.

Part Two—You Know That Play?

- Person A: Hey, _____ you know that play, _____?
- Person B: Of course, I know _____. That's the one about _____.
- Then Person B calls on someone else.

A variation: rather than a single Person A, one person might contribute the names of and relationship between two main characters, another person might say where the play is set, another person might share the play's most famous line of dialogue, etc. Then Person B gives an improvised summary of a play that includes all of those elements.

Spoken Word

(one to twenty people)

Origin of the Exercise

This piece is exactly what it sounds like, an improvised spoken word jam. It is a completely free-form game.

Objectives

- Focus on fully letting go of the temptation to plan.
- Find the "right" words in the moment instead of trying to secure them ahead of time.

- Use the exercise to explore themes and elements of plays-in-progress.

What We Need

- While the game can be played solo, group play adds an element of encouragement.
- This is most fun with some instrumental smooth jazz playing in the background.
- An online suggestion generator, if needed.

How We Get There

- Players create improvised spoken word poems, based on any word that comes to mind.
- When a player is finished with their piece, they snap their fingers.
- If playing in a group, teammates snap along and affirm how amazing the poem was. Statements like, "Truth to power!" "That was incredible," and "Yes, lamps!" (if the suggestion was lamps) are highly encouraged.
- It doesn't matter how good or bad the poem was. It is the team's job to provide over-the-top praise to each poet for merely having had the courage to speak up and share ideas.
- Encourage each poet to gracefully accept the praise, as an acknowledgement that no matter how "good" a first effort or draft is, having the courage to share one's voice is always something to be proud of.

Side Coaching

The poems that players create might rhyme or they might not. They might make sense or they might not. They might be only one or two words. It does not matter. The goal here is just to say something, without having the time to plan it. And whatever is said should be delivered with confidence.

Outfit Monologues

(one to twenty people)

Objective

- This exercise challenges writers to create characters without having their race, gender, age, or other characteristics specified.

What We Need

- For solo players, have students write down five to ten accessories or items of clothing and ten to twenty adjectives on small slips of paper.
- For groups, have one person or several people suggest an article of clothing and two random adjectives.

How We Get There

- Have students fold the slips of paper or turn them face down and randomly choose one accessory/clothing item and two adjectives. For example, if the suggestions are hat, sequined, and old, the player is creating a character who wears an old, sequined hat.
- Ask students to imagine who might wear that item of clothing and what that person would be like.
- Invite students to perform improvised two to three minute monologues in character as the person who would wear that item of clothing. Have students step into the character, embodying posture, body language, and voice.

Reflection: Cultural Competency Challenge

Following the monologues, students should make notes on any themes, lines, or other moments discovered during performance. They should reflect, in writing, on any trends in the way that they imagined their characters. Were they all their same race? Gender? Age? Did they all have the same types of physical abilities? Especially if writers are members of many majority groups and consistently create characters who are reflections of themselves, have them consider what might be added to their piece by intentionally including more characters from traditionally excluded groups.

Writing Diverse Characters with Authentic Voices

These exercises can be used for writing characters based on an outline or character bio, or to gain a deeper understanding of the character during the revision process.

What You Wouldn't Guess: For Characters

(one person)

Origin of the Exercise

- This exercise was adapted from a team-building warm-up created by a software company called Modern Campus.[1]

Objectives

- To consider how characters are *perceived* by others based on their physically observable characteristics.
- To consider how others might *react to* or *judge* characters based on their appearance.

What We Need

- A list of characters.

How We Get There

- For each character in their script, playwrights should complete the following prompt and consider what fact that character would share with the others in their play:
- "My name is _____. My pronouns are _____. One thing you cannot tell just by looking at me is _____. This is important for me to tell you because _____."
- Each introduction should be about thirty seconds long, and no longer than one minute.
- An example might look like: "My name is Sheila McGee. My pronouns are she/her. I'm a partner at the law firm of Warren, Mitchell, & Morris. This is important for me to tell you because when people walk into my office building they usually assume that I'm administrative staff and this really frustrates me."
- Follow-up writing prompt: What does this character think others wouldn't guess, but the character wouldn't want to share and why?

Description Interjection

(two to five people)

Objectives

- To help playwrights discover characters' authentic voices.
- To help playwrights discover what characters need to reveal and what they need to keep hidden.
- To gain insight into how characters might see themselves differently to how they are perceived by others.
- To explore ways characters unintentionally reveal their inner motivations.

How We Get There

- Have the playwright choose a main character from their work-in-progress and answer basic descriptive questions about their looks, personality, mannerisms, attitude, perspective, and role.
- Encourage the playwright to draft and answer at least ten more detailed questions not included in a standard description. Questions might include:
  - How do they wish to be perceived?
  - What irritates them most?
  - What true things would they deny?
- Using the answers to the basic questions, have the playwright quickly free-write a one- to two-paragraph character description. It can be more detailed than what they'll provide with their script and should be brutally honest.
- Invite the playwright to give the written description to a group member to read aloud. Make sure the reader is seated.
- Instruct the playwright to leave the room, and then walk back in as the character.
- When the playwright enters the room, the reader begins to read the description in a neutral tone, exactly as written.
- The playwright, in character, should correct the reader about who they are. They should interject and react to the description in real time, stopping the reader with verbal interruptions. The reader does not respond to these interjections, but pauses to hear them and then continues reading.

- In the following example, Sheila is clearly in denial about certain areas of her life and how she may be either successfully or unsuccessfully hiding her secrets.

Sample Description

Sheila McGee is a 42-year-old Black woman who is desperately searching for a husband. She has dark brown hair, which she wears in locs, and brown eyes. She is 5'7" and always feels like she's ten pounds overweight, even though her BMI is perfectly healthy. She has struggled with her self-esteem after being left at the altar when she was twenty-five. She is an attorney who is wildly successful in the courtroom, but cannot manage to maintain healthy personal relationships. She enjoys reading trashy romance novels, hiking, and being told that she's right. She is loud and confident, but sometimes her responses are more bravado than a genuine belief in herself.

Sheila doesn't have or want children, but she isn't comfortable telling people that because they always say that she'll change her mind, and she finds that annoying. She does genuinely want to be married, though, so when asked when she's having kids, she simply says she'll start thinking about it after she's married. She doesn't tell potential partners that she doesn't want kids, because she thinks that scares men off. However, she loves being an aunt and is a frequent source of support and advice for Erin, who is her niece. When Erin gets stood up at the prom, she leaves early and goes to her Aunt Sheila's house instead of going home and disappointing her mother. Sheila is secretly pleased by this because of her rivalry with Erin's mother Eileen, but she would never say so out loud.

Sample Description with Interjections (in bold)

Sheila McGee is a 42-year-old Black woman **"Wow, so we're really just gonna tell everyone my age? Okay."** who is desperately searching for a husband. **"Um, not desperately. I'm open to it, but I'm not desperate at all."** She has dark brown hair, which she wears in locs, and brown eyes. She is 5'7" and always feels like she's ten pounds overweight, even though her BMI is perfectly healthy. **"Okay, are we just gonna criticize me this whole time? Geez."** She has struggled with her self-esteem after being left at the altar when she was twenty-five. **"Actually,**

I left him. I had already told him that I didn't think things were going to work, but he convinced me that we could work it out, and then he didn't show up in order to get revenge. But I technically broke up with him first. And I don't even think about that anymore. I am over it. Completely over it." She is an attorney who is wildly successful in the courtroom, **"Facts."** but cannot manage to maintain healthy personal relationships. **"Seriously? So you think the problem is me? Because I work really hard to support people, and I am an excellent friend. I just keep attracting flightiness into my life for some reason."** She enjoys reading trashy romance novels, **"Ok yeah, that's true."** hiking, and being told that she's right. **"Because I usually am."** She is loud and confident, but sometimes her responses are more bravado than genuine belief in herself. **"And how did you reach that conclusion? Because I actually am a confident person. I don't think you know me very well."**

Sheila doesn't have or want children, **"Nope!"** but she isn't comfortable telling people that because they always say that she'll change her mind and she finds that annoying. **"Super annoying."** She does genuinely want to be married though, so when asked when she's having kids, she simply says she'll start thinking about it after she's married. She doesn't tell potential partners that she doesn't want kids, because she thinks that scares men off. **"Uh, I don't just think that scares men off. It does. That's a fact. Have you ever dated a single, childless man over forty and told him that you don't want kids? They run. And before you tell me to just date someone who already has kids, stop right there. I don't wanna raise their kids either."** However, she loves being an aunt and is a frequent source of support and advice for Erin, who is her niece. **"Well, I do like teenagers. And she's family."** When Erin gets stood up at the prom, she leaves early and goes to her Aunt Sheila's house instead of going home and disappointing her mother. **"I don't blame her. Eileen can be very judgmental."** Sheila is secretly pleased by this because of her rivalry with Erin's mother Eileen, **"What? I was not secretly pleased. I was just happy to be there for my niece. And I do not have a rivalry with Eileen. We have had some minor disagreements, but I wouldn't call it a rivalry."** but she would never say so out loud.

"Because it's not true. Whoever wrote this description really doesn't know me at all. Well, maybe a little. Some parts of it were true. But a lot of it is wrong. I'm very confident, I love my sister, and I am nowhere near desperate for a husband. I'm just... ready. That's all."

Side Coaching

- If the writer would like a record of the discoveries made during this exercise, a volunteer may record audio or take notes.
- In groups of more than three people, encourage writers to request feedback from others about what they heard in the description versus what they heard and saw from the character.
- If working solo, a writer can play both parts—reading the description and pausing to interject in character. The most important thing is to note what the character protests and/or tries to hide.
- If the character absolutely would not verbally interrupt the reader, have the playwright take notes on what the character would think and feel as they hear the description read.

Reflection: Cultural Competency Challenge

After completing this part of the exercise, writers can revise the written character description, considering the following to check their understanding and appreciation of diverse character creation:

- If they were to do the interjection part of this exercise again, but change only the character's physical description, how would their reactions change?
- If they played the character as an Asian woman, did they suddenly become meek and quiet? If they played the character as a Black woman, were they suddenly loud and sassy? If so, they are playing into stereotypes.
- Consider that changing a character's race doesn't have to mean changing their voice, mannerisms, etc., but do look for how experiences might legitimately be different. For instance, if Sheila is a white woman, she might have more to say about her choice to wear her hair in locs. If Sheila is in a wheelchair, she might interject to describe the challenges of hiking with a physical disability.

Scene Three Ways with Diverse Characters

Origin of the Exercise

- Scene Three Ways is a popular short-form improv game which is said to have been inspired by the classic Japanese film *Rashomon*. Its exact origins are unclear, but I first learned it from a Miami-based troupe called Impromedy and have now adapted it for playwrights.

Objectives

- Explore the same scene from multiple points of view.

What We Need

- A pivotal scene from a work-in-progress.

How We Get There

- Choose a group which has been historically excluded from the greatest benefits of the society in which you grew up.
- Rewrite a pivotal scene from your play so that all main characters are now members of that group.
- For any ways in which the scenes change, cite factual research and your sources.

Reflection: Cultural Competency Challenge

A scene in which a main character is pulled over by the police will likely have a different tone if it's rewritten with a protagonist who is American and Black instead of white. This is appropriate because statistics and facts about the hazards of driving while Black support the idea that the Black character might react differently. On the other hand, if you are rewriting a scene with Black characters and the scene is about an engagement party, the scene may not need to change at all. If it does, ensure that any changes you make are based on research rather than stereotypes.

After rewriting their scenes, playwrights should reflect on the following:

- If most or all of the main characters in their play are white, is whiteness an essential part of their play? Or are they simply reflecting what they find most familiar?
- Research the benefits of diverse representation in media and consider how adding characters of different races might provide additional material and context for important plot points.

Conclusion

Although respectfully writing diverse characters can be challenging, doing so is incredibly worthwhile. By creating stories and characters with worldviews beyond their own, playwrights create opportunities for more audience members to connect with their work.

These exercises are a starting point for diverse playwriting, but they should by no means be the only methods of seeking cultural competency; this work must be considered in every step of the play production process. Great playwrights throughout history have opposed society's worst norms, and the next generation can continue this legacy of progress with plays which intentionally include members of traditionally excluded communities.

Note

1 https://sapro.moderncampus.com/blog/7-easy-activities-that-encourage-students-to-open-up-about-identity-and-privilege

4 Character's *Search for Authenticity*

Improvisation for the Revision Process

Muneeb ur Rehman

Introduction

Writing a stage play is an opportunity like none other to explore and push boundaries of cultural, political, and historical meaning with new stories for a live audience. Your introspective wonderment inspires you to undertake such a creative opportunity; however, the muse's call comes with challenges. The hard labor of a first draft peaks with a series of disconsolate realizations, such as inconsistent themes, shallow characters, or structure that is all over the place. Despite scrambling to solder loose ends alone, a sinking feeling roils in your gut that your creative output is not polished enough, not worthy of sharing for a read, let alone stage-ready for an audience.

A play is for *communal* consumption, so why can't its composition benefit from *communal* collaboration, especially the arduous stage of revision? A first draft may germinate from solitary seeds, but an improvisational hive-mind of peers and colleagues can help a playwright revise more effectively.

Since my foray into improvisational theatre in 2014 as a performer, a basic tenet that has remained foundational for me across its myriad forms is authenticity. The benefits of deeper self-awareness and creative possibilities that come with improvisation gradually led me to explore its applications in schools, communities, and wellness spaces. In 2017–18, when a psychotherapist and I conducted improv/therapy workshops around the theme of "love," participants fluidly explored and expressed their pain around different forms of love in their lives and transformed them, quite organically, into personally derived actionable insights that made them more at ease with themselves.

Encouraged by the utility of improvisation at such a deep and personal level, I continued to explore in my teaching, with non-actors in applied drama and budding actors in the theatre, methods to pursue

DOI: 10.4324/9781003243014-5

personal authenticity through interfaces of therapy and improvisation. While researching psychotherapy scholarship to this end, I came across Claire Hill's three-step framework of psychotherapy. Hill's steps—Exploration, Insight, and Action—are non-sequential stages in a therapeutic relationship between therapist and client, whereby a therapist takes a client through *exploration* of their thoughts, feelings, and narratives to identify their "innate Blueprint," a set of personal potentialities that can be developed[1] but are latent or untapped. From *exploration* emerges *insight*, a shift in perspective or a gain in new understanding of problems, that promotes corrective *action* that leads to desirable change.[2]

Hill's steps follow the same directional process I encountered in my workshops and teaching related to personal authenticity. Characters' struggles to self-actualize, in encounters with themselves and the world, are their *search for authenticity*. This struggle, this search, is true, at a basic level, for every individual, every character, real or fictional. With the lens of *search for authenticity*, richer, more authentic characterization can be achieved in revision.

This chapter offers improvisational exercises along four dimensions of a character's development—existential, past, relationship, and psychological—to establish their *search for authenticity* in the revision stage. Drawing from Hill's model, the framework of improvisation exercises applies the therapeutic approach of helping clients achieve fulfillment in their lives to fictional characters pursuing authenticity in a dramatic story.

Notes for the Facilitator

In a group of playwriting-improvisers, clear decision-making is necessary to move forward in the creative revision process. An individual, referred to here as Head Writer, should guide the process. This approach assumes playwriting-improvisers have a baseline level of experience with long-form improvisation, including "tagging," as well as prior acting experience. Ideally, the group of playwriting-improvisers should remain together for the duration of the revision process.

Some Definitions

Protagonist: In this case, any character under the playwright's focus, not necessarily the leading character of the story. All exercises can be repeated with a focus on different characters.

Side coaching: Prompts or suggestions provided by the facilitator during a scene.

Shadowing: An improviser "shadows" another improviser's character during a scene, playing their essence, id, subtext, or internal representation as the scene plays out.

Multi-Player Shapeshifting: Each tag-in by a player continues the same character, allowing the entire ensemble to contribute to construction of a character's monologue or response to a prompt.

Hemingway: A player narrates the story in addition to playing a character in the scenes.

Split Scenes: Two scenes from different time zones or places play side-by-side on stage.

Posthumous Scene: Set in the future after a protagonist's hypothetical death.

Oscar Moment: Side coaching prompt that invites a player to explore and heighten the in-moment emotional point of view.

Conversational Scene: Centers around conversation between two characters, and does not have to involve movement and object work.

I. Existential Focus

Objectives

To discover the protagonist's innate blueprint from four existential concerns:

- Death anxiety
- Sense of freedom
- Isolation from others and the world
- Meaning in life

Dramatist's Focus

This can be used as an anchoring exercise at different stages of the revision process. Each iteration of this will update and refine the character's innate blueprint. Identify "moments of significance" from the first draft where the character's existential concerns can shed light on their thoughts, actions, attitudes, and words. This can reveal perspectives on specific conflicts, decisions, regrets, and crisis in the protagonist encounters in the play.

Mortality Echo

Origin of the Exercise

- An original exercise exploring consequences of the protagonist's hypothetical death.

Objective

- To specify post-death consequences of the protagonist's decisions in the lives of fellow characters.

What We Need

- First draft has been read by the group.

How We Get There

- Assign roles to each actor.
- Begin a "moment of significance" in the play where the protagonist has to make a difficult decision that challenges their status quo.
- Head Writer calls *Freeze* and a posthumous scene involving the same characters begins, from the same postures, sans protagonist. Head Writer calls *Scene* when the impact of the protagonist's decision is clear from other characters' behaviors.

Time Dash Variation

- Head Writer calls *Freeze* with specific time prompts into the future, such as *a week after the protagonist's death, a year after, ten years after.*

Split Scene Variation

- Assign two groups with the same characters, one on stage right, the other stage left.
- One group plays the "moment of significance" scene with the protagonist in it.
- Other group plays the posthumous scene, sans protagonist.
- The time dash duration should be pre-decided before the scene.
- As the split scene plays, Head Writer calls for switching between the two scenes. As one plays, the other freezes, and vice versa.
- Head Writer has discretion to let the scenes play out to see how the "moment of significance" scene and posthumous scene influence each other.

Reflection Questions

- How do time lapses influence how the protagonist's decisions impact other characters in posthumous scenes?
- How do discoveries from posthumous scenes impact the internal reasoning of the protagonist at "moments of significance" in a revised draft?

Funeral Parlor

Origin of the Exercise

- An original exercise exploring the impact of the protagonist's death on other characters in the story.

Objective

- To bring into sharp perspective the larger impact of protagonist's life.

What We Need

- First draft has been read by the group.

How We Get There

- All characters in the play make a speech at the funeral of the protagonist, regardless of whether the play involves their death or not.
- The protagonist responds as a ghost after each speech to the following prompts by Head Writer:
- "How are you remembered after death?"
  - "What is your impact after your death? How much, if at all?"
  - "What do you wish you could've changed when you were alive?"

Shape-Shifting Variation

- The protagonist can be played with multi-player shapeshifting. Multiple players tag in to continue the protagonist's response as ghost.

Reflection Questions

- How does an encounter with mortality draw out a character's innate blueprint? Describe in abstract terms, as an inchoate dream, and in concrete terms, as behaviors and goals adopted by the character.
- How can the blueprint have "presence" in the play as subtext, environment, or motif?

Resistance Traps

Origin of the Exercise

- An ensemble exercise inspired by representational possibilities of Image Theatre.[3]

Objective

- To accentuate external and internal resistances in the protagonist's awareness and pursuit of an innate blueprint.

What We Need

- First draft has been read by the group.

How We Get There

- After reading, all players build a symbolic prison around the protagonist.
- Each player lays out one external circumstance that entraps the protagonist—abusive relationship, family pressure, etc. The protagonist responds with "I can't…"
- Each player lays out one internal resistance that entraps the protagonist—guilt, shame, regret, etc. The protagonist responds with "I can't…"
- After a series of external and internal obstacles are elicited, Head Writer calls Oscar Moment. The protagonist explores and heightens his emotional point of view with a brief monologue. For example, a young army officer faces external

pressure from war preparations of his brigade and can't be with his ailing mother back home. Internally, he feels bound by patriotic duty and can't request leave.

Shapeshifting Variation

- Multiple players tag in the protagonist's Oscar Moment.

Reflection Question

- How do multiple internal resistances manifest in behaviors, interactions, and words of the protagonist in the revised draft?

Meaning Orchestra

Origin of the Exercise

- Adapted from the short-form game *Story Orchestra*.

Objective

- To evince the protagonist's personal "meaning of life."

What We Need

- First draft has been read by the group. Reflections from prior exercises consolidated.

How We Get There

- Head Writer points at a player and asks one of the questions below. The player answers as the protagonist. When the Head Writer points at another player, the first player quiets and the new player resumes the response. This continues through the series of questions.
  - Do you have something worth pursuing that you feel is bigger than yourself? That would make you feel free?
  - What are obstacles and opportunities for it?
  - If all the horrors and negatives could come true, would your purpose be still worth pursuing? Why?

- Head Writer notes biographical and emotional details from protagonist's past that point to their innate blueprint.

Reflection Questions

- If the protagonist's "meaning of life" is vague or noncommittal, what are the inhibiting factors, internal and/or external? Can the inhibiting factors be clarified as behaviors or attitudes in the revised draft?
- What is revealed from comparing the protagonist's "meaning of life" with their internal and external resistances elicited from ***Resistance Traps*** exercise? Are there any blind spots, contradictions, and/or self-delusions that the protagonist holds? How will they play out in the protagonist's character arc in the revised draft?

Next Steps for the Playwright

- Choose, distill, and consolidate generated material from each run of the exercises.
- Revisit scenarios and scenes from the first draft, considering the distilled knowledge of existential concerns. Notice shifts in urgency, cogency, clarity, resolve.
- What specific pursuits, passions, and motivations emerge in the dramatic world from clarity of existential concerns? Are they essential and intrinsic to the character in the context of the story? If yes, they are constituents of his/her innate blueprint.
- Rewrite the situation, conflict, and relationships of characters, as needed, so that the character's blueprint echoes in the dialogue and action of the revised draft.

II. Past Focus

Objectives

To explore how the protagonist's past experiences have contributed to an innate blueprint.

Dramatist's Focus

This can build backstory to explain how the protagonist's past influences the present. In exploration of past scenarios, look for moments or happenings that hint at the protagonist's initial blueprint. It can be a hunch, impulse, a dramatic incident, environmental exposure, etc. These moments can cast the present inner experience of a protagonist into sharper relief.

Tagging the Past

Origin of the Exercise

- An improvisational exploration of the past using the long-form improv device of tagging.

Objective

- To enrich characterization of the protagonist by exploring the possible origins of their innate blueprint.

What We Need

- Character arc of protagonist is known from the first draft reading.

How We Get There

- Play a scene from the first draft.
- Players can tag out any character other than the protagonist in the scene. Each tag-in should offer something from the protagonist's past.
- The scene, and any subsequent scenes, should shift in light of information revealed by any tag-in. Players should resist the urge to tag scenes frenetically for comedic effect.

Toggle Variation

- Instead of tagging to past, toggle between the present (from first draft) and past.
- Head Writer gives side coaching prompts for switching between the present and past.
- The players in the scene, except the protagonist, become different characters from the past, while initiating the new

scene from the same physical position. Revealed information from the past can intensify the present scenario and raise the stakes.

Reflection Questions

- How can revelations from the past operate as subtext in the revised script?
- How can incorporating the past into the revisions give the character a more layered inner landscape?
- What were some lyrical and textural details from the scenes that the writer can translate into factual details about the character's past?

Past Metaphors

Origin of the Exercise

- Based on the playwriting prompt of imagining a subject, such as a character or a situation, with a metaphor.

Objective

- To explore the protagonist's past for details of their innate blueprint.

What We Need

- Details of the characters' past are known from the first draft reading.

How We Get There

- Head Writer reminds the ensemble of the biographical and emotional details learned about the protagonist from *Tagging the Past*.
- The protagonist steps forward. Head Writer calls the following metaphor prompts, one by one, for each round:
  - As a landscape
  - As a stream-of-consciousness trail of their emotional history

- As an everyday object
- As an everyday place/space
- The protagonist narrates their past as each metaphor prompt.

Multi-Player Shapeshifting Variation

- Multiple players tag in as the protagonist to continue metaphorical narration of the past.

Other Characters Variation

- Other characters narrate, from their points of view, the protagonist's past as above analogies, letting their relationship dynamic with the character affect their descriptions.

Reflection Questions

- What inner world picture emerges with expanded knowledge of the protagonist's past?
- How can understanding the protagonist's past add more weight to the second draft without necessarily including or explaining factual details?

Next Steps

- Choose, distill, and consolidate generated material about the protagonist's past from each run of the exercises.
- Revisit scenarios and scenes from the first draft, rewriting with the distilled knowledge of revelations and history of the protagonist's past.
- Does specific information generated about the protagonist's past deserve separate scenes altogether in the revised narrative arc?
- What specific pursuits, passions, and motivations emerge in the dramatic world from a deeper knowledge of the protagonist's past? Are they essential and intrinsic to the character in context of the story? If yes, they are constituents of his/her innate blueprint.
- Rewrite the situation, conflict, relationships of characters, so that the character's blueprint echoes with the movement of the plot.

III. Relationship Focus

Objective

To explore the influence of the protagonist's relationships with other characters.

"You Make Me Feel" Confessionals

Origin of the Exercise

- An adaptation of the relationship-building exercise whereby both players confess as characters how the other makes them feel.

Objective

- To deepen the tacit influence of emotional exchanges between the protagonist and other characters.

Dramatist's Focus

- Head Writer can choose particular moments from the first or second draft for "You make me feel" confessionals.
- Observe the subtext that keeps the other character from immediately responding to the protagonist's "You make me feel" confessional.
- Resisting another character's "You make me feel" response immediately after the protagonist's can build meaningful tension between them.

What We Need

- Key revisions have been shared with the group, with inter-character dynamics established.

How We Get There

- Players perform a scene from the first or second draft.
- Head Writer interjects a line for the protagonist starting with "You make me feel."

- The other character pauses and responds with body language and facial expressions, without uttering any words, then continues with lines from the script.
- At another point in the scene, the Head Writer interjects a line starting with "You make me feel," spoken by the other character.
- The protagonist responds with body language and facial expressions, without uttering any words, then continues with lines from the script.

Off-Script Variation

- Other character goes off-script and improvises in response to protagonist's "You make me feel…"

Image Theatre Variation[4]

- Choose a character, along with the protagonist, whose relationship is under focus.
- Pick a moment or scenario for exploration of dramatic weight between the protagonist and the other character.
- Both the protagonist and other character shape their bodies, translating what they feel for each other at the chosen moment, into an image.
- Head Writer taps the protagonist. They respond, pointing or looking at the other character, "You make me feel…"
- Head Writer taps the other character. They respond, pointing or looking at the protagonist, "You make me feel…"

Reflection Questions

- Notice tensions emerging from the characters' confessionals for each other, and observe how they coincide or collide with the protagonist's pursuit of the innate blueprint evolving from the *Existential* and *Past* exercises.
- Does emotional content in the exchanges between the protagonist and other character reveal possible scenarios worth exploring with new and/or revised plot points?
- What is the role of the relationship between the protagonist and other character in the emotional trail of the protagonist's inner journey?

Unconditional Positive Regard

Origin of the Exercise

- An original exercise, based on Carl Rogers' concept of "Unconditional Positive Regard", an attitude of open non-judgmental care that a therapist extends toward a client in a therapeutic relationship.[5]

Objective

- To invoke a character's innate blueprint from acknowledgment and support of another's emotions.

Dramatist's Focus

- Usually an approach of therapists for clients, unconditional positive regard provides a safety net for the protagonist to be unfiltered outside the pressure or stakes of a circumstance in the dramatic world. Against a backdrop of resistances and conflicts with other characters, unconditional positive regard from a dissonant character can encourage revelations and confessions that paint the protagonist's innate blueprint clearly.

What We Need

- The protagonist's conflicts, dissonances, and relationship dynamics with another character are clear from the first or second draft reading.

How We Get There

- Head Writer briefly narrates the history of the relationship between the protagonist and another character.
- Keeping in mind all that transpired between the protagonist and the other character, two players begin a conversational scene where the latter extends an attitude of unconditional positive regard toward the protagonist.
- The protagonist improvises in response to other character's unconditional positive regard.
- The other character maintains an attitude of unconditional positive regard toward the protagonist throughout the scene.
- Roles are flipped. The protagonist maintains an attitude of unconditional positive regard toward the other character.

Reflection Questions

- How does unconditional positive regard from another character help the protagonist encounter their innate blueprint drawn from previous exercises?
- Observe the influence of the other character in the protagonist's life. Does it facilitate or inhibit awareness and pursuit of the latter's innate blueprint?
- How do other characters contribute to emotional arc of the protagonist's journey?
- What inner world picture emerges in the protagonist with greater clarity about important relationships?

Next Steps

- Choose, distill, and consolidate generated content about interpersonal dynamics of the protagonist and other characters from each run of the exercises.
- Revisit scenarios and scenes from the first or second drafts incorporating the distilled knowledge of emotional exchanges between the protagonist and other characters.
- What specific pursuits, passions, and motivations emerge in the dramatic world from the influence of the protagonist's relationships? Are they essential and intrinsic to the character in context of the story? If yes, they are constituents of his/her innate blueprint.
- Rewrite the situation, conflict, and relationships of characters, to continue developing integration of the character's blueprint.

IV. Psychological Focus

Objective

To add high-resolution depth to protagonist's interior landscape as they pursue their innate blueprint.

Dramatist's Focus

To coalesce discoveries from existential, past, and relationship explorations into a unified psychological and behavioral manifestation in the protagonist, and create a full picture of the protagonist's *search for authenticity*.

Psyche Spectrum

Origin of the Exercise

- An original exercise, based on the psychodynamic theory of personality,[6] exploring the content of the protagonist's emotional landscape.

Objective

- To broaden and deepen the interior landscape of the protagonist across the spectrum of psychodynamic variables including (from, roughly, most negative to most positive), anxiety, fear, desire, curiosity, awe, and faith.

What We Need

- First draft has been read by the group.

How We Get There

- After the draft reading, the player reading for the protagonist makes statements, starting with:
  - I am anxious…
  - I am afraid…
  - I desire…
  - I am curious about…
  - I am in awe of…
  - I have faith that…
- The experience of each variable has to be backed up by at least one circumstance and/or one relationship from the play. The circumstances and relationships can, of course, extend into more than one emotion.

Counter-Will Variation

Origin of the Variation

- Adapted from Augusto Boal's concept of Will and Counter-Will for interpretation of an actor's role.[7]

Directions

- Many times, two psychodynamic variables can be felt concurrently but in different measure. To our will, there is a counter-will, so the monologue can also begin with subordination of

one psychodynamic variable to another. Try the following prompts:
- I am anxious... but I have faith that...
- I desire... but I am afraid...
- I am curious... but I am in awe of...
• Again, the experience of each variable has to be backed up by at least one circumstance and/or one relationship. Try different combinations of psychodynamic variables together.

Scenes Variation

- The Head Writer chooses "moments of significance" from the draft.
- As improvisers play scenes, the Head Writer side coaches with psychodynamic prompts at "moments of significance."
- The protagonist breaks into a mini-monologue delineating the prompted feeling corroborated by a circumstance and/or relationship, and other characters improvise off-script in response.

Reflection Questions

- Observe if, from anxiety and fear, further negative emotions of shame, guilt, and pain also emerge. If they do, how do they link to events generated from *Past Focus* exercises?
- How do the protagonist's passions, pursuits, and motivations (the innate blueprint discovered in previous exercises) affect management of negative emotions?
- How do the protagonist's "awe" and "faith" contribute to the innate blueprint?

Polar Emotions: First Encounter with Innate Blueprint

Origin of the Exercise

- An original exercise, based on the process of exploring a client's feelings in a therapeutic relationship.

Objective

- To highlight the protagonist's first encounter with their *search for authenticity*.

What We Need

- First draft has been read by the group.

How We Get There

- This exercise intensifies a protagonist's first moment of self-awareness regarding their innate blueprint, the beginning of their *search for authenticity*. At moments of significance, which have long-term impact, a character may experience polarized emotions—emotional dyads.[8]
- Head Writer picks a "moment of significance" that challenges the protagonist.
- The protagonist plays the scene, but the Head Writer calls *freeze* at the designated "moment of significance." The protagonist breaks the fourth wall and starts a soliloquy with any of these emotional dyads:
  - I fear—I wish
  - I love—I hate
  - I'm angry—I accept
- The protagonist then returns to the scene, and other players improvise post-soliloquy.

Story Orchestra Variation

- Head Writer orchestrates a soliloquy with playwriting-improvisers, all of them responding, in turn, as the voice of the protagonist.

Reflection Questions

- The intense inner response at a "moment of significance" serves as a signal to a protagonist about their intrinsic passion, pursuit, and motivation, as well as the struggle to actualize their innate blueprint, their *search for authenticity*.
- Can the writer strengthen plot points and scenarios by raising the stakes through a focus on the protagonist's growing self-awareness of innate blueprint?
- Can this exploration of the protagonist's emotional contours guide more focused scene-writing for a revised draft?

Protagonist Hemingway

Origin

- Based on one of the rules of a very loose-structured improv format, JTS Brown.[9]

Objective

- To revisit the entire story from the perspective of the protagonist.

Dramatist's Focus

- Allow the character to be reflective at each stage of the story as they encounter their values, obstacles, relationships, and desires.
- Consider the character's lived journey in the story versus point of view as narrator of the story to explore potential perspective shifts in the play.

What We Need

- First draft has been read by the group, and the innate blueprint of the character has been clarified through prior exercises.

How We Get There

- Head Writer directs the ensemble to stop and listen whenever the protagonist breaks the fourth wall and addresses the audience.
- The protagonist introduces the play from a personal point of view, and then continues to interrupt scenes to narrate.
- Other characters stick to the first-draft script dialogue; only the protagonist can veer from the script and improvise.

Free Flow Variation

- The protagonist's narration can change the direction of upcoming scenes and veer away from the script's first draft. Other players agree to these changes and can add more, improvising in response to the protagonist's narration and dialogue.

Reflection Questions

- How does a singular focus on the protagonist's perspective open up new responses, vis-a-vis their innate blueprint, both in scenes and narration?
- In the free-flow variation, did other characters and plots change or new themes emerge that could be explored in the play's next draft?
- Can language and insights from the character's narration be worked into dialogue?
- Would the character as narrator be an effective device in the overall construction of the play?

Decision Island

Origin

- An original exercise, inspired by the dramatic device "Conscience Alley,"[10] to explore the complex internal processes involved in making critical decisions.

Objective

- To clarify/deepen/advance/enrich character's decision-making in relation to their *search for authenticity*.

Dramatist's Focus

- Can articulate resistances and obstacles to a character's choices in pursuit of authenticity.
- Can reveal stakes should those choices not be pursued.
- Can reveal doubts about character's choices.

What We Need

- First draft has been read by the group.
- The protagonist's innate blueprint and moment of crisis in the play is clear from prior exercises.

How We Get There

- Head Writer, collating new discoveries from previous exercises and in discussion with the ensemble, decides on possible decisions the protagonist can make at different stages of the story.
- Small groups of players take their places, with distance between groups. Each group of players is treated as an island, representing a decision, course of action, a potential point of no return for the protagonist.
- The protagonist moves "into" each island.
- Players on opposite sides of a Decision Island explore "what if" scenarios, and then the protagonist improvises a short monologue that sums up the choice, possible way forward, and effects on relationships and other circumstances.
- The monologue serves as an opening for a scene exploring the consequences of the decision. The process is repeated with each Decision Island.

Reflection Questions

- What language is most effective to express urgency, crossroads, resolve, confusion, hope?
- What new information about the protagonist's inner experiences emerges from the monologues?
- How does the protagonist's innate blueprint, as generated and explored through previous exercises, affect decision-making?

Next Steps

- Choose, distill, and consolidate generated content about the inner landscape of the protagonist from each run of the exercises.
- Conduct a discussion with the players about new discoveries from the improvisations.
- Choose from discussion, communally, which details from existential, past, relationships, and psychological dimensions aggregate as the protagonist's innate blueprint.
- Summate and prioritize notes for changes/additions to the protagonist's *search for authenticity* in the second draft revision.
- Keep a separate column for notes on innate blueprint, and keep revising from material generated from each run of the exercises.

- What specific pursuits, passions, and motivations emerge in the dramatic world from the protagonist's psychological exploration? Are they essential and intrinsic to the character in context of the story? If yes, they are constituents of his/her innate blueprint.
- Rewrite the situation, conflict, and relationships of characters with developing themes, so the character's blueprint echoes throughout the play.

Conclusion

In honing a protagonist's *search for authenticity* through improvisational exercises that lead to written revisions, you will likely make discoveries about other elements—plot, secondary characters, storyline, style, theme—which you should also consider in the revision process. The protagonist's *search for authenticity* through discovery and pursuit of their innate blueprint does *not* have to result in complete achievement, the supposed state of self-actualization. The protagonist's s*earch for authenticity* is a continuous search that takes new shapes and meanings with the changing circumstances of the character and the story. It is the *search* itself, and unanticipated discoveries along the way, that make a protagonist's inner drama as compelling as the outer drama, their negotiation with and navigation of the external world dramatic. As you undertake the enterprise of revising your play, brace yourself for this process, as, like in every authentic personal endeavor, it will also echo the trials and travails of your own *search for authenticity*.

Notes

1 Hill, p. 90.
2 Hill, p. 36.
3 Image Theatre is a form of theatre that explores meaning through image-making with participants' bodies, invented and popularized by Brazilian Theatre Practitioner Augusto Boal. For more information, refer to his book *Rainbow of Desire*.
4 Image Theatre is used in multiple contexts to different ends. For more information, refer to Augusto Boal's book *Rainbow of Desire*.
5 Hill, p. 34.
6 Hill, p. 212.
7 Boal, *Games for Actors and Non-Actors*, p. 43.
8 Hill, p. 154.
9 Armstrong.
10 Edmiston, p. 181.

References

Armstrong, Nick. *JTS Brown: An Improv Journey.* J.T.S. Brown: An Improv Journey - The Improv Network, 2013. https://www.theimprovnetwork.org/j-t-s-brown-an-improv-journey/.

Boal, Augusto. *Games for Actors and Non-Actors.* 2nd Ed. Routledge, 2002.

Boal, Augusto. *Rainbow of Desire.* Routledge, 1995.

Cole, Toby. *Playwrights on Playwriting.* Cooper Square Press, 2001.

Edmiston, Brian. *Transforming Teaching and Learning with Active and Dramatic Approaches.* UK: Routledge, 2014.

Hill, Clara E. *Helping Skills: Facilitating Exploration, Insight, and Action.* 5th Ed. American Psychological Association, 2020.

Welsh Jenkins, Linda. *The 90-Day Play.* 90 Day Novel Press, 2017.

Part II
Body and Mind

5 The Picture Project
Originating Story through Movement

Sarah Kozinn

Introduction

Over the years, my approach to teaching performance has become more directed towards cultivating artist-creators. I see it as my obligation to not only teach technical skills, but also to empower students to make their own work. For the students who want to become professional actors, it is important to me that they leave knowing that their creative process need not depend on being cast by someone else—especially in this new paradigm of multi-platform digital media consumption and production. It is easier than ever to get work out into the world through a large array of channels, and the means of production are much more accessible. (We can now record and edit fairly good quality movies on our smartphones, for instance.) With this landscape in mind, I want students to leave the studio envisioning themselves as creators and agents of their own artistic process, and to be able to find creative fulfillment even when they are between gigs. In many ways, it seems obligatory to teach students how to become multi-hyphenates; the boundaries between actor, writer, director, and producer do not have to be absolute.

The Picture Project is a jumping-off point for creating a larger piece through deep character exploration that encourages writers to experience themselves as performers and vice versa. The exercise uses an embodied approach to creating character through explorations of movement qualities, body comportment, and physical relationship to space to reveal how someone who moves in a particular way experiences the world. Starting with physical exploration of character, the exercise eventually leads to writing a monologue that students perform. From there, students and instructors can take the project in a myriad of directions. Currently, my class adapts their pieces into filmed adaptations.

The central idea of this work is that how we hold and move our bodies shapes our perception. During Lucid Body Actor Training at

DOI: 10.4324/9781003243014-7

the Michael Howard Studio, my teacher and creator of this method, Fay Simpson, made us consider how the way we hold ourselves—with an exploded 4th Chakra[1] (chest open) or with an imploded 1st Chakra[2] (pelvis tucked), for example—is the armor we put on to survive in the world. Using this idea, then, we can approach character forensically, examining physical cues to piece together the story of a particular person. We can identify her armor, and then creatively explore the need for protection. The armor can tell us who this person is. Someone whose shoulders turn in and who holds their arms around their chest may be protecting their heart or grieving. I can speculate that this protection may have come from an early rejection, but then I go deeper by putting that shape into my own body. When I turn my shoulders in and wrap my arms around myself, I feel like I am shielding myself from something. What could that be? Why? I then can write from this point of view, creating scenes and worlds that were seeded from an embodied experience. That is the initial framework for the exercise.

Origins

The Picture Project originated in a need to find ways into character that had their starting point in physicality, rather than psychology. I found great freedom in methods I studied such as Lucid Body work, Meyerhold's Biomechanics, Viewpoints, Laban Analysis, Rasa Boxes, and Balinese dance and puppetry. What all of these had in common was an awareness of one's body in space, that movement has meaning, and an attention to the way movement can stir up a host of emotions, experiences, and revelations.

Approaching character through physical explorations has always been a central component in my classes, but the current iteration of *The Picture Project* evolved after coming across Larry Schreiber's "Spoon River Exercise" in his book *Acting: Advanced Techniques for the Actor, Director, and Teacher*. In this exercise, students read *The Spoon River Anthology*, a poetry collection by Edgar Lee Masters that tells the stories of a town's deceased citizens, and pick one of the poems to perform as the character in the poem. Because these are short poems, the actors must do the legwork of creating backstories, conducting research on the time period, and accessing the "character's psychological and emotional base."[3] The actors use the poems to mine the given circumstances of the characters' lives and imagine what their characters want. Actors look for the "compelling emotion" behind the characters, and that becomes the core of everything the characters experience. Once they have done their analysis, they let the poetry work on them, experiencing these words now loaded with knowledge of exactly why they are said.

I wanted to see what would happen if, instead of beginning with words—with a poem being the engine of discovery—we begin with something else. I thought of Roland Barthes' *Camera Lucida* and his description of the "punctum," the thing in a photo that "pricks" the viewer: "A photograph's *punctum* is that accident which pricks me (but also bruises me, is poignant to me)."[4] It is totally subjective, personal, even private, and completely undeniable. What if we start from there? What if we begin from this point of bruising, of pricking—from a subjective response to visual stimulation? What if the beginning source of inspiration for character creation could come from an untapped source, a nascent feeling awoken by this visual?[5] The visuals I landed on were documentary photographs, and the process unfolded like this: Find a photo that "pricks," explore the subject of the photograph, put yourself into the person's physical posture, shape, and comportment, and then develop the language the character uses to express wants and desires. This is basis of *The Picture Project*.

Why a photo?

Artists for millennia have employed ekphrasis, using one art form to illuminate a piece of art from another, and it is not uncommon to find photographs as the source material for a play.[6] Playwright Maria Irene Fornes often used photographs to inspire story, inviting the images to spur her and her students' imaginations as they crafted their plays.[7] I assign documentary style photographs because one can easily recognize that there is an actual person, caught in a particular moment in time, who may or may not still be alive, but who nonetheless existed. The circumstances surrounding the image are real, material, and consequential.[8] I find that I can more easily persuade students to find the truth in the subject's worlds and avoid caricatures, especially for students new to writing and acting. Even though the students imagine the given circumstances for everything that is beyond the frame, I situate the exercise as a kind of resurrection of this person during which the students are trying to be as faithful as possible to them. By doing one's best to get to know this person without judgment, meaning they are writing *as* this person and not *about* this person, the actor's writing and performance can develop a deep respect for the subject, even if that person is someone the student imagines makes bad choices or does heinous things to hurt someone else.[9] Of course, this does not mean that they cannot dream big and expand, but they have to ground the story of this person's life in the truth of the circumstances they deduce from the image.[10] For example, if the actor recognizes a look of defiance in the eyes of the subject and surrounding the person is broken furniture, torn documents, and a police officer, the actor may not know what exactly just happened, but they can intuit from the person's look that they are defying something; perhaps it is the authority figure or some kind of expectation they are resisting. The actor will never know exactly what this is about (dramaturgical research may help them flesh out some of the circumstances), but they can lean into the truth of the feeling they recognize in that person's eye, and imagine everything else from there, returning to the clues in the picture to validate their creative impulses.

Physical Preparation

To prepare the class for the exercise, spend time building physical awareness as a group. For the goal of developing proprioception and kinesthetic awareness, I lead students through ensemble-building exercises informed by *Viewpoints*.[11] After ensemble work, I turn the class's attention to gesture work by bringing in modern dance instructor Francisco Martinez, who works with a method developed by choreographer Alwin Nikolais. While Nikolais may be best known for decentralizing movement (and the dancer/actor), most relevant for this work is his emphasis on conveying meaning through movement. In Martinez's adaptation of Nikolais techniques, he leads the students through movement isolations, followed by exercises that ask the students to apply metaphor, symbols, abstractions, and words to movement. For example, he may have students randomly select from a stack of descriptive words and translate their chosen words into qualities of movement. The words reflect tempo, shape, and texture; a student might select "lugubrious," "jagged," and "languid." Martinez layers on "expansion" and "contraction," so movement sequences incorporate these qualities as transitions. After students embody their selected words in movement sequences, they draw or write in order to record abstract ideas and impulses, reinforcing the connection between physicality and psychology. Martinez's work resonates well with Michael Chekhov's physical-psychological exercises.[12] For example, in Chekhov's work with "Action with qualities," actors explore the influence of descriptors on physical actions. The simple addition of "with caution" changes not only an actor's movement but the experience of the movement. "Coloring" action with qualities invites feelings to arise.[13] It is important that, no matter the method an instructor uses, some experience in moving with qualities and physical expression is introduced before the exercise begins. Once the class has a basic grasp of these ideas, it is time to start.

The Picture Project

Objective: To use physical exploration to build complex written and performed characters.

1 **Read Excerpts from *Camera Lucida: Reflections on Photography***
   The objective of this step is to introduce Barthes' conception of the *punctum* in such a way that the students will be able to find a photograph that stimulates a strong and personal response. It is essential that the picture they choose can ignite their imagination and spark curiosity. Gauging their choice using the idea of *punctum* will lead them to the right selection. First, students read selected sections on their own. Have them think about an image that has "pricked" them that they can discuss. During class, read excerpts out loud, and then break into small discussion groups where they define *punctum* in their own words and share the image they thought about—if they had one. Once they understand this idea, they are ready for the next step.

2 **Photo Selection**
   Engage the class in the following questions before choosing a photo:

   - Why are we using a photo and not a painting? (See endnotes 4 and 5.)
   - Is a writer/actor's photo selection limited by his/her/their own identity? In other words, can an actor play a character that has a different gender, race, ability, or ethnicity from his/her/their own?[14]

The process of selecting a photograph to work with is personal, so this exercise should be an invitation to all artists regardless of how they identify. To do this, provide students with a list of documentary style photographers whose pictures represent people from a wide variety of subject positions. Some of those photographers may include Oscar Castillo, Nan Goldin, John Edmonds, Henri Cartier-Bresson, Michael McCoy, Daniel Arnold, Texas Isaiah, Catherine Opie, Robert Frank, Zanele Muholi, Dorothea Lange, Aston Husumu Hwang, and Diane Arbus, as well as photos from the Library of Congress Digital Collection. The above photographers and their subjects include people with a range of gender identities, ethnicities, classes, races, disabilities, and ages. After having the discussion about photo selection, emphasize that they should embody the character, not impersonate them. With the latter, the actor comments on the person being portrayed, maintaining, and even amplifying, the distance between the actor and the character. The former, embodying, implies an attempt to collapse that distance – to really act as *if* they are that person.

Then instruct students:

- Select a photo that "pricks" you.
- Make sure you can see the person's face and a significant part of their body.

Over the past eight years that I have taught this exercise, I have found it to be extraordinarily inviting to students. They can find a photo of someone like them or someone who is vastly different. Of course, there is a long history of appropriation and harmful stereotyping of people from the global majority, people with disabilities, and people with non-heteronormative or non-cisgender identities. Having transparent conversations about the work helps students play characters outside their own subject position in ways that approach character through movement and not through stereotyped impressions of what a person would do and say.

I think a lot about how the work I did with Anna Deavere Smith when I was in graduate school influences this project. She has often said that her work on verbatim theatre was influenced by something her grandfather told her: "If you say a word often enough, it becomes you."[15] Her work explores the revelation of character not only through language, but also the way language is used and what happens when language breaks down. As actors in her class, we investigated this idea by interviewing and performing the words of other people. In many ways the task was like painting a portrait, but instead of using paint, we used our voices, with language as a way to respectfully access character. In the class's final show, I performed Smith's hairdresser, Grant, a white man in his forties, who was sitting in the audience, and I remember wanting him to recognize himself in my performance. I felt profoundly close to him. This method is extremely powerful, because you get to know someone intimately by adopting their cadence and words, by using your own body and voice as a way to present another. In many ways *The Picture Project* is an experiment in discovering whether the same kind of intimate knowledge that comes from getting inside another's words can occur when adopting a character's physical expression and movements.

3 **Physical Exploration**
Objective: To make discoveries about the character through physical exploration.

Directions

- Students bring a physical copy of their photograph into class. Each student discusses what "pricked" or "bruised" them and why. Prompt students to use specific details.
- After vocal and physical warm-ups, students find a space in the room, then tape their pictures at eye level on the wall.
- Give students at least one minute of silence to study the picture. Then ask them to comport their bodies into the same position as the character, as if looking into a mirror. Coach them by asking questions: Where is there tension or ease? Where and how do they hold their weight? How do they hold their shoulders and arms? How do they hold their pelvis (tilted forward or back)? Is the person's body making curved or angled shapes—or both? Does a hip jut out to the side? How do they hold their head? Where is their center of energy? Students may be unaware of what their bodies are doing, so you can guide them into shifting their shape to better match the photo through verbal prompts or mirroring.[16]
- Once students have found their character's position, ask them what they are experiencing? What emotions, feelings, or images are coming up for them? What information are they getting about this person and their experience in and of the world?
- Give students five minutes to write down their discoveries, listing the qualities they saw in the picture and experienced living in their posture. This journaling can be in words or drawings, realistic or abstract, as long as it has meaning for them. Perhaps they discovered their character is rounded, twisted, smooth, bumpy, jagged, angled,

horizontal, vertical, spiral, diagonal, and so on, calling back the work they did during movement exercises. They can jot down associations they made or feelings they experienced. (Perhaps the experience felt like an ice cream sundae or like being a puppy. Maybe a song or specific place came into their heads. Let the ideas flow. There is no wrong idea.)

- Students return to the shape of the character for a few moments, and then they activate it. Give them fifteen minutes to move through space exploring which part of their body initiates locomotion. Once they have established a lead, coach them to integrate qualities into the movement. What does it mean to move smoothly or jaggedly? Explore tempo. At what tempo does this person move? What is their rhythm? Do they walk normally or roll or swim through the space? Experiment with levels. This is a period of discovery.
- Students return to their journals for a few moments to note any discoveries they made. What did moving like this make them experience? What did they learn about this person?

This first part of the movement work is abstract, without the desire to express a specific idea. Next, students will bring these qualities back into the everyday through movements that express distinct meanings through gesture.

- Students return to their photograph, and they determine a gesture (a movement with a beginning, middle, and end) that the character might have just made or be about to make, such as waving hello, shooing away a fly, or fixing their hair, for example. The gesture comes from the circumstances of the photograph. They explore that gesture, simply at first, and then they color it with the qualities of movement and tempo. A quick and jagged wave "hello" will be different than a slow and slippery wave.
- Once they have landed on a repeatable gesture that is executed in a way that expresses their character, they add text. What would their character say? As they wave hello, do they say, "Mom? It's me!"? Or as they fix their hair, do they say, "I look like shit"? How would they say it? Is their voice also jagged and quick? What does that sound like? This is time for exploration, and marrying voice with movement.[17]

Establishing a movement with a beginning, middle, and end that is grounded in the given circumstances of the photograph and executed while voicing the character's thoughts gets the students ready for the next stage: writing their world.

4 **Scene Detectives: Pre-Writing**
This is when students determine the who, what, where, why, and when of their scene. Have students answer the following:

- Who are you? This question narrows in as you go; start broadly and then get more specific. Some questions could be: What do you do for work/pleasure? What are your likes/dislikes? Are you married? Single? Divorced? Do you have children? Pets? How old are you? Has life been easy/hard? How do you take of yourself? Where are you from? Fill in the details. This question is ongoing, and the answers will evolve.
- Who is your character talking to? What is their relationship to this person? (It is important that the actor chooses a strong relationship to this other person. Even if it is a stranger, the stakes of the encounter need to be high. In other words, the character has to need the other person to do or say something in order to get what they want—and they have to do it now.)
- What are you doing? This has two levels. The first is what the character is actually doing in this scene. Are you folding laundry, applying makeup, waiting for an elevator, getting dressed? The second level is about what you want from the other person. What are you doing to him/her/them to get what you want? For example, are you begging for forgiveness or teaching someone a lesson? (This can be thought of as the character's objective.)
- How are you doing it? Threateningly or seductively? (This could be thought of as the tactics the character uses to achieve their objective.) This will evolve in rehearsal.
- When is this? What time of day? When in your life?
- Why? Why is this moment important? Why are you doing what you're doing *right now*? Encourage students to raise the stakes. Why must this happen now? What's at stake if the character does not get what they want?

After exploring answers to these questions on paper, students decide what just happened—not five minutes ago, but the second before the photo was taken. Think of this moment as the "catalyzing event," the thing that leads to a significant reaction, just like how baking soda added to a cup of vinegar causes an eruption. Perhaps the person you love just said "no" to your marriage proposal or your boss just told you you're promoted. The first line of text will be in response to this moment.

5 **Character Interviews**
Objective: To discover how the character interacts with others and to imagine how they respond to personal questions.

This is the first time the actors perform in character and the last step before they write their monologues. The amount of time you give each interview will depend on the size of the class. Five minutes per person is sufficient.

Directions

- Ask students to bring in essential costume pieces. For example, if the character wears heels or a hat or ill-fitting pants, the student should wear them for the exercise. Costume will help them connect with their characters.
- Have the class make a semi-circle with an empty chair for the interviewee placed in the stage area. The semi-circle creates a more supportive feeling.
- The student interviewed enters from offstage, moving as the character, and takes a seat.
- Give each student the opportunity to ask the character a question. Coach them to ask questions that will deepen the performer's understanding of who they are. After each question, the interviewee responds in character. Some questions could be connected to the character's background (Where are you from? Do you have any siblings? When was the first time you fell in love?), others to their likes or dislikes (What's your favorite food? What's your pet peeve? What's your favorite TV show?), and others can pry more deeply (What is your relationship to your father/mother? What are you most afraid of? What were the circumstances of your birth?).
- At the end of the interview, the character has to find a reason to leave, justify it, and exit. (Maybe she has a plane to catch, or he left the stove on, or they receive a text that a patient needs to see them right away.)

- Give students time to write about what they learned (or assign for homework).

At this point, the students have done a lot of discovery. To keep track and synthesize what they have learned, I ask students to create a collage for their character using a digital platform called MURAL.[18] They can add words, music, images, videos, and more to express the character's qualities, personality, needs, moods, home, and environment, and ultimately create a map of the character. The collages become references for the students, as well as a way to get ideas and feelings down in other mediums before they turn to text.

6 **Write**

Using all this information, the students begin writing a three-minute monologue. Provide the following instructions:

- The monologue has to have a beginning, middle, and end.
- There needs to be an obstacle—something you have to get past to get what you want. (If you want to borrow the car, the obstacle could be that your dad doesn't trust you and won't lend it to you.)
- There has to be an action. You have to make a choice about what your character wants. For example, your character might want to earn his/her/their father's trust.
- The first line is in response to the "catalyzing event."
- By the end, you either get what you want, don't get what you want, or resolve to want something else. The dramatic tension has ended... for the moment.

7 **Perform**

Objective: Through performance, figure out what revisions need to be made.

Directions

- Students bring in their monologues and their photographs. Their pieces do not have to be memorized yet, but they need to know the text very well.
- To provide a rehearsal (and calm nerves), first have them perform the piece for another student.
- Then, one at a time, students perform their drafts as the characters. They should have only essential costume pieces and props. Give them a moment with their photograph

to "step into" character, to physically assume that person's comportment and physical expression.
- As the actor performs, be aware of physicality and qualities of movement. Notice if the stakes need to be raised and if the obstacle is significant. Guide them to make strong, specific choices. I have found that students often need to deepen the relationship to the other character; I guide this by asking questions about its significance. This is also a time to heighten the moment before or raise the stakes. For example, if the character needs to borrow a car, there should be an important reason. Maybe their girlfriend is about to get on a plane before they can tell her they love her and convince her to stay. Maybe a friend needs a ride for a private reason that can't be shared, but time is of the essence.
- After all have performed, students go back to revising.
- Students memorize their revised drafts and perform again, adding costumes and props to fill out their worlds, until they have fully realized characters who speak their truth about their situations, wants, and desires.

Reflection

Students walk away from this exercise with pieces they have created born from embodied practice. They can expand them into one-act plays, or they may envision their characters as part of larger stories and develop full-length pieces. The people outside the picture frame might become realized. The moment before and the moment after might expand into their own scenes. In class, there are many directions an instructor can take. In my course, students collaborate with film students to adapt and translate their staged monologues into short films. Sometimes they keep the text exactly as written, and other times, because the piece is being translated into a visual medium, words are replaced with images and montages.

For example, Thomas Mercogliano, who was in my class in the Fall of 2021, used a picture from the Library of Congress archive.[19] In the photo, Major Fred W. Sladen, a career military man and the commanding officer of West Point from 1922–1925, sits in uniform atop a horse and looks directly into the camera with unwavering focus, his mouth turned slightly down at the corners. His posture is erect, his neck long, and his hands look like they are gripping the reigns. Thomas connected to what he read as Sladen's sense of duty and saw in his eyes that his commitment was wavering. This led him to write a piece opining the price of war. Thomas's directors worked with him to create the adaptation, and the short film took an expressionistic approach, imagining the character speaking from the grave, with cuts between dirt shoveled on a coffin and red-saturated shots of the character demanding recognition of his sacrifice. Covid restrictions during filming required Thomas to keep his face covered, but he translated the tension in the photograph into his own body, and his look of determination echoes the soldier's eyes in the original picture. He let this posture and tension guide the story.

Performance and writing go hand in hand in *The Picture Project*, like a feedback loop, as students explore characters through movement, interviews, monologue-writing, and portrayal. The resulting monologues can stand alone or be the springboard for other creative projects. The possibilities are vast.

Notes

1 The 4th Chakra is the heart chakra, and it is associated with love and grief.
2 The 1st Chakra is located at the base of the spine and is thought of as our center of survival and rage.
3 Schreiber, p. 87.
4 Barthes, p. 21.
5 Of course, other acting teachers invite students to wander through art galleries and birth ideas from their response to a painting or sculpture, so this is another route into this inspiration.
6 For example, in the anthology *Snapshot*, a group of eighteen playwrights, including Tanya Barfield, Lynn Nottage, and David Lindsay-Abaire, all respond to Lee Friedlander's photograph, *Mount Rushmore, South Dakota, 1969*, with their own short play.
7 Svich, pp. 1–32.
8 Of course, an actual person could be the subject of a painting that captures a real moment in time, but we see in the brush strokes the already subjective interpretation of that person on the canvas. Yes, the photograph expresses subjectivity as its maker is a photographer who chose the angle, moment, quality, and the exposure, but that feeling of "truth" and "reality" often belies the fabricated parts of capturing an image. It feels as if we are having unobstructed contact with the subject, especially in moments when the subject is unaware of the camera. This is obviously a gray area, and one could argue that abstract paintings and images reveal truths in ways that photos cannot. For this exercise, keep it simple; there is a real person, caught in a moment in time, in a real space that once existed.
9 Developing the habit of not judging one's character is useful when performing scripted characters as well. Actors need to have the character's point of view and understand his/her/their motives.
10 Students could of course work with a painting of a fictional character and go from there, but as an initial exercise in deep listening and attention to details, this method creates a standard in character creation that they will apply to the

performing and writing of fictional characters. My objective is that they will treat these characters born from fiction with the same respect they develop for the actual people they are performing and writing in this project.

11 Viewpoints is a technique for dance and movement composition originally developed by Mary Overlie. Anne Bogart and Tina Landau furthered Overlie's innovations, applying the viewpoints to staging with actors. Viewpoints exercises develop both the ensemble and awareness of bodies in space. Through these early exercises, students become aware of how they respond to stimuli reflexively (I drop to the floor when I get close to another person), creatively (I will now roll to locomote), and emotionally (when I move this way, I feel excited and happy). Their sensory awareness develops as they move at top speeds and avoid collisions, or play with proximity and distance from another actor. They note their experiences so that we can apply these movements deliberately later on.

12 Chekhov, p. 58.

13 Ibid., pp. 36–37.

14 Having a discussion prior to photo selection about who can play what character will give students more clarity on class expectations. You may find that this discussion shifts from class to class, but I recommend that the instructor remind the students that the actors are performing the person and must avoid stereotypes and assumptions.

15 Smith, p. XXIV.

16 I rely on verbal instruction to guide students, and I sometimes use my own body to demonstrate. If I think they would benefit from a physical adjustment, I always ask permission and specifically detail what I am going to do and where I am going to touch them.

17 Vocal work prior to this stage will be helpful. At the least, do a vocal warm-up at the beginning of class.

18 Mural.co/education has free accounts for students and professors.

19 To see the photo of Maj. F. W. Sladen and Lt. H.D. Higley, go to the Library of Congress: https://www.loc.gov/item/2014693125/# (accessed 7/25/22).

References

Barthes, Roland. *Camera Lucida: Reflections on Photography*. Translated by Richard Howard. Farrar, Straus and Giroux, 1982.

Chekhov, Michael. *To the Actor: On the Technique of Acting*. Harper Collins, 1991.

Schreiber, Terry, et al. *Acting: Advanced Techniques for the Actor, Director, and Teacher*. Allworth Press, 2012.

Simpson, Fay, and Eleanor Boynton. *The Lucid Body: A Guide for the Physical Actor*. Second edition, Allworth Press, 2020.

Smith, Anna Deavere. *Fires in the Mirror: Crown Heights, Brooklyn, and Other Identities*. 1st Anchor Books ed, Anchor Books/Doubleday, 1993.

Svich, Caridad, et al. "The Legacy of Maria Irene Fornes: A Collection of Impressions and Exercises." *PAJ: A Journal of Performance and Art*, vol. 31, no. 3, 2009.

6 Physical Expressions in Devised Playwriting

Luane Davis Haggerty and Aaron Kelstone

Introduction

It may seem counterintuitive to think that stripping away formal spoken language can foster student growth as they develop plays. However, while language and diction are important elements, the driving force of all plays revolves around character, plot, and ideas. When teachers introduce a physical approach to playwriting, it creates a visceral reaction to physicality that supports students with varying levels of language ability and comfort with the writing process. Being able to concretely visualize the play's plot and the resulting sequence of actions enables actor/writers to express themselves in a creative manner.

We have found through the iterative application of specific curriculum outcomes that a physically based, hands-on approach offers a firm foundation for student success. In an ASL playwriting classroom, where the students may seem to be at a disadvantage due to differences in cultural experiences, learning styles, social skills, and physical ability, the integration of physical exercises into the curriculum can guide a diverse student group towards the discovery of specific concepts to support the creative writing process.

We use a series of theatre exercises that help students identify and use specific dramatic elements, as well as demystify the process of writing by providing alternative ways to develop their plays. These alternative physical approaches to playwriting allow students to physically explore and present their plots in a visual format. This process of physically scaffolding the play development process supports the eventual transfer of their stories into traditional written formats.

DOI: 10.4324/9781003243014-8

Visualization

Early in the process students are introduced to improvisational game play which enables them to develop their work in small segments that support the creation of a series of scenes. To begin the physical process, students explore exercises that support their understanding of visualization skills, character types and development, the one-act concept, and approaches to plot analysis. These visualization exercises are introduced to the actor/writer progressively through several exercises.

Visualization Exercise One: Where?

The origin of this adapted exercise lies in Stella Adler's techniques.[1] It is designed to build the actor's imagination.

Objective

- To develop the actor's imagination by first observing the world around them in detail

How We Get There

- Divide students into groups of two to five students. Have each group create a list of different room locations such as kitchens, libraries, bedrooms, classrooms, and offices.
- From this list, they then choose one room location. Each group identifies important pieces of furniture for their chosen room and then visually create the room for the rest of the class, taking on the roles of family members, roommates, or married couples as they mime bringing in specific furniture objects.
- Encourage students to discuss how the addition of character and relational context helps in understanding space and how it is used for stage. In many cases, no literal setting is needed if the relationships are clear.
- The class will guess the specific type of room based on the mimed action and relational interaction. This exercise introduces students to the structural aspects of play development based on location and setting as a part of the story development process, as well as the need for context in interaction and communication within the group.

Visualization Exercise Two: What's Beyond?

This exercise originated with Uta Hagen's work[2] and is similar to common exercises that ask actors to choose moments in their lives and recreate them.

Objectives

- To develop an actor/writer's personal connection to the work.
- To provide a platform for the actor to add layers of character depth and application of personal observation in their stage work, which in turn will influence their writing.

How We Get There

- Each group uses the room location developed in Exercise One; however, half the group leaves or turns away, while the other half re-create the "room."
- The group members who created the "room" reenter the "room" improvising specific behaviors, such as coming inside after shoveling snow, getting the morning newspaper, or walking the dog. All action is still mimed, with no dialogue.

The other group re-enters the room, observing how the added antecedent action helps provide additional context to the created location and scene. This exercise helps students see how specific character choices and physical actions influence the storyline, can occur without dialogue, and influence subsequent scenes.

Visualization Exercise Three: What's Next?

Objective

- To create context through physical expression.

How We Get There

- Have the two groups switch. The new creating group will have a moment to discuss and agree on how to express their

characters' exits from the scene through gesture, movement, or mime, establishing where they are going and why they need to leave, perhaps miming that it's time to go to work, or escaping from an argument, or tending to a problem seen through a window.
- The new observing group must now identify what the implied action of the person is who is leaving the room.

Through this exercise, students learn the difference between an ordinary action, such as simply exiting with no underlying context, and a dramatic action, such as an exit that is a reaction to an event within the scene. The actor/writers can reflect on how goals are physically expressed and how those goals need to be clearly presented to help others visualize specific destinations without relying on dialogue.

Drafting by Phone: Three Dimensions to Two

After students successfully complete these three improvisational exercises, they are then allowed to reenact the scenes and use their phones to video record.

- Assign each group to transfer these video recordings into a formal script format.
- Introduce traditional storyboard techniques and online storyboard templates that allow them to include specific dramatic images, colors, and other information.
- Allow the actor/writers to find their own approaches to documenting the three-dimensional video work into a two-dimensional written form.
- Encourage the writing group to use the proposed tools to help them through the editing process as they transfer the physical and visual elements into dialogue, stage directions, and descriptions of setting and location for their scenes, ten-minute vignettes, and one-act plays.

This process of "drafting by phone," coupled with the use of storyboard techniques, provides an effective way for students to flesh out the visual and physical elements of their scenes as they create a cohesive written draft of their work.

Character Building

Another challenge for playwrights, especially those new to the craft, is to develop characters that are not limited by dialogue or depth of background, natural psychology, and relationships. To support this process, a series of character-building theatre exercises are introduced to the actors/writers.

Character Building Exercise One: Safe Place to Play

Michael Chekhov originated a psycho-physical approach to acting that nurtures the imagination while grounding emotion in physical action.[3] For students who struggle with written English, these exercises help to create a psychological shift to viewing their "writing" as something they do as naturally as having a conversation, to understand that they have already "written" the piece; they are simply copying from their natural communication method into English.

Objective

- To shed self-consciousness and find ownership of the stage.

How We Get There

- Ask the actors/writers to wander about the room to find their best place to work. Ask them to remain aware of how they knew which space to choose. Which places are most comfortable? Least comfortable? What do they notice about the places others are choosing?
- Move, sit, kneel, roll, and/or jump into the chosen spot. Use the space to express an emotion or a character.

Reflection

At the end of this exercise, discuss with the class the role of control and safety, how a person chooses to move in space, and what internal emotions influence their choices. Also, how is the space affected by their choices and the movement of the rest of the group? Physical safety needs to be monitored by all involved, but the dramatic elements of conflict that arise as each person moves in and out of various comfort zones can be especially useful to the actor/writer. This helps students comprehend that characters do not deliver lines. They respond, through dialogue, to their chosen actions and the actions of others.

Character Building Exercise Two: Stream of Consciousness

This work is inspired by Tadashi Suzuki techniques.[4]

Objective

- To develop three crucial aspects of the actor's body: energy production, breath calibration, and center of gravity control.

How We Get There

- Invite students to move about and locate themselves anywhere in the room.
- Encourage them to choose their own preferred warm-up exercise and begin.
- Instruct them not to judge what is going on around them, but to simply observe and allow for their own stream of consciousness to take their focus.
- Suggest that they respond to emotions and thoughts that emerge by reflecting them in their warm-up. For example, if mind is racing, then run; if depressed, then huddle; if happy, then jump.

Reflection

After the exercise, ask students to discuss and analyze how their warm-up represents a potential symbolic or metaphorical movement on stage.

Character Building Exercise Three: Breathing Together

Breathing exercises are a foundation of Yoga and Tai Chi. This exercise pulls in positive energy and lets go of negative (distracting) energy in order to provide emotional grounding to help center the actor and create a calm place from which to begin developing the life of a character.

Objective

- To calm down, focus on the work, and alleviate stage fright or self-consciousness.

How We Get There

- Have the students form a circle.
- Instruct a volunteer to make eye contact with another person in the circle and exhale.
- Have the receiving person inhale.
- The second person then makes eye contact with a third person and exhales. This process continues until everyone in the circle has participated.
- Context can be added to the process through mimed gestures, which the receiving person must respond to before sending their breath and a new gesture to the next person. For example: Joe mimes smoking, so Julie coughs as she inhales. Then Julie makes eye contact with Jack and changes the gesture to blowing bubbles. Jack pops the bubbles with his finger as he inhales, and so on.

Reflection

This exercise physically demonstrates the power of focus. Paying attention and respect to each participant's choices expands awareness from individual to group dynamics. In Deaf culture, eye contact, the length of time directly shared in eye contact, and the withholding of eye contact are part of the relational foundation of American Sign Language and interpersonal communication. Even the simple process of inhaling and exhaling can have context and a corresponding response.

Character Building Exercise Four: Handshape Hand-Off

This work originated with Sanford Meisner. His theories on imagination are fused with Deaf cultural and linguistic gestural play, resulting in the creation of elementary Sign Language poetry. In the creation of an American Sign Language poem, one of the most basic forms is a handshape poem. By using the shape of the hand that forms letters or numbers, you can create a variety of stories or images that follow poetic structures of rhyme (in English, rhyme is defined as words that sound the same, but in ASL, it is hand shapes or signs that look the same); imagery (use of the five senses to create a picture in the mind of the receiver of the communication); and many other literary techniques.

For example, a description of a Clayton Valli poem using only handshapes, titled "Hands," might be described in as follows: by using an open palm you can create the shape of the world; the sign for express (hands open out on chest); all (one hand circles the other); spring (one hand open up and out from the other); summer (create the image of many growing plants); fall (open palm used in the sign for tree while the other hand mimics the movement of a leaf falling from the tree); and snow (open palms mimic the movement of falling snow). This poem suggests that all things in the world can be expressed using your hands (a metaphor for Sign Language) and then illustrates all four seasons. Compare this with a Meisner exercise where an object is employed by each actor in a different way. For example, a stick becomes a golf club, a toothbrush, a baseball bat, a back scratcher. Clearly the ASL usage is more complex, but in playing with language in a Deaf cultural way by using handshapes rather than an object, the approach to creating a story—by handing off either the shape of a hand or an actual object—is similar.

Objectives

- To expand natural gestural vocabulary.
- To help students become aware of their fundamental strengths when using language or expression.
- To encourage students to play with language and alternative forms of expression.

How We Get There

- Form a circle and explain how to use the shape of your hand as an object (open palm or point on finger, etc.).
- Each student must use this handshape to communicate differently. For example, the leader may start with a full open hand as might be used for the natural gesture representing the concept *stop*. Each subsequent person retains that handshape

and creates a new representational meaning. The open hand could then slap the forehead as in *duh*, or put the hand over their mouth as in *uh-oh*, and so on. The exercise can include accepted grammatical handshapes used in American Sign Language. However, at more intermediate levels, the exercise can include universal gesture or mimed movements, as well.
- At more advanced levels, each of the handshapes can be connected to create a complete thought as produced by the whole group. In other words, as the shape is passed to the next person the thought and images need to be connected by acting and reacting. For example, after the natural gesture *stop*, the next person shakes this shape to indicate no, the next person reacts by putting hand over mouth as if shocked, the next person shows what is shocking through gesture of an open palm, and so on.

This exercise helps the writer see how physical qualities of the body can support the underlying context of their dialogue and assure that the audience clearly understands the intent and meaning behind spoken or signed dialogue.[5]

Movement, Posture, and Gesture (MPG)

The goal of MPG is to physically feel the change of inner emotion with the alteration of physical presence. In this way, the student can inhabit characters who might otherwise be inaccessible on a visceral level, potentially leading to shallow representations in both performance and writing. The exercises that follow are adapted from François Delsarte's codified movement studies. Delsarte created charts mapping out nearly every part of the body and analyzing it for emotive communication.[6]

MPG

1 Movement
- Instruct the class to line up on one side of the classroom.
- Have students individually walk across the room using a variety of movements (skipping, crawling, hopping, short steps, long steps, tiptoes).

- Initially, each person uses the same type of movement. For instance; all of the students skip. But each student needs to find a reason to skip in a different way (one might be acting as a character who is a four-year-old, one might be tripping over something, and so on). As you continue, ask them to choose their own sequence of movements: a hop, skip, and jump perhaps.
- View the "choreography" and discuss with the class. What sort of character might move in this way? What does the sequence of movements suggest as a story?
- Finally, place two actor/writers side-by-side to do their movement sequences. Many times, the actors will start to find ways to use the movement sequences to communicate and connect. Often a story or relationship organically emerges, simply from the movements.

2 Posture

- Add movement sequences to the posture choices. For example, bodies that are expanded, contracted, maintain a low center of gravity or high center of gravity.
- Ask how those postures affect the perception of the characters and the movement dialogue.
- Discuss how it felt to present the movement piece in a different posture. For instance, did the character age? Did a human character become animalistic?

3 Gesture

The last level of this exercise is to permit communicative gestures into the movement pieces. It adds specificity to the scene and provides a foundation for writing the scene down in proper playwriting format. Suggestions for natural gestures could be *Hello, Stop, No, Yes*, all added while the actor/writer preserves original movement and posture choices.

4 Consolidation of MPG

- With the final cross, have all students incorporate the three elements (MPG) by using their choices to build a character (person, animal, spirit).

- In the follow-up discussion, analyze what these specific MPG choices could represent. Human, spirit, animal, or magical? Which MPG provided a clear identification of character? What could be modified to help make some MPG actions clearer?
- This exercise can also be completed in reverse to enhance character analysis by naming a commonly known character. For example, individual students might represent Little Red Riding Hood using their different MPG actions. As the class sees different MPG actions for the same character, it effectively demonstrates there is no one right way to establish character.

Next Steps

For the final stage of this exercise, have students use this process to write character monologues from the perspective of a commonly known character (such as Mary Poppins or a superhero) with the intention of revealing their inner truths. For example, how does Mary Poppins really feel about having to move on every time she is able to heal a family? Does a confident superhero have identity issues? The goal is to translate the work with MPG into the ability to show characters we think we know in an unusual or unexpected light.

Conclusion

Although most conventional approaches start with the writer confronting the blank page, we suggest a parallel method can also be used. Allow the work to begin, develop, and arrive in a printed format by creating dramatic works physically and imaginatively, first through the embodied language of the actor/writer using American Sign Language (ASL), universal gesture, mimed movement, and Sign Mime techniques as described in our chapter. These exercises encourage writers to visualize their work beyond the confines of print and paper. Exploring visual aspects of play development can lead to making the abstract concrete, moving ideas from physical expression into plays written, even in first draft, with stronger action, language, and plot elements, as well as more creative development of memorable characters.

Notes

1 Spolin, *Theatre Games for the Classroom*, as seen through the eyes of a practitioner of Stella Adler's acting technique during a class in 1981 at Hunter College.

2 Hagen, *Respect for Acting*. Although this information appears in her book, much of this information is received knowledge by the writer through practice in a class with Ms. Hagen in 1978.
3 Chekhov.
4 Suzuki.
5 Handshapes and gesture are clearly foundation elements of American Sign Language. Using handshapes in this way parodies a Deaf children's game of poetic language play (Padden and Humphries, 1988: 91). It is also similar to the Meisner acting game of taking an actual object, a pole for instance, and having each actor use it in a different way (Meisner, 1961: 10). Michael Chekhov discusses a similar process in which he suggests that the process helps in "molding the space around the actor" (Chekhov, 1953: 8).
6 For instance, in Delsarte's chart describing the emotion connected with the shapes of the hands, having your hand clutched is the same handshape used in the sign "anger" as well as being the same handshape used by Delsarte to naturally express anger. Delsarte's expressive analysis shows that body movement and ASL vocabulary using the same body language, handshape, or facial expression match up nearly exactly. This matching of observation and technique led us to use the idea of motion, posture, and gesture or MPG (easier for the student to remember and apply in analysis and practice). See *Every Little Movement*, T. Shawn.

References

Adler, Stella, and Howard Kissel. *Stella Adler: The Art of Acting*. Applause, 2001.
Chekhov, Michael. *To the Actor: On the Technique of Acting*. Routledge, Taylor & Francis Group, 2002.
Hagen, Uta, and Haskel Frankel. *Respect for Acting*. Wiley, 2003.
Padden, Carol, and Tom Humphries. *Inside Deaf Culture*. Harvard University Press, 2006.
Meisner, Sanford, and Dennis Longwell. *Sanford Meisner on Acting*. Vintage Books, 1990.
Shawn, Ted. *Every Little Movement: Book about Francois Delsarte*. Dance Horizons: N.Y., 1953.
Spolin, Viola. *Theatre Games for the Classroom: A Teacher's Handbook*. Northwestern Univ. Press, 2000.
Suzuki, Tadashi, and Kameron H. Steele. *Culture Is the Body: The Theatre Writings of Tadashi Suzuki*. Theatre Communications Group, 2015.

7 Active Group Playwriting

Psychodrama Techniques Adapted for Theatre-making

David Kaye

Introduction

Psychodrama was created by Dr. Jacob Moreno in the 1920s as a form of group therapy. This approach explores a pivotal story in a person's life by recreating that episode using an array of specially designed improvisational techniques. It evolved when Moreno carried over what he had learned from the formation of his Stegreiftheater[1] (Theatre of Spontaneity) to his psychiatric practice.[2] As psychiatrist Dr. Adam Blatner writes:

> Although preferably performed in a group format, [psychodrama] focuses on the particularities of the individual as the intersection of various relational roles, (e.g., being a son and a spouse) and roles related to difficulties and potentialities (e.g., fears, like fear of flying; or doubts, how the next job interview will be). For this reason, it is said to be an individual therapy in a group format, centered on the protagonist, and the action may take place around the various roles that s/he assumes throughout life.[3]

Blatner's overview of psychodrama as a form of group therapy is striking in its relevance to the playwriting process. The world of a play is ultimately the world of roles, relationships, and the actions that impact those relationships over the designated timeframe of the script.

Over the last thirty years, I have been applying psychodrama techniques as a fully physicalized approach to playwriting and play devising. The image of isolated playwrights, hunched over their blank pages as they try to bring forth a play, is fairly accurate. Zerka Moreno, Jacob's wife and collaborator, notes that, in psychodrama, the body remembers what the mind forgets. It is through the body that we have a greater capacity to connect with our emotions and our subconscious thoughts. It also offers us a far enhanced ability to communicate with others.[4]

DOI: 10.4324/9781003243014-9

Psychodramatic techniques can be highly effective when applied to group playwriting.

The following exercises are laid out in the pattern that I use to create ensemble devised work that bases fictional characters and stories on personal experiences. However, the exercises can be used in any order, and single exercises can target specific needs in the playwriting process. These techniques are designed for group writing. Even if the purpose is the creation of an autobiographical solo-play or a fictional play by a single playwright, this process engages a creative ensemble to explore character(s), relationships, actions, and other story elements.

A facilitator or guide is required. The guide can be the director, the playwright, or any designated person from the group. I refer to the other participants in the process as group members, the ensemble, or players.

Warm-Up Exercises

For any theatrical endeavor with an ensemble, a good warm-up is crucial to get both mind and body ready for the work at hand. In this case, the warm-up also begins with an important premise; I use this technique to help discover and expand the depth and fullness of truth and authenticity in the playwriting process. Therefore, I begin with developing comfort with sharing truthfully and authentically within the ensemble. I use exercises related to *sociometry*, a term coined by Moreno, to provide a method for exploring group dynamics. Sociometry illustrates how members in a social group interact toward or away from each other based on spontaneous emotional responses.[5] This technique allows an ensemble to see, through movement and/or the physical placement of each participant in a designated space, their relationship to each other on any range of questions. It can also show patterns in the ways individuals work together as a group toward a specified end or goal. These exercises can be used by writers to develop the points of view of individual characters and the group dynamics that exist within the fictional world of a play.

The Missing Chair

This game was developed by Moreno as one of a series of sociometry exercises created to reveal various points of commonality, or lack of commonality, among members of a group. Arrange chairs in a circle. There should be fewer chairs than participants; if you have ten participants then you should have only nine chairs in your circle. If possible, keep at least two feet of space on either side of each chair. One person stands in the center of the circle, and everyone else takes a seat. The guide gives a simple prompt, which the person standing repeats and then completes with an honest response.

Guide: I really like...
Person in the Middle: I really like... taking long walks on a sandy beach.

Now, every person sitting who also likes taking long walks on a sandy beach must get up and find another seat as quickly as possible. The person who was in the center, as well as all the people who get up, can sit in any of the vacated seats. The only rules are that everyone must be truthful in their responses and no one can return to the chair they just vacated. As in the game of musical chairs, one person will be left standing. That individual now uses the same prompt but completes it differently.

New Person in the Middle: I really like... watching football on Sundays.

If no one gets up, then the person in the middle states another "I really like..." until there is movement. "I really like" is a safe way to start. The group will build trust as they reveal simple truths about themselves. Once trust has been established, the guide can move on to prompts with more depth. For example:

What really makes me angry is...
What I am really scared of is...
What I never want to hear is...

And so on. The exercise will reveal various elements of agreement and disagreement among the group. Factions of various sizes, group consensus, or a single outlier will appear with each question and change with the next. The questions can also be used to transition the group toward the actual subject matter of the play being developed. For example, if the ensemble is developing a play where the characters will be dealing with care for an elderly parent suffering from Alzheimer's, the prompts might be:

What I fear most about aging is...
I will always be grateful to my mother for...
Please don't ask me to...

Hands On

The group is spread out evenly in an open playing space. The guide poses a question that starts with the phrase *who would you*. For example: "Who would you want to be in charge if all your lives were in danger?" Each participant moves to their choice and places one hand on that person's shoulder. The only rules are that they must make a choice and they can choose only one person. (Occasionally, I allow participants to choose no one.)

A graphic representation of the group will evolve. Many may cluster around one or two people. A chain of people may form. The group can observe the unique patterns and shapes and what the composition says about the interpersonal relationships within the group.[6] This can also lead to an exploration about why people made their choices. These questions work best when they are simple and specific rather than vague. A low-risk question like "Who would you choose to cook a meal?" may reveal more about the chooser than the chosen person. The chooser may think that person is the best cook. Or the chooser may be a bit germophobic and trust that person to wash their hands.

The guide can then build to more complex questions like "Who would you trust most to keep an extremely personal secret?" Questions can also be posed that pertain specifically to the play being created. For example, if working on the play from the previous exercise, the players can respond from a character's perspective, exploring their responses to questions like "Who should assume power of attorney for Dad?" or "Who would be the best person to take Dad to the nursing home?"

Linear Sociogram

This may be the most familiar form of sociometry. A specific statement is posed. For example: "I love going to auditions." The guide establishes two points on opposite sides of the room. The point on one side represents the greatest level of agreement with the statement ("Auditioning is the best!"), and the point on the other side represents the least amount of agreement with the statement ("I'd rather pass a kidney stone than audition."). An imaginary line runs along the floor between these two points.

Everyone in the group moves to the spot between the two points that best represents their response to that question. Two or more people can occupy the same point on the line by standing to one side of the other of the person on the line. The group will begin to see where there is agreement, where the group is bifurcated, where there is a wide range of responses, or where an individual may be alone. The guide can lead discussion after observing the results, and then a new question can be posed.

Applying this exercise to statements specific to a fictional play being written, where the group assumes the play's characters, will help reveal a deeper understanding of their various points of view and their relationships to each other. For example, in our fictional play about a family coping with their father's condition, statements might include: "Children have a responsibility to care for their aging parents." Or more specifically, "Dad should be placed in a nursing home." These questions may reveal where there is the greatest potential to build conflict, or conversely, where to enhance the shared opinions between characters. It may also reveal where some points of view need to be altered to strengthen the dynamics of the interpersonal relationships.

Psychodramatic Exploration

Moreno calls the next step in a psychodrama session the *action phase*, where a specific scene will be enacted.[7] In a group therapy session, participants would share actual stories from their lives, and the one that most resonated with the group would be selected. The same process I described in **Hands On** could be used to determine whose story the group explores.

I use this process for autobiographical devised plays. In a play created for incoming students at the University of New Hampshire, for example, the ensemble shared stories of their struggles during their first year of college. About half the students were willing to share a story. After the last person finished, the storytellers stood and spread out in the playing space. The rest of the ensemble then placed a hand on the shoulder of the group member whose story most resonated with them. When there was no majority choice, then the individuals in the smallest group moved to their second choice. This continued until one story received a majority.

If a fictional story is going to be explored, then the guide can simply describe the scene from the work-in-progress. In the telling of the story, there must be a clear protagonist and at least one additional character who provides an obstacle that the protagonist must confront. In this case, these roles can be selected by the playwright, if the goal is to develop the script, or by using the *Hands On* technique for a fully ensemble-driven process.

The Interview

For the first step of the exploration, the guide takes the protagonist for a walk around the playing space; the simple act of walking engages the body. The guide asks questions to dig deeper into the story and the characters. If autobiographical, the protagonist simply answers truthfully. If fictional, the protagonist improvises as truthfully as possible from the character's point of view. The rest of the ensemble listens intently to learn details about the story and its characters. The guide plays the role of a trusted confidant who knows only as much of the story as has been told to the entire group. For example:

> So, I understand your father was really unhappy about you wanting to study art and not something like business.

- Can you tell me more about your father? When did it all come to a head?
- Can you tell me more about your mother? Did she support your decision?
- How would you describe your parents' relationship?
- You said your sister is still in high school. Is she aware of this rift with your dad?
- How important is it to you that your dad supports your decision?
- Do you think he understands you and what you want in life?

By the end of the interview, everyone in the group should have a firm grasp of the story and the various characters both directly and indirectly involved with the protagonist's struggle. If a fictional story is being explored, the interview is followed up with a step I call *corrections*. This phase allows for any problems that came up to be addressed. These may be character or story elements. Two improvised facts about a character might contradict each other, or inconsistent plot details or timelines may have been introduced. The group decides to drop, alter, or change elements as needed to strengthen the overall storytelling.

Setting the Scene and Assigning Roles

The guide now asks the protagonist to set the location where the scene takes place. Perhaps the living room of her parents' house when her father announced that if she wanted to study art, he would not pay her tuition. She sets up their living room, using chairs and other objects in the space. The guide now asks the protagonist to choose who she wants to play each role and place them in the scene. These are normally the important people in the protagonist's life, relevant to the scene being explored.

Non-human roles can also be cast. Perhaps a family dog was present when this event happened or a TV was on. Ensemble members can take on those roles and have conversations (using words) with the protagonist. In this case, these interactions are not technically heard by the other characters. For example, there may be a fireplace where the protagonist often stands to feel safe and warm. A group member may be chosen to play the fireplace. They may just stand in the specified place in the room, always offering a warm smile when the protagonist is near. But they can also speak to the protagonist, or the protagonist to them, should either choose to do so. The guide may also prompt such an interaction. Non-human characters offer unique pathways to better understand and flesh out the protagonist, as well as the other characters, the given circumstances, and the story itself.

The Enactment Begins

The guide asks the protagonist how the scene should begin and then the enactment gets underway. At any point during the enactment, the guide can pause the action and utilize the tools of psychodrama to delve more deeply into the characters' behaviors, actions, and interpersonal relationships. A pause can also be called by any of the players if they feel unsafe while participating in the enactment. Everyone stops and takes a breath, and then the person who paused the action cues the guide to either restart the scene or call for a break. The guide will determine at what point to end the exercise. When I feel the exploration is at a good stopping point, I ask the group to pause, take in a breath, and on their exhale, release the role they have been playing.

Psychodramatic Tools

Role Reversal

A core therapeutic tool used by Moreno was role reversal, a method where two individuals swap roles. Both players try to behave and speak as truthfully as they can from this opposing character's point of view before they return to their original roles.[8] Its use in therapy is largely to allow the protagonist the opportunity to gain insight, and often empathy, for the other individual. Its use in the play development process is to give the protagonist the opportunity to better illustrate the behaviors and traits of that other role. This is particularly important if the play being created is autobiographical. It also offers an active technique for infusing more critical information about a character into the script.

Continuing with our example, perhaps an important aspect of the father's past has come up. Rather than the protagonist stopping the psychodrama to tell the ensemble these important facts, she can instead assume his role and communicate these aspects of his story in character. The reversal also gives the protagonist the chance to see her role played by another person and vice versa. This often leads to the revelation of actions, tactics, and lines that had never occurred to either player.

If there is a point when the guide perceives that an exploration between the protagonist and another character needs a new perspective, the guide can pause the action and have the two players reverse roles. The guide uses a line that was previously spoken to restart the interaction, and the scene continues with the players in their reversed roles. When the guide determines that this exploration has achieved the benefits it was able to provide, the players are paused. The guide returns them to their original roles. The scene can be repeated, or it can continue from where it left off. Overall, I have found role reversal very effective in exploring new and often unexpected directions scenes or character relationships may take. The infusion of this instantaneous reverse perspective often jump-starts spontaneity.

Doubling

In Moreno's psychodrama, a participant can be given the role of the protagonist's double to support the protagonist by joining the inner world and adding voice to inner thoughts.[9] In the playwriting adaptation of psychodrama, this interwoven collaborative technique allows members of the group not currently playing roles in the scene to support the process in a critical way. By doubling the protagonist, they contribute deeper insights into the character and the creation of dialogue.

Either the protagonist or the guide chooses the double. The double should be next to or directly behind the protagonist. If the protagonist moves, the double moves. As a reenactment of a fight between the art student and her father takes place, the double could speak such possible inner thoughts as "I keep repeating myself" or "I need to stand my ground." The person doubling always speaks in first-person singular and in the present tense.[10] No other characters engage with the double or appear to hear the lines. If motivated to do so, the protagonist may choose to repeat any of the lines offered up by the double. For example, the double may voice inner thoughts the protagonist is having about her father, such as "You don't know the first thing about me" or "The reason you are so miserable is you hate your work." If the protagonist repeats the inner-thought line, then the other character(s) in the scene have now also heard the line and respond accordingly. While a traditional psychodrama would focus only on the protagonist, I allow doubling for other important roles in the scene; this allows the technique to be utilized for the development of other characters as well. To keep the scene from being overwhelmed by too many people speaking at the same time when there are multiple doubles, the inner-thought lines may be spoken quietly into the character's ear.

Doubling roles greatly magnifies the amount of brain power invested in the scene development process. It also allows these new players to move from passive observers to active participants. An alternative to doubling is to simply allow any observers to yell "pause" if they want to offer an inner thought they feel is important to the moment. After freezing the action, the observer runs up onto the stage and behind the intended character, and then speaks the line. The scene continues as the observer returns to the group. The new line is heard by the other characters if the player chooses to use it. The downside of this approach is that the participants are not as fully invested in the action as they are when they are doubling. It is, however, an excellent way to generate additional line possibilities if working with a small group.

Divided Double

A divided double is a variation of doubling created by Moreno. Here, the double is assigned a specific part of the protagonist's psyche, made explicit by the guide. The double may take on such roles as the defiant part, the obedient part, or the fearful part of the character.[11] As is the case for any doubling technique, these roles are extensions of the protagonist or other characters being explored. The main difference is that the divided double actually engages in a scene with the individual they are doubling. For example, when the double voices the inner-thought line "you never stand up for yourself," the guide may pause the action and have the double and the protagonist engage with each other, utilizing that line.

> Double: You never stand up for yourself!
> Protagonist: It's not that easy.
> Double: Not that easy? Just tell him to screw off!
> Protagonist: But... maybe he's right.
> Double: I can't believe this. You are such a doormat!
> Protagonist: I know. I know... I guess... I'm scared of him.

At this point, the guide could introduce another divided double, a third participant who could take on the part of the protagonist that is scared of her father. The protagonist (and playwright) can now observe a battle between these two parts of her. One is strong and determined, and the other is frightened. Moreno believed that every role has two sides.[12] Divided doubles can be used to develop this duality in characters.

Divided doubles can also be drawn from different time periods of the character's life. For example, it may surface that the art student and her father had a very different relationship when she was a child. A double of her as a child can be cast (ideally by the protagonist), and they can explore an interaction. It may surface that a specific event forever changed that relationship when she was in her teens. An additional divided double could be added to allow the protagonist to engage with both her child and teen self. The ensuing improvisation may develop and illuminate critical past actions and events that help shape and clarify the present behaviors and actions of the character.

Surplus Reality

Moreno defined psychodrama as the science which investigates the truth by dramatic methods.[13] In theatre, one could argue that truth is relative to the special world of the play. Art is by its very nature artificial (human-made), and thus we can alter aspects of that world at will. Moreno appears to have embraced this idea as part of his "dramatic methods" in the form of surplus reality. This idea is related to Stanislavski's "magic if:" Using the power of one's imagination, how would one behave if these were the circumstances? The goal of exploring truth is not in any way diminished. It is simply acting truthfully if we make a change to the reality of that world.

I witnessed a powerful exploration of surplus reality as applied for artistic purposes during a character development exercise for *The Glass*

Menagerie. Guided by Dr. Eberhard Scheiffele, actor Pamela Arkin was playing Amanda Wingfield. In the character interview, she revealed how tired she was from constantly having the responsibility to keep her family afloat. When asked if there was someone she wanted to talk to, she immediately said "my father." Amanda's father is not in the play, but in this surplus reality, she was able to bring him back to life and into the world of the play. A profoundly touching scene was played out on a park bench where we saw how much she longed to have someone take care of her, like when she was a child. This "as if" scenario was a wonderfully humanizing moment for the actor and the character.

In a traditional psychodrama, surplus reality can serve as an experiential therapy. It allows the protagonist the opportunity to create and then experience a reality impossible in real life. In the playwriting sphere, this technique allows for the exploration of multiple story possibilities as well as additional character development. If the father in our art student scenario always shuts the daughter out, a surplus reality can be created where he will finally listen. It is possible that by the time this altered reality scene plays out, he has said how much he loves her, and all he really wants is for her to be happy. This may alter the direction of the play's plot. Surplus realities can also be used to explore a character's past through improvised scenes that exist outside the new play's timeframe. Doubling, divided doubles, and role reversal can also be applied to a surplus reality scene. It is a tremendously useful structure that can enhance experimentation and discovery of character and story.

Conclusion

Throughout all of these exercises, script material is being generated. The ensemble should decide how to capture these explorations. I sometimes record them (with everyone's permission), and I always ask participants who are observing to "scribe" the scenes by writing down lines and moments that resonated with them. These are shared at the end of each session.

There are many more psychodramatic techniques developed by Moreno. The ones I have described are those that I have found to be the most useful in this active playwriting process. A cautionary note: when applying these techniques to autobiographical work, it is important to always keep the goal of creating an artistic work front and center. Using psychodrama to explore fictional characters and stories may touch on many personal aspects of the participants' real lives, but the goal is not therapy. It is highly recommended that participants using these tools have come to terms with the subject matter. Issues that remain volatile and/or unresolved in any individual participant's personal life should be considered out-of-bounds for these exercises. The ability to embrace that the circumstances are simply pretend and part of the artistic experience is critical to virtually any approach playwrights and other theatre artists use to create a fictional play of truth, depth, and authenticity. Moreno's innovations, with a shift in focus from therapy to the creation of art, have provided me with a powerful method to actively engage a group in the creation of a play.

Notes

1 Moreno, J.L., *Das Stegreiftheatre (Theatre of Spontaneity).*
2 Blatner, pp. 23–30.
3 Moreno, Z.T., pp. 178–186.
4 Pepinsky, pp. 262–286.
5 Hoffman, pp. 3–16.
6 Ibid.
7 Richard and Garcia.
8 Yaniv, pp. 70–77.
9 Moreno, Z.T., pp. 178–183.
10 Hollander.
11 Blatner, pp. 1–15.
12 Moreno, Z.T., pp. 178–183.
13 Moreno, J.L., *Psychodrama First Volume (Fourth Edition).*

References

Blatner, Adam. *Acting-In: Practical Applications of Psychodramatic Methods.* New York: Springer Publishing Company, 1996.
Blatner, Adam. "Psychodrama: the state of the art." *The Arts in Psychotherapy,* 24, pp. 23–30, 1997.
Hoffman, Chris W. "Sociometric Applications in a Corporate Environment." *Journal of Group Psychotherapy, Psychodrama & Sociometry,* Vol 45, pp. 3–16, 1992.
Hollander, Carl. *A Guide to Auxiliary Ego Development,* 1974, June. Retrieved from asgpp.org: https://asgpp.org/wp-content/uploads/2020/02/hollander-aux-ego-dev.pdf
Moreno, J.L. *Das Stegreiftheatre (Theatre of Spontaneity).* Berlin: Gustav Kiepenheuer Verlag, 1924.
Moreno, J.L. *The Theatre of Spontaneity.* Beacon, NY: Beacon House, 1973.
Moreno, J.L. *Psychodrama First Volume (Fourth Edition).* New York: Beacon House, 1972.
Moreno, Z.T. "Psychodrama, Role Theory and the Concept of the Social Atom." *Journal of Group Psychotherapy and Sociometry,* 42, pp. 178–186, 1989.
Moreno, Z.T. "Clinical Psychodrama: Auxiliary ego, double, and mirror techniques." *Sociometry: A Journal of Inter-Personal Relations,* 9, pp. 178–183, 1946.

Pepinsky, C.P. "Sociometry." *American Sociological Association*, 11(3), 262–286, 1948.

Richard, D. and Garcia, A. *Psychodrama in Individual Therapy.* N.d. Retrieved from Psychodrama Training Assocaites: http://www.psychodramatraining.com/article1.htm

Yaniv, D. "Dynamics of Creativity and Empathy in Role Reversal: Contributions from Neuroscience." *Review of General Psychology*, 16, pp. 70–77, 2012.

Part III
Playing Games

8 Building the World of the Play Through Collaborative Performance

Mike Poblete

Introduction

Creating a setting that doesn't just serve a play but drives it forward can be challenging for any Playwright. Often worldbuilding requires revision during the workshop phase because collaboration may be needed to fully flesh out complex theatre environments and anticipate actor challenges. I have benefitted from employing collaborative performance exercises in my writing process, and in this chapter, I will share my favorite worldbuilding exercises inspired by improv and devised theatre methodologies. Those who might benefit from these exercises include Playwrights open to recruiting actors to assist in their writing process, theatre collectives interested in developing a new play with a Playwright, writing groups where the collective takes turns assisting one Playwright at a time, and introductory playwriting classes.

The exercises in this chapter are provided in a recommended order that begins with a Playwright's loose ideas about characters and plot, and builds toward a more detailed and refined world. They can, however, be used out of order or individually. Because the exercises are structured to assist a *single* Playwright who already has a sense of certain basic elements of their play, the role of the Performers is a little different than in most rehearsal rooms. Their explorations are not aimed at better understanding character or working towards a performance, but are narrowly focused on assisting the Playwright in their creative process, so they must listen carefully to what the Playwright is looking for from each exercise. Communication is, of course, a critical component of any rehearsal room; these exercises have suggested prompts to help the Playwright move the collective from one task to the next, but the exercises are meant to be flexible, and the more the Playwright is able to trust the Performers to play and make discoveries at their own pace, the more informative the generated material will be. Having a director

DOI: 10.4324/9781003243014-11

in the room, although not required, can be very useful in assisting communication between the Playwright and Performers.

What is Needed

- A basic knowledge of the principles of improv and devised theatre are required for many of these exercises. There are excellent books on both topics; for improv, I recommend *Truth in Comedy: The Manual for Improvisation* by Charna Halpern, Del Close, and Kim Johnson; and *Impro: Improvisation and the Theatre* by Keith Johnstone. For the basics of devised theatre and collaborative storytelling, *Devising Theatre: A Practical and Theoretical Handbook* by Alison Oddey and *The Performer's Guide to the Collaborative Process* by Sheila Kerrigan provide good foundational theory and accessible exercises.
- At least two Performers are required. I believe that the heart of Western drama is conflict between at least two opposing viewpoints, and to that end these exercises are largely structured around two Performers, although they can be modified to allow for more Performers to embody additional characters, objects, and/or concepts.
- I recommend video recording the exercises, which is a common practice in devised rehearsal rooms to capture "happy accidents" that spontaneously emerge.[1]
- Be certain to leave time to debrief with the Performers as their insights will be crucial.
- It may be necessary to have a thorough conversation establishing creative boundaries, and potentially even legal documentation. The role of the Performers in these exercises might be considered a form of collaborative dramaturgy; Michael M. Chemers, Professor of Dramatic Literature and Theatre Arts at the University of California, Santa Cruz, warns that anyone working within a dramaturgical context must be careful regarding their creative input toward a Playwright's work and not make a "copyrightable contribution."[2]

Definitions

As we are discussing worldbuilding, I must explain how I distinguish the terms space, location, setting, world, and set.

- "Space" refers to the playing space of the Performers in the rehearsal room or on stage.
- "Location" refers to where a play takes place, such as in an apartment or a gym.

- "Setting" is similar to location, but is more conceptual as it refers to the surroundings of a play, and considers theme and tone. (For example, a setting might be a pleasant rural town with one stop sign, as opposed to the locations of different homes and businesses within this town, where the specific actions of the play take place.)
- The "world" of the play is more conceptual still, referring to not just the setting or location, but the society in which the play exists, and considering elements of environment and morality.
- Finally, a "set" is what is physically created by a designer to house the world on a stage. Getting specific with these exercises can be very useful, but the outcome should not be a specific set. Remember that a play may be performed on different types of theatre stages (e.g., proscenium, thrust, or in the round) or performances may be site-specific, immersive, or touring.

Brainstorming the World

While the world of a play is deeply informed by physicality, it is not in and of itself physical; rather, it is defined by the rules that dictate the cause and effect of the action on stage. For example, in Moses Goods' *Lovey Lee*, a powerful play about a queer Hawaiian man navigating identity in the 1970s, performed at Honolulu's Kumu Kahua Theatre in 2020, the protagonist moves to many different locations, but the world follows him because of consistent rules: that family are those that support you, that being queer is a capital crime, and that running away cannot change who you are. John Cariani's *Almost, Maine* takes place in a variety of locations within the same setting, a small town, and pushes the limits of plausibility by embracing magical realism. The world is believable and consistent, however, because it follows rules such as: love is a powerful force, what is broken can be fixed, and, of course, that magic is real. Although many of these exercises can help shape detailed play locations, the larger purpose is for the Playwright to identify patterns that reinforce the story they are trying to tell and to develop those patterns into rules.

The exercises in this section can assist a Playwright early in their process. The Playwright should observe how the rules of the world are clarified when Performers encounter obstacles. Pay particular attention when a Performer takes on the role of a central character: note mannerisms, habits, physicality, and vocality, as well as how other Performers react to this character. Try to distinguish between rules that are particular to the character and rules that are consistent for larger groups of people within this world.

The Monologuist

A good place for a Playwright to begin is to explain, to the Performers, what they know about their play so far. There are a number of widely used improvisational long-form structures that involve mining true stories, like *the Harold* and *the Armando*.[3] For *the Armando*, a Performer receives an offer of a word from the audience and begins to tell a true personal story inspired by that word; the other members of the troupe will then create scenes inspired by that story. Aspects of this methodology can also be used by a Playwright to brainstorm locations and rules for their story.

Objective

- To brainstorm potential locations for a play through character embodiment.

How We Get There

- The Playwright begins by telling the story of their character or characters in a third-person monologue format. There are no rules, but some sense of character backstory, as well as the present moment, should be conveyed. The monologue can be written ahead of time or not, but preparation will ensure pertinent information is communicated.
- One Performer picks a character described by the Playwright and begins moving around the space as they believe the character might move: big or small steps, quickly or slowly, taking up a lot of space or perhaps being cautious or sneaky.
- Once the first Performer has had enough time to settle on a physicality, perhaps thirty seconds or so, a second Performer enters the space and begins to move as they believe a second character in this world might move.
- Slowly, the two Performers begin to interact, reacting to each other's physicality and establishing some non-verbal communication. The relationship that the Playwright has established should begin to emerge. Are they long-time friends? Colleagues? The Performers' physicality should try to reflect the characters' power dynamic. The Playwright can provide additional guidance by asking questions, such as, "Are you happy to see each other? Are you afraid of her?"

- To further define the characters' relationship, the Performers begin to converse with each other as their characters when they feel compelled to do so. The Playwright can prompt this by asking, "What do you two have to say for yourselves?" The Playwright can also skip this step if they feel that non-verbal interaction is sufficient for the Performers to understand their characters well enough to begin creating a location.
- Once the Performers seem comfortable conversing, perhaps after a minute, one Performer should begin to establish a location that feels true to the characters' relationship, such as a character's home, a place of work, or a busy street where they must sidestep passersby. Performers should physically interact with their surroundings: lean on walls, sit on furniture, look out at the horizon, etc., and verbally comment on those surroundings. The Playwright can prompt this by asking, "Performer One, why don't you show us around?" The second Performer should accept and build on the first Performer's offers (choices that expand the scene, such as declaring that there is an old wicker rocking chair in the corner).
- Once the location has been established, other Performers may join the scene to play additional characters, inanimate objects, or concepts.
- If the Playwright is comfortable with performing, they can join the scene as well by embodying an additional character, object, or concept that fits the location, making offers and building on other offers made. I would only recommend this approach if the exercise is being video recorded, as the Playwright cannot take notes while performing.
- When the Playwright has taken enough notes on this location, the Performers reset. They go back to interacting physically before starting a new conversation, and, when the time feels right to the Performers, or when the Playwright prompts, a new location is established. They can, of course, play different characters if the Playwright wishes, but I have found that observing the same characters allows the Playwright to focus on how various locations affect those characters differently.
- The process is repeated until the Playwright feels they have observed as many locations as they need to help them in the next stages of their writing.

This exercise also builds rapport within the collective regarding ways to initiate, describe, and build a setting together, which will be useful as the Playwright and Performers explore subsequent exercises.

Active Worldbuilding

Having considered locations based on character choices, the Playwright can now consider worldbuilding based on those characters' physical *actions*. A play centering on divorce, for example, could take place in the living room, where cherished memories and a contested house are front and center, but if the play is set on the front lawn where characters are constantly in motion, the threshold of the house becomes a meaningful barrier between who lives there and who no longer does.

Objective

- To create a world as a consequence of the characters' actions, rather than just a place to house those actions.

How We Get There

This exercise starts like **The Monologuist**, but now the first Performer introduces an activity.

- The Performer engages in a physical action that feels right for the character based on details offered by the Playwright (for example, if the character values fitness, the first Performer might start curling barbells).
- After thirty seconds, the second Performer joins the activity in a way that suits their character (perhaps they are at a different exercise machine, or mopping the floor, or are dropping off a package at the gym).
- After another thirty seconds, additional Performers may join, further defining the location through detailed activities.
- As with **The Monologuist**, the process is repeated with different activities and different locations, with the Playwright carefully noting what might work well for the play. The Playwright can, of course, also suggest activities that might occur in the world of the play.

Power Play

Now that the actions of characters have been considered in shaping a world, the Playwright can take things a step further by considering the power dynamics of the characters as they perform those actions. Does a particular character feel powerful or weak in their world? In control or out of control? Is the world scary or comforting? How does the world react to a character's power in it?

Objective

To further brainstorm locations based on characters' power dynamics.

How We Get There

- The first Performer plays the protagonist, moving around the space as they believe that character would move.
- After thirty seconds, the second Performer enters the space as a second character or an aspect of the world, such as looming responsibilities or opportunities. They engage with the first Performer, adjusting their physicality based on power dynamics. For example, if a Performer plays an oppressive element, such as a landlord demanding rent, they might try to be physically bigger, louder, and dominating. If a Performer plays a character that needs assistance, such as a child or a car with engine trouble, they might speak softly or weakly, but they might also be defiant while addressing the more powerful character. Remember that dominance and submission can take many physical and vocal forms.
- After another thirty seconds or so, additional Performers can enter the space one by one, embodying further characters or concepts and engaging with the first Performer accordingly. The Playwright can prompt this by saying, "Why don't you go show them what you think of them?"

Understanding how power dynamics are established can offer great insight into the world. What patterns emerge from these power dynamics? Are these patterns consistent with other established rules of the world? Is it *too* oppressive? Does the main character have *too* much control over the environment?

Shaping the World

Having considered a setting with rules crafted by the characters that inhabit it, the Playwright can direct collaborative exercises that help shape the details of that emerging world.

Shaping a Remembered Space

Modified from a common creative writing prompt, this first of two exercises asks the Playwright to create a space based on a memory. The Playwright chooses a real location they know very well, ideally with emotional resonance, such as their grandparents' living room. The location does not need to be indoors, but a literal confined space can help with specificity and vividness.

Goal

To develop a language to describe and shape a real location.

How We Get There

- The Playwright enters the space and defines its parameters (the total playing area) by walking around as if it is the remembered location, describing any physical elements they touch, such as furniture or walls, in as much detail as possible. A childhood bedroom, for instance, may include the bedposts, the dresser, the stuffed animals—pick one up, squeeze it, show how soft it is.
- After perhaps a minute or two of description, the Playwright welcomes the Performers into the space. The Playwright should guide them, telling them to watch their step, don't walk into the door, etc.
- To picture the location as clearly as possible, the Performers challenge the Playwright to provide more details by asking clarifying questions about elements that interest them, such as, "What is this?" or "What is over here?" The Playwright must answer; if they don't remember, they must make something up.
- Once the Performers have a strong sense of what the location looks and feels like, perhaps after two minutes, they should begin to make offers to define the location further, such as

telling the Playwright what they see in this corner, over on that bed. The Playwright can also prompt this by asking, "What else do you see?" Of course, much of what the Performers "observe" would not be found in the actual remembered location; they are describing items that fit the *world* that the Playwright has described, therefore the Playwright must listen to how the remembered world is experienced by the collaborators. This rapport will inform how the following exercises are carried out.

Shaping an Unknown Space

The Playwright and Performers can now shape a new fictional space that will serve as a setting for the play. This is effectively the same as **Shaping a Remembered Space**, but now the Playwright describes a fictional location connected to one or more of the established characters in the play. This can be executed independently of **Shaping a Remembered Space**, but I have noticed that wonderfully unexpected things can happen when they are completed one after another.

Goal

To use the skills built in **Shaping a Remembered Space** to create a vivid fictional location that will serve the Playwright's world.

How We Get There

- The Playwright enters the space and describes what they see, hear, touch, smell, and taste. Bear in mind that the character(s) may not have a strong connection to the location until the *end* of the play, so be open to different possibilities.
- As in **Shaping a Remembered Space**, after the Playwright describes the location, the Performers enter the space and interact. The difference is that, because this location is not based on a real place, it is being shaped in the moment.
- The Performers ask the Playwright questions to further define the location. They must poke and prod delicately; the fledgling world might collapse under too much pressure, but

they must be persistent enough to force the Playwright to make decisions. The Playwright, in turn, must be open to exploring and changing the world being crafted. Again, video recording can preserve details that might otherwise be lost.

- After a couple of minutes of clarifying questions, the Performers should make offers of what they see in this location, building on what the Playwright has established. Offers should be bold, but fit the emerging rules of the world. The Playwright can, of course, correct the Performers so that they will better understand the initial vision of the location, but, again, the Playwright would do well to observe how the Performers interpret and build upon their descriptions.

Inhabiting the World

With locations brainstormed and shaped, the Playwright can now consider what other elements occupy the world of the play and how characters interact with them.

Magical Objects

Objects can ground scenes and orient focus. They can be literally magical, like a shattered heart in a bag in *Almost, Maine*, or metaphorically magical, like Booth's stocking of cash in Suzan-Lori Parks' *Topdog/Underdog*.

Goal

To add details to a location, and the characters that inhabit it, by defining its objects.

How We Get There

- All Performers walk around the space until someone feels the impulse to touch an object they believe exists within it. The Playwright can prompt this by asking, "Would you pick that up and tell us what it is?" The Performer picks it up, feels the weight and shape; other Performers stop and pay attention.

- The Performer that chose the object explains to the group what it is and why it is meaningful.
- Slowly, the Performers pass the object around. Performers may offer personal connections with the object, reminisce with the first Performer about the object, or validate each other's sentiments, building on previous offers.
- The process repeats as a different Performer selects a new object.
- The Playwright should note how each object subtly affects how the Performers interact with the location as a whole.

Entrances and Exits

With a detailed location now largely defined, the Playwright can consider how characters enter and exit. A common improvisation game called **Entrances and Exits** is based on the conceit that the way a character enters and exits a scene affects the entrances and exits of other characters.[4] This exercise is important for Playwrights because, in live performance, entrances and exits are big events, potential ruptures of the world. Entering a crowded train station, for example, has different implications than entering a bedroom during a party. This exercise examines the draw and attributes of locations by exploring how characters react to entering them from the outside world.

Goal

To explore cause and effect by asking what it is about a location that *makes* characters enter and exit.

How We Get There

- The first Performer enters and exits the space, then repeats the process, trying different ways they believe consistent with the character, perhaps experimenting with different days, different moods. The Playwright should notice how the feel of the location changes in the transition from empty to occupied, and how those changes are affected by the Performer's choices.

- Once the Playwright has observed various entrances and exits, they can dismiss the first Performer and invite a second Performer to enter and exit the space. The Playwright should pay attention to how this character changes the feel of the space. This can be repeated with additional Performers as the Playwright deems appropriate.
- After individual entrances and exits, the process is repeated with two Performers: one Performer is already in the space when the Playwright invites a second to enter. How does the second Performer react to the first? The first to the second? How does this dynamic change with heavier or lighter footsteps, more or less energy, anger, or joy? Is it the location, each other, both? Why do they stay or not stay?

Climate Change

At this point, the Playwright can consider where the characters are coming from when they enter, and where they are going when they leave. What is the larger world, and how does it affect what happens? In Viola Spolin's excellent handbook, *Improvisation for the Theatre*, she points out that, in creating a location for a scene, not only do the immediate surroundings need crafting, but the larger environment as well.[5]

Goal

To define a location by exploring the effects of its immediate surroundings.

How We Get There

- The Performers should first consider the surroundings immediately outside the location. This may or may not be outdoors (the location itself can, of course, also be indoors or outdoors), but if attention has not yet been given to the outdoors of this world, this would be a good time to explore that.
- The Performers enter the location either together or one at a time, depending on what serves the Playwright best. They might shiver, wipe their brows, or perhaps be relieved to have entered a comfortable atmosphere. Do they need a drink of

water right away? Do they need to take off wet clothes and warm up? Is it darker or lighter in this location? Louder or quieter? Is this a typical day or is it unusual? How does this affect their interactions with the other characters as they enter?
- The Performers should interact with the location, emphasizing its contrast with its outside surroundings. Is the location itself too cold, warm, dry, or wet? How does this affect the relationships between the characters? Who is comfortable and who is not? Who has the power to make other characters more or less comfortable in this space? What does a more or less comfortable location say about the people who live or work within it?
- The Playwright should note how the Performers' choices emphasize what the location is and is not. Again, as with all of these exercises, the Playwright looks for patterns that emerge in the Performers' actions, and by cross-referencing notes against video footage, it should become much easier to identify rules of the world that support the story, as well as specific attributes of each location within it.

Additional Considerations: Fragility and Speech

The roles of fragility and speech are deeply embedded into the DNA of any world. The Playwright should consider how these two elements inform the environment of the play. Is the environment strong and stable or is it fragile? Perhaps the characters are on a moving boat, or the slippery side of an icy mountain, or recovering from an earthquake. Looking back to the **Entrances and Exits** exercise, consider what a rupture to the space means and whether fear of rupture affects the rules of the world. Might one, or several, of the rules be bent or broken by such a rupture? Consider the difference, for instance, between a woman confronting her partner about an affair in a café versus in the back row of a church during a hellfire sermon. Or the fragility of a hideout for a criminal when the police might burst in at any moment.

Language and speech patterns reveal a lot about characters, such as where they come from and what challenges they might face. During the exercises, the Playwright can ask Performers to experiment with different speech patterns: quick, methodical, musical, hesitant, high- or low-pitched. If Performers speak second languages, they can introduce them into the environment. Characters might need to code switch with some other characters, revealing power dynamics. What speech rhythms and patterns emerge, and how do they affect the rules of the world?

Conclusion

Whether these exercises are used exactly as written or modified to fit an existing play-building methodology, guided collaborative performance can be a very useful tool in helping Playwrights, whether working alone or with other writers, to create vivid locations and clear rules that define robust worlds. These worlds will drive the action of a play as much as any character and make the director's and actors' jobs of interpreting the play much easier. Be playful and imaginative as you collaborate to create your play's setting; anything is possible as long as the rules of your world are consistent.

Notes

1 Graham and Hoggett, p. 35.
2 Chemers, p. 132.
3 Halpern, p. 39.
4 Salinksy and Frances-White, p. 395.
5 Spolin, p. 87.

References

Bogart, Anne, and Tina Landau. *The Viewpoints Book: A Practical Guide to Viewpoints and Composition*. New York: Theatre Communications Group, 2004.
Cariani, John. *Almost, Maine*. Rev. ed. New York: Dramatists Play Service, 2008.
Chemers, Michael M. *Ghost Light: An Introductory Handbook for Dramaturgy*. Carbondale: Southern Illinois University Press, 2010.
Goods, Moses. *Lovey Lee*. Unpublished, 2020.
Graham, Scott, and Steven Hoggett. *The Frantic Assembly Book of Devising Theatre*. Florence: Routledge, 2009.
Halpern, Charna. *Art by Committee: A Guide to Advanced Improvisation*. Meriwether Publishing, 2006.
Halpern, Charna, Del Close, and Kim Johnson. *Truth in Comedy: The Manual of Improvisation*. Englewood, CO: Meriwether Publishing, 1994.
Johnstone, Keith. *Impro: Improvisation and the Theatre*. London: Taylor and Francis, 2018.
Oddey, Alison. *Devising Theatre: A Practical and Theoretical Handbook*. London: Routledge, 1994.
Parks, Suzan-Lori. *Topdog/Underdog*. New York: Theatre Communications Group, 2001.
Salinsky, Tom, and Deborah Frances-White. *Improv Handbook: The Ultimate Guide to Improvising in Comedy, Theatre, and Beyond*. Bloomsbury Publishing, 2013.
Spolin, Viola. *Improvisation for The Theatre: A Handbook of Teaching and Directing Techniques*. Third edition. Evanston, Ill: Northwestern University Press, 1999.

9 It's All About Play

Locating the Game in Embodied Playwriting

John P. Bray

Introduction

Sheldon Patinkin—who was a Chicago-based theatre director, educator, and artistic consultant at Second City—once said:

> When you drop all the life problems and just invest yourself in solving problems within the rules of the game—and since the rules are always about getting what happens next off the person that you're responding to—it creates a sense of community.[1]

In my *Theatre Topics* article, "Playing Together! How the New York Writers' Bloc Created Camaraderie, Community, and Great Stories," I discuss how playwrights Jeffrey Sweet, Donald Margulies, Michael Wright, and Jane Anderson, as well as actors including Jerry Stiller and Anna Meara, formed a community of theatre artists known as the New York Writers' Bloc (or, the Bloc) which sought to bring Second City-based improvisational theatre techniques into the world of new play development.[2] The key factor in improvisation is the game—that is, the rules and structure in which players of the game must solve a problem. The result was a form of embodied playwriting, shaking writers out of their heads and embracing the corporeal nature of live performance.

The Bloc's approach to embodied storytelling practices can guide how our students (undergraduate, graduate, high school, etc.) approach writing for the stage. As Michelle Hayford writes in *Undergraduate Research in Theatre*, "Theatre [is] a collective experience of embodied storytelling, where performers tell stories and audiences bear witness to what it means to be human."[3] Therefore, it is essential to dramatic writers to learn quickly that they are writing something that will be embodied and seen, and the idea of the game can help your students create action-oriented scripts with a focus on human bodies moving

DOI: 10.4324/9781003243014-12

through space. The exercises (games) below have proven invaluable not only as warm-ups, but as tools for creating and revising scripts, as writer-performers find plays in the *doing*, the performing of a physical action, while solving a problem within the rules of the game.

Exercises

Stay

In his book *Acting One*, Robert Cohen offers "contentless scenes," which are "so called because they are devoid of fixed plot or characterization."[4] These scenes are meant to demonstrate objectives (or, as Cohen calls them, "goals;" more on objectives in Exercise Two), as well as "obstacles, vulnerability [of the actors], projection, and the person-to-person contact and tactical interplay that characterize dynamic relationships."[5] These scenes are also excellent *games* for writers who are just learning how to write for live performance as it forces them to get up out of their seats and *perform* in front of their classmates.

Stay

Objective

- To limit the number of words a character can speak and focus on their behavioral patterns
- To illustrate and clarify the importance of objectives, obstacles, and tactics

What We Need

- Two writer-performers
- A performance space with a door (classroom, etc.)

How We Get There

Use a classroom space to double as a performance space where there is a door the writer-performers can access.

- Ask for two writer-performer volunteers, whom you will endow as A and B.
- B's objective is to leave the room. A's objective is to have them stay.

- B moves to leave.
- A shouts "STAY!"

Note: they cannot physically touch each other and can only speak one word to each other at a time. They must find a way to achieve their goal without touching, both for physical safety reasons, and to make sure the writer-performers are comfortable.

Each word must be its own complete sentence; for example, A can't chop up the sentence "I want you to stay" as five lines. So, it may look like:

A: WAIT!
B: CAN'T!
(At this point, A might block the door.)
A: Please!
B: Move!
A: Never!

Side-coaching

If B is moving towards the door, you can say, "Stop them!" If A pauses too long, remind B, "You want to leave! They're just standing there, head for the door!" The stakes should be high, so the writer-performers don't have time to get stuck in their head.

On top of justifying why they're using one word at a time, the writer-performers have to figure out why they aren't physically touching. That's another layer: the two writer-performers are using one word each, trying to get something, and not physically holding each other back. The imaginary situation can be tricky if the characters supposedly know each other well. Writer-performers can get creative; for example, A might say, "Locked," and mime locking the door.

Writing

Now that the writer-performers have physically demonstrated the way in which characters actively move to pursue an objective, the writer-performers will now create a similar situation on paper: two characters, one wants to leave, one wants the other to stay. Each character has an objective, each character provides an obstacle, and each must use some tactic to get what they want.

With this game, the writer-performers quickly learn the nature of dramatic writing: a character has an objective, the second character provides an obstacle via their own equally important-yet-opposite objective, and they both employ tactics to get what they want. They do so, however, not by sitting at a desk, but by physically moving around the room in hot pursuit of their goals, experiencing how much the body is engaged when performing—and therefore, writing—theatrically, as well as in real life circumstances. According to former Second City program director Michael J. Gellman, "Most of what you communicate in life and onstage is determined by your behavior, not by what you say. A grunt can communicate much more than poetic speech. A shrug can be more meaningful than a witty one-liner."[6] With *Stay*, the writer-performer fully experiences the movement with minimal dialogue, which they then use to create a new short scene.

I Need You

One of the first lessons I learned as an undergraduate actor in the 1990s was "acting is reacting." The very notion of "reacting" suggests that at least two people must be present. At SUNY New Paltz, one of my acting professors was Dr. Beverly Brumm, who had studied with Sanford Meisner.[7] Brumm told the class that our story took place in our scene partner's eyes. As a result, whether in scripted scenes or during a repetition exercise, we needed to be fully invested in our partner. The investment had nothing to do with bringing in off-stage imitations of life to create an illusion of Realism; rather, as argued by David Saltz, the Meisner approach asks participants to "commit illocutionary acts within the theatrical context," which we can consider a game.[8] In other words, participants in a Meisner activity were bound together by the game that required their entire focus to be on their partner. Each moment was created in the present, and the past was quickly left behind.

In addition to Meisner activities, Dr. Brumm borrowed from teachings of other Group Theatre members to give us the vocabulary to identify the building blocks of drama within a given scene:

> Objective: What does a character want from another character in a scene?
> Block:[9] What stands in the way of the character getting what they want?
> Tactic: What does the character need to do to get what they want?

The objective-block-tactic approach is an excellent tool for analyzing a script, as well to ensure that psychologically driven drama written by students remains active and embodied.

In 1999, I attended a workshop offered by Professor Simone Federman. She led an exercise, **Come Over Here**, in which two people compete to convince a third person to join them, making the third person an object of negotiation. There are many plays in which a third character becomes an object of negotiation (Yasmina Reza's *Art*, James McLure's *Lone Star*, etc.), and this exercise requires writer-performers to embody those circumstances. This exercise was similar to the Meisner technique, given its repetition of only one line ("come over here") and focus on the partner, but movement was grid-based, akin to exercises in Anne Bogart and Tina Landau's *Viewpoints*. Something not explicitly stated was that the two competing characters were using tactics meant to make the third person *feel* something. The object of negotiation should *feel* the need to choose one or the other. It's the "tactic" part of the game that is the focus of **I Need You**.

I Need You

Objective

- To learn that characters viscerally react to the needs of other characters.

What We Need

- Three writer-performers

How We Get There

- Ask three writer-performers to form a triangle with some distance.
- Person A is the object of negotiation ("head" of the triangle, if you will).
- Persons B and C are the other points of the triangle and will negotiate over person A.
- B begins.
  - B: I need you!
  - A: I need you!

- When A repeats "I need you," they not only repeat what they hear, but also the energy, gestures, and vocal inflections given to them. In other words, they don't just repeat the phrase, they repeat *everything* received from B.
- Then, C speaks.
  - C: I need you.
- A repeats what they hear, feel, and see when giving the line back.
- This continues until A is convinced to join either A or B.

Side-coaching

If a writer-performer is stuck, remind them to focus on their partner and repeat what was just communicated. "How did she say it? How did he move? Look at their hands—what are their hands doing?"

Follow-Up Questions

When the exercise is over, ask why A decided to join B or C. Focus on the way B or C made them feel:

> "I felt like they needed something from me. I felt like I needed to help."
> "I felt threatened."
> "I felt loved."
> "I felt safe."

Writing

Now that the writer-performers have played this game, their task is to write a quick scene in which two characters negotiate over a third character. The objective could be "I want you to come with me instead of that guy," vs. "No, no! Come with me!" The writer-performer can then have A (the head of the triangle/the character being negotiated over) feel compelled to join either B or C dependent on what emotions B and C make A *feel*.

When a character wants something, they must convince another character to let them have it by making the other character *feel* something. Now, this sort of approach does not *always* work in everyday life.

Once too often, I told my dad his workouts were really paying off as a way of buttering him up to borrow the car keys; the last time I tried this, he asked, "What do you want?" When employing tactics, our efforts may have the opposite effect.

Six Movements

When discussing the history of the Bloc, Michael Wright, a playwright who began his career as a stage manager at The Actors Studio, wrote:

> After we had met for about a year, some of us nonwriters began to want to try some writing without going through the horrors of critique. That was when the six-line was introduced. The six-line was based on a simple theatre game used for improvisations.[10]

Writer-performers create "six lines between two characters, with each character having three lines. ... A line can be one word or five pages ... and is the sum of one character's thoughts as spoken in that one response."[11] A prompt would be given one week prior and would feature a "negotiation," in which the characters each had a clear objective.[12]

After attending the Artistic New Directions Improvisation Retreat in 2001, I developed an exercise called **Six Movements**. At the retreat, Gary Austin, founding member of The Groundlings, asked improvisers, in teams of two, to come up with movements, and then to create dialogue that justifies the movements. We would name our movements out loud, taking turns, perform the movements, and then the dialogue would come last, justifying the behaviors. Sometimes the behaviors were outlandish! But the key was to follow and trust our acting partners.

A hybrid of the six-line and Austin's exercise, **Six Movements** focuses on telling a story without using any spoken dialogue.

Six Movements

Objective

- To create short scenes without dialogue.

What We Need

- Two performers
- A space to explore (preferably with a door to reference, such as a classroom)

How We Get There

- Have two writer-performers stand in front of the room (A and B). B creates the environment, demonstrating that they have something that really shouldn't be dropped: a tray of cookies out of the oven, something expensive that must be handled gingerly, etc.

Movements:

1. B creates the environment and object.
2. A enters abruptly, startling B.
3. B drops the object, and it breaks.
4. A approaches B.
   (Here it changes—A can help B clean up, making further choices—hectically, as if expecting the boss to enter? Sympathetically, because B is about to cry?)
5. Based on the previous beat, B either accepts help or tries to correct A on how to clean the mess.
6. The last movement belongs to them both: if the scene has taken a sweet turn, they might join or touch hands. An angry turn, one might storm off. If they agree on it (nonverbally), they can look towards the door as if to say "oh, no, they're here!"

After several pairs of writer-performers have performed the exercise as outlined above, they can begin creating their own six-movements, so long as there is a sense of confidence in the room. One key ingredient to this game is *stakes*: each moment should raise the stakes until the end. The last beat could serve as a button to the scene (holding hands), or the stakes might get even higher (looking at the door).

Writing

Once the writer-performers have experienced these physical exercises, they can apply what they have learned to a new script: two characters, one room.

- Each character will say their movement out loud and perform the action.

- Then, using the "strike-through," remove their out loud moments. What the writer is left with is a series of movements via stage-directions.
- If something isn't clear, now the writer-performer can add dialogue, but only for clarity, not to over-explain the scene.

Conclusion

The key takeaway from this chapter is that theatre games created by members of the improvisation community can teach playwrights how to embody behavior, thereby gaining a stronger understanding of how that behavior communicates volumes without a character needing to speak a single word. Or, as Michael Wright says, "When a playwright uses behavior, he is recognizing a crucial element of theatre: the actions of a human being help define and move the story along."[13] With the embodied playwriting approach, student-written scripts become active, as students (whom I've addressed as writer-performers throughout this chapter) are learning that characters are constantly *doing*. Professor Michelle Hayford concurs, offering:

> Writing for the stage means accounting for a work that will live off the page in three-dimensional space, with all the accoutrements of theatrical design artistry. Too often, students conceive of playwriting as dialogue among characters, and their hyperfocus on the text is to the detriment of imagining how the embodiment of the production will live in the space of a theatre with an audience.[14]

By learning how to embody their characters' objectives via improvisational games, students (now, writer-performers) will better understand the best practices for writing theatrically.

Notes

1 Qtd. London.
2 Bray, p. 1–10.
3 Hayford, p. 1.
4 Cohen, p. 39.
5 Ibid.
6 Scruggs and Gellman, p. 55.

7 Sanford Meisner (1905–1997) was a member of The Group Theatre and an acting teacher whose most popular exercise involved "the repetition," in which two actors would focus entirely on each other, make an observation about each other, and repeat what they heard from the other person until there was an organic change. This approach to acting became known as The Meisner Technique, and did not rely on the sense memory or affective memory exercises of fellow Group Theatre alumnus, Lee Strasberg, father of Method Acting in the U.S.

8 Saltz, p. 73.

9 Not to be confused with a "block" as it's used in improvisation, which means to deny an offer given by a scene partner to the detriment of the game.

10 Wright, p. 15.

11 Ibid.

12 Ibid.

13 Ibid., p. 6.

14 Hayford, p. 89.

References

Bray, John Patrick. "Playing Together! How the New York Writers' Bloc Created Camaraderie, Community, and Great Stories." *Theatre Topics*, 24(1), pp. 1–10, 2014.

Cohen, Robert. *Acting One*. Boston, MA: McGraw-Hill, 2008.

Hayford, Michelle. *Undergraduate Research in Theatre: A Guide for Students*. New York, NY: Routledge, 2022.

London, Todd. "A Brief History of Improvisation: Spolin and Sills Laid Down the Rules." Spolin Games Online – Improvisational Library and Training, September 29, 2020. https://spolingamesonline.org/a-brief-history-of-improvisation-spolin-and-sills-laid-down-the-rules/.

Saltz, David. "The Reality of Doing: Real Speech Acts in the Theatre." Essay. In *Method Acting Reconsidered: Theory, Practice, Future*, edited by David Krasner, pp. 61–79. New York, NY: St. Martin's Press, 2000.

Scruggs, Mary, and Michael J. Gellman. *Process: An Improviser's Journey*. Evanston, IL: Northwestern University Press, 2008.

Wright, Michael. *Playwriting in Process: Thinking and Working Theatrically*. Newburyport, MA: Focus Pub./R. Pullins Co., 2010.

10 Folkgames as Creative Stimulus for Devising

The Case of *Chaskele*

Solomon Y. Dartey

Introduction

The majority of a child's life is full of play, but through this play life lessons are learnt which contribute to the child's development. Africans, for instance, teach morals of life, collaboration, care, and understanding through folk culture. Our folk activities, especially games, promote reconciliation, cooperativeness, good sportsmanship, and unity. In fact, folkgames are integral to the survival and growth of a child in the African setup, serving not just as recreational activities, but as a critical avenue for the transfer of morals and tenets. As N.K. Lowe wrote, in an article for *Science and Technology Education*, "Play is not just a filling of an empty period, or just a relaxation or leisure activity, but it is an important learning experience."[1]

Interestingly, these folkgames are rarely explored by creatives, unlike folksongs and folktales, which are regularly explored in Ghanaian theatrical performances. Practitioners may employ folkgames as warm-up activities during rehearsals and interludes or breaks during workshops, but few recent practitioners have ventured to use folkgames in performance. However, theatre is a dynamic tool for advocating for and advancing social and developmental change, and there is a need to engage new mediums to promote and preserve the essential folk culture of old, to transfer the knowledge of a community's past and current values. Theatre for Development, Theatre for Education, and other applied theatre practices mostly hinge on what is prevalent in the community and create out of it, acting as a tool for communication with the ability to transcend language and cultural barriers, as well as advancing positive initiatives, such as the Sustainable Development Goals (SDGs), promoted by the United Nations Agenda 2030 for Sustainable Development, which aim to end poverty, protect plants, and ensure prosperity for all.

It important for creatives whose focus is mainly to provoke change or advance community development to approach their creativity by engaging

DOI: 10.4324/9781003243014-13

with what is familiar to people, something that is dear to them or resonates with them, something like their food and folklore. For instance, Ghanaian playwrights like Efua Sutherland, Mohammed ben Abdallah, Yaw Asare, and Martin Owusu started their creative journey by relying heavily on the culture of the Ghanaian people. Their plays relied heavily on folktales, especially Ananse tales. The character Ananse is a Ghanaian original but found in tales from Africa, the Caribbean, and some Black American communities.[2] His descriptors include intelligent, cunning, witty, dubious, and mythical. Plays such as *The Marriage of Anansewa* (1975) by Efua Sutherland; *Ananse in the Land of Idiots* (2006) by Yaw Asare; *The Story Ananse Told* (1999) by Martin Owusu; and *Ananse-Kweku Ananse* (2004) by Efo Kojo Mawugbe are examples of plays woven around the folkloric character Ananse. This phenomenon led to the coinage of the term *Anansegoro*, a Ghanaian theatre form which is rooted in Ghanaian folk stories, especially the tales of Ananse. Playwrights deconstruct folktales, reconceive them, and create newly relevant plays or performances.

My own work on devised performances such as *Wise Up* (2014),[3] *Body Words* (2014),[4] and *Facta Non Verba Reloaded* (2013)[5] relied heavily on folklore. My quest to engage the use of folkgames in my performances came after the success of *Body Words*, a devised performance by students of the School of Performing Arts at the University of Ghana, which used improvisation, folksongs, and folkgames as tools for creation and development. This led to extensive research into folkgames and how to engage them conceptually and as a resource to create performances. The research revealed the need to always deconstruct the folkgames to enable participants to appreciate the embedded meaning of the game alongside the peripheral meaning. After deconstructing, the innate meanings derived become as integral to the creation of the performance as the aesthetic appeal.

Most Ghanaian folkgames seek to develop the focus, precision, collaboration, bonding, and reflexes of the participants. For devisers, using folkgames as stimulus is useful and reliable for story development, as they can excite imaginations and develop interest. For example, Calabash Farm used the Chaskele game as a stimulus to create a theatrical performance promoting the SDGs in Ghana. Chaskele's concept, approach, and outcome became the basis for devising, using research and community participation, to focus specifically on SDGs 3 (Good Health and Wellbeing), 6 (Clean Water and Sanitation), and 15 (Life on Land). Chaskele as a Ghanaian folkgame is similar to baseball or cricket, but for the purpose of devising, the people playing the game were categorised under two broad groupings: *Cleanliness* and *Anti-cleanliness*. The *Cleanliness* characters are those who pick up waste materials in their surroundings and aim at dropping them in a bin, in this case a used tire, basket, or bucket. The other team, who normally are very close to the bin, try to keep the cleanliness team from achieving their aim; they kick the waste about haphazardly. These characters could be classified as anti-progressives, for they suggest that it is somebody else's duty to clean up the environment. For our performance, after playing the Chaskele game, the character Striker stepped out and said the following:

> And that's Chaskele. This is the game they are playing. Everybody wants to throw something into the tire but this guy (*points at the guy with the stick*), standing there, doesn't agree. Some were able to throw the rubbish into it, some couldn't. That's the moral of this game. Many of us over here in this Madina don't like development. So, we have become stumbling blocks to the progress of the community. Like this guy who is hitting away the positive vibes of the others who are aiming at their goal, many of us do not want to come together as a unified force, to clean up Madina, to develop Madina, and to progress Ghana as a whole. Please let's change our attitudes, and it starts from today. Thank you!

Figure 10.1 Performers setting up for the Chaskele game at Alliance Française d'Accra. The stage is littered this way before the performance starts, and the performers through the playing of the game clean the stage. Photographs by the author.

Through the game, the attitudes of individuals towards their environment were established through the playing of Chaskele. Though the message was established allegorically, the narrative by Striker after the game performance deconstructed the essence of the game to the audience. Through improvisational gameplay, folkgames can be used as a stimulus for creating performances that seek to address societal themes or promote social actions. While Chaskele is ordinarily played on an open field, the game can easily be adapted to a performance space by performers while developing their original stories. Of course, while exploring how such a game can be used by creatives, it is important to know how the game is originally played.

The Chaskele Game

Chaskele is a folkgame which derived its name from the sound an empty tin can makes when hit with a stick and then drops on the ground, hence it is non-syllabic. It is very common in the coastal regions of Ghana but has permeated other regions over time. Usually played in an open field before sundown for relaxation, Chaskele promotes social cohesion, sense of belonging, and fraternity. The folkgame is played

Figure 10.2 Calabash Farm performers playing the Chaskele game. The defender is holding the stick behind the used tires and the other players are aiming to throw the used plastic bottles into the tires.

mostly by males in Ghana, but audiences who normally watch the Chaskele game from afar sometimes become active participants, having learned the rules while observing, so females join the game in some communities. The game is very flexible and evolving, depending on the surroundings and materials available. Like baseball or cricket, the game is normally played with sticks, crushed cans, buckets, or used tires. Focus and precision are the hallmarks of this game, as a little loss of focus or concentration can lead to injuries due to the objects used in the game. When engaged competitively, teams are challenged to strategize and use semiotics as a communication tool to outwit the opponent.

A minimum of two players can play the game, with one trying to hit the bin and the other as the keeper/defender. The players start the game from a neutral position, thus an agreed line is drawn away from the bin, and each participant aims to first get their can into the bin to determine who becomes the defender. Once that is determined, it now becomes the duty of the defender to ensure his opponent's thrown cans do not enter the target (the tire or bucket). The defender typically stays close to the target to prevent scoring, with some rules providing only one opportunity to deflect an opponent's can. Players try to make sure each can enters the tire or bucket. The closer the player is to the target, the better the chance of dropping the object in the bin. The beauty of

Figure 10.3 The defender is focused on preventing the waste bag from entering the tire, while the other players are focused on throwing.

Figure 10.4 The defender attempts to hit a plastic bottle that has been thrown by another player.

the game is that wherever the object (crushed can) falls during a missed shot becomes the spot to stand to try again. The game can be varied depending on the number of people playing and the quest of the teams. It could be a defender against a few other players, two defenders against several players, etc. If there are multiple players, they all keep trying till the last person hits the target or there is a consensus to end the game. In some instances, the last to hit the target naturally becomes the defender of the new game. This game can last for hours provided the defender is effective, because it comes to an end only when all the players' cans are in the bucket or tire.

Engaging Chaskele for Performance Purposes

The Chaskele game can be played as a warm-up activity as well as be explored as a stimulus for creating original pieces through the use of improvisation. To start, one needs to get the following materials: paper or papier-mâché balls, a used tire or bucket, sticks (to use as bats), and paper and pen to record discoveries that can be integrated into the devised performance or play. To promote recycling, it will be good to use waste or recycled products, and using a paper ball or papier-mâché is a good replacement for crushed cans, as they sometimes cause injuries. Another advantage of paper or papier-mâché is that words or ideas can be written on them or hidden inside them. The facilitator can also number the balls and link them up with activities hidden from participants. Whenever participants score, they get to individually perform a hidden activity or lead the team in a collaborative task. The record-taking is to be done by the teacher or facilitator. Students should be encouraged to record their reflections after every session, as well as write about connections to their environment or community.

The Setup

It is important to position the basket, bucket, or tire at the centre of the stage, at an angle that allows for ample throwing distance from a starting line, as shown in Figure 10.5. The sticks and balls should be within range, and participants should each pick up a ball and stand behind the line to signal their readiness for the game to commence.

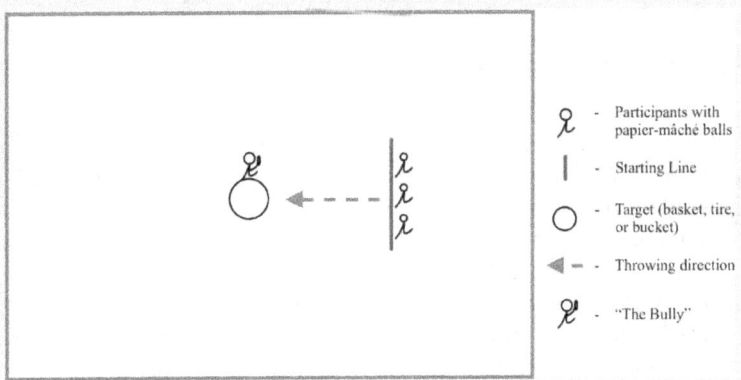

Figure 10.5 A diagram showing how to position "The Bully" and other team members when starting the Chaskele game. It is important for all to start at a neutral position.

Chaskele as Metaphor

In playing the game as metaphor, it is important for the facilitator to establish a subject matter for group deliberation. The subject matter should be community-centred; for example, perhaps the group is going to explore the problem of bullying. Participants should begin by researching the issue to better understand the effects and consequences of bullying in their own schools and communities. Then participants can engage in an improvisational approach to the game. Participants take their positions for the game, with one person standing by the bin (see Figure 10.5). This person becomes "The Bully" and prevents the other participants from hitting the target. Any time participants' throws are deflected by "The Bully," they share how they feel about being bullied. The game can be repeated, with participants improvising and telling the team future consequences of being bullied. After this, "The Bully" should allow participants to successfully make the target and reflect on the experience of being helped instead of obstructed. Participants can reflect on their personal experiences, both in and out of the game, and develop them into monologues, which they can read to the group. These monologues can further be developed into a performance with bullying as the subject matter. This exercise can be used to engage performers and writers in the initial exploration of many other contemporary subjects or pressing issues in the community.

Environmental Police

To play *Environmental Police*, the Calabash Farm adaptation referenced earlier in this chapter, with students, the facilitator should make sure that the space is filled with tennis balls, plastic balls, sensory balls, and other things that can be thrown and will not cause injury, but these objects should represent recyclable or waste materials. The tire, basket, or bucket should be placed at the centre of the stage or where students can throw from a distance. At the beginning of the process, the facilitator should document the reactions of students when they enter the space, perhaps by taking pictures or asking questions. Questions can be asked (such as: Who caused this? Why did the person do that? What happened here?) and the facilitator can enlist the students' views on what should be done to clean the room.

At this point, the facilitator informs the class about how the room should be cleaned. Participants can only pick up one item at a time and must throw from the place where they pick up the object, and they must take turns. The facilitator can act as an anti-cleanliness agent or delegate someone to take up that responsibility. The anti-cleanliness agent needs to hold a stick or a bat to use to prevent thrown objects from entering the target. Whenever participants miss the target or have an object deflected by the agent, they have to make the next throw from the spot where the object lands. Participants should continue playing until most of them succeed in reaching the target, and whoever gets the most objects in the tire or bucket becomes the winner of the activity.

The facilitator should ensure that students reflect on their experience with the activity. They should consider the role of the anti-cleanliness agent and how those actions affect society. They should also reflect on their own roles and how they can positively affect their communities. Students can use these reflections as the basis for written monologues, which can be combined into a performance that had its beginnings in a game.

Conclusion

Cultural folkgames, such as Chaskele, afford creators, devisers, and writers the opportunity to explore urgent societal issues and community concerns by combining gameplay and improvisation to develop original performances that tap into cultural folklore and shared knowledge, enhancing the effectiveness of a performance and encouraging the embrace of positive social actions.

Notes

1 Lowe, p. 1–89.
2 Juang and Morrissette.
3 Directed by Solomon Yaw Dartey and Alfred Elikem Kunutsor, *Wise Up* was a devised performance with the environment as its subject matter, commissioned for Clemson University Scholars to the School of Performing Arts, University of Ghana.
4 *Body Words* was a devised performance which relied heavily on improvisation, folkgames, and folksongs for its creation. Directed by Solomon Yaw Dartey and performed by students at the School of Performing Arts.

5 *Facta Non Verba Reloaded* relied heavily on the use of miming and shadow theatre as key elements in the performance creation. Directed by Solomon Yaw Dartey with students of the School of Performing Arts, University of Ghana.

References

Juang, Richard M. and Noelle Morrissette. *Africa and the Americas: Culture, Politics, and History.* California, ABC-CLIO, Inc, 2008.

Library, Ypsilanti District. *Folk Games.* 2021, March 17. Retrieved 23 August 2022 from: https://www.ypsilibrary.org/2021/03/folkgames.

Lowe, N.K. "Games and Toys in the Teaching of Science and Technology." *Science and Technology Education*, pp. 1–89, 1988. Document S.

Part IV
Changemaking

11 "Laughter that Shatters"
Improv Techniques for Social Justice Comedy Playwriting

Elspeth Tilley

Introduction

Humor is a powerful tool for social justice playwriting. Comedy can break stale categories to allow new ways of thinking, release stress, and undermine power imbalances. However, many writers lack confidence in their ability to be "funny", thinking that comedy is innate rather than learned. Others may worry that humor is incompatible with serious political issues. Neither is true: I am not funny in real life (at all), but I can write politically purposeful plays that, to my astonishment, audiences guffaw at and reviewers describe as "hilarious"[1] and providing "the biggest laughs."[2] At the same time, these plays have "fired spiky, uncomfortable questions" (which is my real aim) about social issues from climate change to feminism to animal cruelty, "delivered in a completely enjoyable manner – great fun … somehow!"[3]

I can trace this surprising ability to generate humorous insights into thorny issues to my improvisation background. At the improvisation training program at La Boite Theatre, Brisbane, Australia, in the 1990s, I was fortunate to work with skilled trainers (including Deb Frances-White who would go on to worldwide fame with the "Guilty Feminist" podcast),[4] who imparted the fundamental mechanics of comedy embedded in physical play, word play, and status play exercises. Brisbane was experiencing a political renaissance under its first Labor Premier in thirty-two years, who ushered in a new era of civil liberties, homosexual law reform, conservation, and labor rights. The environment of progressive change was reflected in the improv culture at La Boite, where both training and performances were politically astute and imbued with a strong sense of demanding, celebrating, and cementing social change. It's only with hindsight that I realize how fortunate I was to be part of it and how deeply it has influenced my playwriting and teaching.

This chapter shares a playwriting workshop design in which I present key aims of social justice comedy playwriting, then take participants through improvisation activities in each of the three areas of playfulness—physical, linguistic, and status—that I first learned at La Boite. These categories, as I later discovered, correspond well with the main structures of humor identified by Sigmund Freud—body humor, mind humor, and spirit humor.[5]

Understanding body humor, including the lineage of many improv exercises to classic slapstick and commedia dell'arte, helps writers find the "funny" in (safe forms of) failure and celebrate all kinds of bodies. Mind humor helps writers build creativity through divergent thinking and imagining different versions of our world, including very different possibilities for our social and political arrangements. Spirit humor (drawing particularly on Keith Johnstone's work on status) helps us learn how to build differentiated characters and involve those characters in bespoke narratives in which underdogs triumph and tyrants receive their just deserts, delivering audiences the empowering experiences of justice that they crave.

Context: The Aims of Social Justice Comedy Playwriting

I only know two jokes, both involving bad puns that make people groan, not laugh. Nothing could have surprised me more than the first time I sat in an audience listening to people laugh at one of my plays. So, get rid of the idea that you have to be a "funny person" to write comedy, or that it's about jokes. You can get jokes out of a joke book, but jokes alone won't make your play a comedy.

The plays of mine that people laugh at are the ones with illogical characters, flipped perspectives, and silly status reversals. For example, I often put more-than-human characters on stage to share their views on humanity: horses that give a horse-eye view of the racing industry, penguins who poke fun at Antarctic-adventuring humans in giant puffy jackets, or a talking lipstick that compares human use of cosmetics to baboons reddening and inflating their bottoms. My human characters are also often not what they first appear to be—roadworkers who stage a de facto climate protest by stopping traffic for hours, or hospital staff who gleefully encourage patients who can't cover their medical expenses to pay their way by participating in a reality TV show about their health.[6]

Audiences laugh at the sheer ridiculousness of it. Then they write to me later to say that unexpected concerns stirred in their consciousness after they'd left the theatre: Why don't humans look after each other to the same extent penguins do? Where exactly are we heading with the privatization of public health? How do horses feel about being whipped and drugged and castrated for human entertainment? Something about comedically disrupting the boundary between reality and ludicrousness prompts people first to laugh, then to look at themselves and their assumptions afresh.

One explanation for this can be found in the work of Michel Foucault. In his great work of social justice, *The Order of Things*, Foucault exposes the ways human systems of thought arbitrarily prioritize concepts—humans over nature, capital above labor, and many more hierarchies and power schemas encoded into culture.[7] The book was conceived in response to a comedic passage in an essay by Jorge Luis Borges. In the essay, Borges imagined an encyclopedia that classified animals by comedic categories such as whether they had just broken the water pitcher or were depicted using a fine camelhair brush.[8] The Borges passage is problematically Orientalist, but it is the disruptive effect it had on Foucault that is useful here. Foucault wrote of his:

> laughter that shattered, as I read the passage, all the familiar landmarks of my thought—our thought that bears the stamp of our age and our geography—breaking up all the ordered surfaces and all the planes with which we are accustomed to tame the wild profusion of existing things, and continuing long afterwards to disturb and threaten with collapse our age-old distinction between the Same and the Other.[9]

Foucault felt his thinking take a great leap to see the arbitrariness of humanity's supposedly rational categories of hierarchy, separation, and difference. This same sense of a "leap" is what I feel when I encounter a play that uses humor to make me see social justice issues differently. For example, in Anders Lustgarten's *The Hamster*, a hamster that never stops growing offers a hilarious yet shockingly unsubtle metaphor for the unlimited-growth mentality of capitalism.[10] Or *Brackendale* by Elaine Avila, in which two Bald Eagles living at a dump poke fun at humans for our obsession with shiny plastic things.[11]

There is a brain science explanation for how this works. Disruptive comedic devices are often deliberately naïve or childish; they take us back to a time before we learned to accept all the ways that (non-Indigenous) humans order things to place ourselves at the pinnacle of separated ecologies. Cognitive psychologist Melanie Joy argues that children are naturally empathetic and non-hierarchical, but in Western cultures we are trained in empathy inhibition to serve egoistic motives or cultural beliefs.[12] We may be taught, for example, to dissociate the living pig from the tasty bacon. We might be socialized to think that people in menial jobs are uninformed. We may learn to cognitively block awareness of the five hundred years it takes a plastic bag to decompose when we close the garbage can lid. To cope with our exploitative, hierarchical world we are trained, Joy concludes, to become very good at psychic numbing.

Johnstone described a comparable numbing process in *Impro* when he discussed losing the sense of connectedness with the world that he had as a child, because "school had been teaching me *not* to respond." Laughter, though, is the opposite of numbing. Laughter is a "positive and arousing affective experience:"[13] our heart races, breathing increases, endorphins flow. Improvisation techniques are invaluable because they retrain us in accessing a childlike state of play, in overcoming what Johnstone called the "violence" of "categorizing and selecting"[14] in order to re-enter a "wild and aberrant"[15] state in which we can re-embrace our earlier empathy, spontaneity, and creativity. The writing that comes out of such a process is often both playfully funny and disruptive of the status quo.

Warming up with Improv

It may seem counterintuitive to begin a writing workshop with activities in which no writing happens, but kinesthetic and verbal improvisation exercises are invaluable for activating the "pre-rational" mindset necessary for writing social justice comedy. My workshops begin with a simple "Pointing at Things" warmup, adapted from Johnstone[16] by Tom Salinsky and Deborah Frances-White,[17] to break the ice, activate presence and focus, and dispel inhibition. Johnstone identified this activity, in which people point at things and name them, then point at things and misname them, as one of his favorite ways to swiftly re-access "the amazing intensity of the world I'd lived in as a child."[18] It also introduces a fundamental tenet of humor theory: incongruity.[19]

Pointing at something and naming it something else inevitably leads to laughter, which provides an immediate opportunity to explain humor studies' concept of "Misattribution Theory," in which playful incongruity (disrupting the "rules" of language as a form of representation) activates mirth.[20] Participants can suggest and discuss examples of incongruity (e.g., Cassandra the cleaning lady who is also a Greek soothsayer in Christopher Durang's *Vanya and Sonia and Masha and Spike*) or misattribution (e.g., the mistaken identity of classic farce in *One Man, Two Guvnors*,[21] or *Date Night*, in which Tina Fey and Steve Carell's mild-mannered characters are mistaken for mobsters,[22] or *Miranda*, in which the title character is repeatedly mistaken for a man[23]).

After an activity at which everyone can succeed, I move to a warmup at which everyone will fail, to introduce the role of pleasurable failure in comedy. When I first learned this exercise, I recall it being credited to Anne Bogart, although I have yet to find it in her written works. David Farmer's *101 Drama Games and Activities*[24] and Inside Outside Theatre's website both include versions.[25] My adapted version is deliberately more chaotic than theirs as failure, not success, is my aim.

Number Ping-Pong

Directions

- Ask participants to pair up and face each other. They can stand or sit.
- Ask the pairs to count to three, taking turns to say each number, then start at one again, bouncing the numbers back and forth as fast as they can, like a ping-pong game.
- As soon as you notice participants beginning to master the flow, ask them to replace the numeral one with a silly noise/action combo (I like to use a loud meow and paw-swipe like a naughty kitten).
- After another minute, replace the numeral two with another silly noise/action combo (I use a donkey braying and swishing its ears).
- Then, in turn, swap out the numeral three (e.g., for a gull crying and flapping).
- Move the pace of change just fast enough to force mistakes.

When everything has dissolved into chaos and laughter, it's time to stop and ask people what made them laugh. They quickly diagnose that it is the "stuff ups" that are funny. When the activity is going well, it's serious, but when they cannot help but fail they involuntarily begin to laugh together. A continuation activity for a longer and more physical warmup is 'What are you doing?', in which partners take turns getting each other to mime activities while explaining that they are doing something completely different.[26] Both exercises create laughter through failure, as well as demonstrating incongruity. We can connect this to humor theory tenets that are useful for playwriting: disruption of rigid control is funny (known as relief theory—energy used to try to manage a situation is released as relieved laughter when we give up the attempt at control)[27] and for an audience watching a play, witnessing a controlling character come undone provides the same sense of relief.

If the workshop is the start of a long sequence of participants working together, this is a good moment to elicit shared ideas about what makes a brave space. What safeguards do we need to ensure that people can take risks? Or, for participants coming together just once, discuss how the concept of failure-as-success can be used in playwriting to create situations in which rule-bound characters must surrender control. Either way, it's a good demonstration of the relationship between relinquishing control and generating humor, and participants will be able to offer examples from plays or films. Yasmina Reza's *God of Carnage* comes to my mind, in which four buttoned-up parents gradually unravel into tantrums and recriminations as they try and fail to rationally discuss a playground altercation between their children.[28] Plato warned against laughter as a dangerous emotion that overrides rational self-control,[29] but the opposite effect is useful to playwrights: a character's loss of rational self-control generates laughter. Errors, failure, and disruption of power and control are the lifeblood of comedy.

Because this warmup uses body play, it is also a useful reminder for playwrights that the goal of our writing is ultimately to be theatricalized by performing bodies, and that bodies can be funny. Most of us never quite lost that childish impulse to laugh at fart sounds. Braying and making donkey ears is, as Shakespeare well knew with Nick Bottom,[30] classic clowning territory. Asked to suggest other clowning devices that use body humor, participants may identify big shoes that make the body clumsy or red noses that honk when touched. Psychologists have connected this celebration of physical unruliness to a sense of liberation associated with bodies that refuse to be disciplined. There's an important power element in the humor though: if a stern and forbidding teacher is yelling at kids who haven't done their homework and that teacher's bottom lets out a ripper fart, or their false teeth fly out as they shout, the kids will probably laugh about that for weeks. But if a kind and beloved teacher becomes critically unwell, and that's why they're tripping over their own feet, losing their teeth, or stinking up the room, suddenly it's not funny at all, just sad. So, there's more to body play than just rejoicing in undisciplined bodies. It's the set-up or context that makes it funny, or not—which we'll come back to in discussions of spirit humor and punching up, below. Next, in my workshop, I move to an activity that develops skills in linguistic comedy, but simultaneously shows that language doesn't need to be clever to be funny.

Da Doo Ron Ron Compliments

This twist on a classic "improv" warmup continues to pick apart "what makes things funny" and simultaneously builds participants' confidence in their own comedic abilities.

Directions

- Practice singing along to "Da Doo Ron Ron" by The Crystals as a group (with groovy hip sways and clapping to inject body humor) until you've got the rhythm and melody.
- Then, turn the song off. Go around the circle and say your names. The whole group repeats names back to cement familiarity.
- Turn the song back on, karaoke-style with backing track but no vocals.
- It's helpful if you lead off by way of demonstration. Sing the first verse of the song (singing it badly is even better—see the humor of failure, above).
- Pick a person from the group, use their name, and make the verse about them—but it must be a compliment. "I met them on the corner and their name was Dwight, da-doo-ron-ron, da-doo-ron-ron. Their name was Dwight, and they're… all right! Da-doo-ron-ron, da-doo-ron-ron."
- Everyone repeats the verse together, then it's Dwight's turn to create a compliment about someone else.

It doesn't look particularly funny written down but, in the moment, participants often generate spontaneous compliments for each other that have the room in stitches. Why? Because we're deploying what Freud called "mind humor". We're using word play, such as rhyming, puns, and sometimes double entendre or layered meanings, but often it's the lamest contributions (rhyming "right" with "Dwight") that get the biggest laughs, reinforcing that *not* trying to "be clever" is an important route to humor (or, as Johnstone put it, "be obvious").[31] Plus, as Johnstone pointed out, improvising in verse sabotages the need to control meaning and enables words to come "of their own accord" based on sound alone.[32] The shift from letting our *cognition* lead our language generation to letting our *body* lead the language (by allowing the mouth to physically form the sound without thinking), often releases unexpected jokes. From Aristophanes' comedies to the witty dialogue of contemporary plays such as Beth Henley's *Crimes of the Heart* or Patrick Marber's *Closer*, many plays use wordplay to comic effect, yet also address more serious issues. Playing with verbal language generation can help playwrights access a brave space in which wordplay flows more spontaneously. Wordplay is also a useful tool for playwrights who need to cloak subversive intent when open criticism of authority is prohibited.

A discussion about why the exercise specifies only compliments is also important. Johnstone used insult-trading as an effective form of rigidity disruption in his training, and I acknowledge that in some contexts that might be useful. However, in customizing his exercises to my own values and to our climate-and-pandemic-altered world (in which young people in particular are very stressed and vulnerable), I prefer to use feminist ethics of care concepts which focus on kindness and lifting others up.[33] Interestingly, participants often comment that this feels more compatible with the ways they cared for and related to each other as very young children (prior to internalizing the authoritarian/hierarchical tenets of patriarchy). They find games in which cooperation is the goal more conducive to reactivating a childlike sense of wonder, play, and untamed laughter than those based on competition, and thus can more quickly enter a naïve mindset that generates highly imaginative playwriting. Thus, no matter what games we play in my theatre and playwriting classes, nobody is ever "out" when they make a mistake. Having established that stuffing up is the point, we cheer and applaud the mistake (not the person, because a person is not their mistakes) and carry on.

Which brings us to "spirit humor". Anthropologists tell us that one of the evolutionary functions of humor is to help us cope with "subsistence stress."[34] We evolved as animals who laugh, because laughter helps us cope with things we feel threatened by. This is what Freud means by spirit humor: humor that delivers the audience the justice they crave, by setting up the premise of a superior or conceited character on a pedestal, who is then fodder for a lowlier "fool" to disrupt. Our experience witnessing a disruption of power can be either a release valve, providing a safe way to defy authority when we cannot wield power in our own lives, or serve as a model, motivating and inspiring us to actively seek justice in the real world because of the joy we've experienced in seeing it happen on stage. Johnstone and Freud essentially agreed that comedy is about reversals of power or, as Johnstone called it, status.

Improv for Writing Justice

Status is well documented in many places[35,36] and Viola Spolin's exercises are a particularly great resource[37] so I won't repeat the basics here.

What is useful to add is how helpful status work can be for social justice comedy playwriting. Here, I use an adaptation to status work in which the low-status character receives a written "secret weapon."

Status Work: The "Secret Weapon" Activity

Directions

- Provide two participants with a simple setting and scene starter, e.g., waiting outside a closed door for a job interview, with the characters unsure who is next in line.
- Coach one to play high-status and aim to psych the other character out and get through the door first.
- Coach the other to play low-status and aim to be liked by the high-status character.
- The interactions will quickly fall into a binary of intimidation/flattering, controlling/acquiescing, in which one character competes and wins over the other, while the other wins the audience's sympathy.
- Let it run for a few minutes then coach the low-status actor to let the high-status character get what they want, end the scene, and ask the group for observations. Most people will say that it was not funny at all—interesting, but more as a tragic scene that elicited feelings of pity for the low-status character and dislike of the high-status character.
- Ask the actors to play the same scene with the same dialogue and characters.
- Write the low-status character a "secret weapon" to spring when they feel the moment is right. I write this "secret weapon" on a scrap of paper and slip it into the low-status character's hand after I've watched the first scene and have a sense of the characters. It is context-specific, but has included such things as the low-status character revealing that they are in fact the hiring manager and that was the job interview, that they are the daughter of the hiring manager and already have the job but other people are being interviewed to give appearance of due process, or that only people who are shorter than a certain height are eligible for the job for safety reasons (seeing the high status character suddenly slump down in their seat to seem shorter elicits an immediate laugh). Any form of context-relevant triumph for the low-status character will have the same effect: laughter.

152 *Elspeth Tilley*

Ask the group to discuss the differences between the two scenes. They will note that when a dominated character quietly or even accidentally foils a domineering character's aims, we find it funny. The more frustrated the "top dog" is at being thwarted, the funnier it gets: justice is being served and relieved laughter results. Any clip from Abbott and Costello (Abbott plays the devious straight man with Costello as the comic fool who subverts him) or *Blackadder,* a UK television series that sustained four series on this single comic setup (an unlikeable high-status character constantly thwarted by a revolving cast of underlings who subvert his lust for power)[38] will illustrate the concept, as will the opening scene of Aristophanes' *The Frogs,* or any scene from commedia dell'arte in which the braggartly Il Capitano is brought low by the trickster servant Arlecchino. This simple device can sustain lengthy comedic opportunities when used as a "see-saw"—the power shifting to and fro between the characters and creating a moving dynamic that is fascinating to watch and generates multiple comedy pay-offs. It's worth emphasizing that when the unlikeable character's own trait or behavior creates their undoing (an "own goal"), and all the low-status character must do is knowingly let it happen, it's even funnier. The underdog's triumph helps the audience cope through laughter with things we too feel threatened by.

Participants can then practice playwriting using the mechanism by grouping in threes. Two improvise new characters and premise. Any setting with clearly status-differentiated characters (intern and senior executive, hotel cleaner and self-indulgent rock star, etc.) with competing goals will work.[39] The third watches, then writes the "secret weapon," and sees their offer immediately tested in the story as physically represented by the others. Rotate until everyone has had the chance to write a disruption and see it embodied. This is excellent training for writers in how to design spirit humor contextually: the humor only works if the threat is first clearly established, and if the threat and the secret weapon that defeats it are matched, like two sides of a coin. This is also a good moment for discussion of foreshadowing, and how dramatic tension and the audience's satisfaction at the payoff can both be heightened by hints that presage the specific nature of the power reversal to come.

Character Generation

It's now time to translate all of the physical improvisation learning into writing. Everyone will need paper and pen. Coach the participants not to pause to think but to "be ordinary" and avoid self-censorship, writing instant answers as you rapidly read out the following prompts:[40]

- You are generating a character. The character should not be based on yourself or any real person.
- Your character has exaggerated status. Are they very high or very low?
- What is one item of clothing they are wearing right now?
- What is their name? Gender? Age?
- What is a physical mannerism (gesture, gaze, tone of voice) that deliberately signals their status?
- What is an involuntary physical mannerism (tic, posture, etc.) that they don't realize is also signaling their status?
- What did they have for breakfast?
- Where does their money come from (work or otherwise)?
- Where do they live?
- Where did they wake up this morning?
- What is something they lack in life?
- What is a secret desire they have?
- What achievement in their life so far are they most proud of?
- What are they least proud of?
- How did they vote (or did they vote) in the last election?
- Who is their favorite person in the world?
- Where do they want to be in ten years' time?
- What is their worst childhood memory?
- What is their greatest fear?

Pause only for a moment then ask participants to create another character, one with opposite status. Use the same prompts. Then have participants visualize the two characters in the same place. There is one object in the place that they both want.[41] Ask the participants to quickly write answers to the following prompts:

- Where are the characters at this very moment?
- What is the object they both want?
- What is the high-status character doing at this very moment?
- What are they thinking or saying at this very moment?
- What is the low-status character doing at this very moment?
- What are they thinking or saying at this very moment?
- How is the high-status character being oppressive?
- How is the low-status character responding?

- What comes next?
- What is the low-status character's secret weapon?
- What comes next?

You may want to coach the writers to have the low-status character find out something about the high-status character's fears, goals, or dreams, and use that information to prevent them from getting their goal. Suggesting that they have the high-status character increasingly display their frustration can also be productive. When scenes are shared at the end of the exercise, typically every single scene is funny, and some are very, very funny. You can also usually deepen the comedy by asking the writers to go back through their scene and add foreshadowing.

Of course, not everything that comes from this exercise will be useable in a play; it's a blunt instrument that invokes power dynamics without complexity. But as well as increasing participants' confidence in their ability to write comedy using status, often what is created here becomes the core of something more subtle and layered. Further writing can build towards redemption narratives or deeper character motivations. Characters who behave badly can themselves be victims, and in the wider context of a play this can be revealed, but for writing a single comic moment, the bursting of a pompous bully's balloon by a mild-mannered victim will always get a laugh. It's built into our psychology.

Punching up: The Ethics And Risks of Social Justice Comedy

Not all improvisation or theatrical comedy enacts justice (some quite the opposite). It's important to diagnose the difference and develop systematic ways to monitor, predict, and evaluate the ethical impact of your social justice comedy playwriting.

"Punching up" is a useful concept in humor. There's a 1990s Larry King interview with old-school comedian George Carlin on YouTube, where they talk about a third man whom, they both agree, does not punch up. This third man, they say, makes jokes at the expense of women, immigrants, and LGBTQI+ people. He attacks people who, as King points out, are vulnerable. He punches down with his humor. But then, as Carlin points out, maybe for the audience this forgotten third man is addressing, it's not punching down in their eyes, because they feel threatened. Carlin says, "his targets are underdogs, and comedy traditionally has picked on people in power, people who abuse their power." King asks, "Why does he get away with it?" Carlin replies:

> I think his core audience are young white males who are threatened by these groups. I mean, a lot of these guys aren't sure of their manhood, because that's a problem when you're going through adolescence ... and women who assert themselves and are competent are a threat to these men, and so are immigrants in terms of jobs... I think that that is what is at the core of what takes place in these arenas: there's a certain sharing of anger and rage at these targets.[42]

So, in other words, comedy is *always created by a sense of punching up*. If a play is demeaning vulnerable people yet getting laughs, then you need to take a hard look at the audience the work is appealing to and ask what they feel threatened by and why, and how unaware they (and therefore you if it's your play they're laughing at) are of their privilege. It's important to think about privilege as intersectional and multi-faceted, too. While Carlin may have insightfully diagnosed his colleague's misogyny and homophobia, and spoken about white privilege late in his career, he was apparently unaware of his own racism early in his career when he created a deeply offensive Native American character.[43] Performing for almost exclusively white audiences at that time, Carlin himself lacked any feedback from outside a very small cultural echo-chamber to help him see his own privilege.[44]

There are several means by which we can reduce the risks of being similarly blind to offence. The first is to collaborate and ensure authentic diversity and inclusion in those collaborations. Even when playwriting seems solitary, play *production* is inherently collaborative. What does the demography of your network of collaborating directors, producers, casts, technicians, etc., look like? Whose voices do you hear every day when you work? How much do you let those voices change what you write?

The second is to formally consult with paid advisors and test audiences. If you use script-advising services, find out how different those readers are from yourself. Request diversity. If scheduling a reading, recruit an audience from well outside your usual circle of friends and acquaintances. Advertise the reading in places you don't normally go. Get readers and development audiences who are well outside your echo-chamber and listen to their feedback.

Third, if you're writing about a social issue, make sure it's one you're qualified to comment on (such as one you also take real action on).

Make sure your test audience includes people who live this issue and ask them not only whether you've avoided offence but also whether you've made any contribution to advancing solutions. Sometimes, aestheticizing serious issues can trivialize them or result in a catharsis that reduces audiences' impetus to act in the real world.[45] Test audience responses can help identify that risk.

Fourth, do your research. Read up on stereotypes, microaggressions, practical decolonization, ableism, anti-racism, and more, so that you know what you're up against and what other people are already doing about it.[46]

Finally, join an improv group. Nothing has taught me more about the mechanics of mind, body, and spirit humor than engaging in ridiculous tomfoolery with beloved co-conspirators in the brave space of a good improv group. Because the things that make you laugh, when you improvise, will also make your audience laugh, when you write.

Notes

1. Levine, Litwak and Bilodeau.
2. Boyland.
3. Harlow.
4. https://guiltyfeminist.com/
5. Freud.
6. Scripts available at: https://www.playmarket.org.nz/playwrights/elspeth-tilley/
7. Foucault.
8. Borges.
9. Foucault, p. xv.
10. https://archive.org/details/anders-lustgarten-the-hamster
11. https://www.canadianplayoutlet.com/products/brackendale-by-elaine-avila
12. Joy.
13. Warren, Barsky, and McGraw, p. 43.
14. Johnstone, p. 16.
15. Ibid., p. 78.
16. Ibid., p. 13.
17. Salinsky and Frances-White.
18. Johnstone, p. 13.
19. Incongruity occurs when two normally unconnected things are linked. In *The Act of Creation* (2nd ed., London: Hutchinson, 1976), Arthur Koestler identified it as a key basis of humour.
20. Zillman, p. 37–57. Misattribution theory is more complex than just misnaming (there is also negative misattribution) but this is a good place to start.
21. Bean, https://www.dramatists.com/cgi-bin/db/single.asp?key=4690
22. Klausner [writer] and Levy [director].

23 Hart [writer].
24 Farmer.
25 http://www.insideoutsidetheatre.com/resources/warm-ups/
26 https://www.dramanotebook.com/drama-games/what-are-you-doing/
27 Torres-Marín et al.
28 Reza.
29 Plato.
30 Shakespeare.
31 Johnstone, p. 88.
32 Ibid., p. 104
33 Tong and Williams.
34 Minc, 39–113.
35 Johnstone, 33–74.
36 Giebel.
37 Spolin.
38 Curtis, Atkinson and Elton [writers].
39 New Zealand novelist Pip Adam has a great version of this, at https://www.thebigidea.nz/stories/falling-in-love-with-the-beginning-middle-and-end
40 There are many versions of this rapid character-generation exercise in different playwriting texts but mine is influenced by a character template I was generously given by Philip Braithwaite (https://www.playmarket.org.nz/playwrights/philip-braithwaite/), and by Noel Greig's *Playwriting: A Practical Guide* (Oxon: Routledge, 2005).
41 María Irene Fornés reportedly used a related but not identical activity involving two characters and a contested object, see Caridad Svich (2009), The legacy of María Irene Fornés: A collection of impressions and exercises. *PAJ: A Journal of Performance and Art, 31* (3), 1–32.
42 *How George Carlin became George Carlin.*
43 Healy, 137–142.
44 C.f., Willett and Willett.
45 Tilley, 3–32.
46 I find the website https://everydayfeminism.com/ brilliant.

References

Bean, Richard. *One Man, Two Guvnors*. New York: Dramatists Play Service, 2011.

Borges, Jorge Luis. "The Analytical Language of John Wilkins." Translated by Ruth L. C. Simms. In *Borges, Other Inquisitions 1937–1952*. Austin: University of Texas Press, 1993.

Boyland, Stuart. The British Theatre Challenge at Brockley Jack Studio Theatre. *The Upcoming*, 2019, October 11. https://www.theupcoming.co.uk/2019/10/11/the-british-theatre-challenge-at-brockley-jack-studio-theatre-theatre-review/

Curtis, Richard, Rowan Atkinson, and Ben Elton [Writers]. *Blackadder*. London: BBC Television, 1983–1989.

Farmer, David. *101 Drama Games and Activities*, 2nd ed. Raleigh, N.C.: Lulu Press, 2011.

Foucault, Michel. *The Order of Things*. New York: Pantheon, 1970.
Freud, Sigmund. *Jokes and their relation to the unconscious*. New York: Norton, 1905.
Giebel, Jean Dobie. "Improvising tactical choices based on status or 'Who's driving the dramatic action bus?" In *Objectives, Obstacles, and Tactics in Practice: Perspectives on Activating the Actor*. Valerie Clayman Pye, and Hillary Haft Bucs (Eds.) (New York: Routledge, 2020.
Greig, Noel. *Playwriting: A Practical Guide*. Oxon: Routledge, 2005.
Harlow, Lisa. *Sky Blue Theatre Review*, 2018, September 2. http://fairypoweredproductions.com/sky-blue-theatre-review/
Hart, Miranda [Writer]. *Miranda*. London: BBC Television, 2009–2015.
Healy, Cori. "Reexamining political correctness through feminist rhetoric in the stand up of George Carlin." *Comedy Studies*, 7(2), pp. 137–142, 2016.
How George Carlin became George Carlin. Interview, Larry King Live. CNN, 1990. https://edition.cnn.com/videos/entertainment/2017/01/09/george-carlin-1990-larry-king-live-interview.cnn/video/playlists/larry-king-live-interviews/
Johnstone, Keith. *Impro: Improvisation and the Theatre*. New York: Routledge, 1979.
Joy, Melanie. *Why we love dogs, eat pigs and wear cows: An introduction to carnism*. San Francisco: Conari Press, 2010.
Klausner, Josh [Writer], and Shawn Levy [Director]. *Date Night*. Los Angeles, CA: 20th Century Fox, 2010.
Koestler, Arthur. *The Act of Creation*, 2nd ed. London: Hutchinson, 1976.
Levine, Julia, Jessica Litwak and Chantal Bilodeau. Propelling Climate Action through Theatre. *The Lark*. 2017, December 5. https://www.larktheatre.org/blog/propelling-climate-action-through-theatre/.
Minc, Leah D. "Scarcity and survival: The role of oral tradition in mediating subsistence crises." *Journal of Anthropological Archaeology*, 5(1), pp. 39–113, 1986.
Plato. *The Collected Dialogues of Plato*, translated by E. Hamilton and H. Cairns. Princeton: Princeton University Press, 1978.
Reza, Yasmina. *God of Carnage*, translated by Christopher Hampton. New York: Dramatists Play Service, 2008.
Salinsky, Tom, and Deborah Frances-White. *The Improvisation Handbook: The Ultimate Guide to Improvising in Comedy, Theatre, and Beyond*. New York: London: Continuum, 2008.
Shakespeare, William. *A Midsummer Night's Dream*. Oxford: Shakespeare Head Press, 1997.
Spolin, Viola. *Improvisation for the Theatre*, 3rd ed. Evanston, IL: Northwestern UP, 1997.
Svich, Caridad. "The legacy of María Irene Fornés: A collection of impressions and exercises." *PAJ: A Journal of Performance and Art*, 31(3), pp. 1–32, 2009.
Tilley, Elspeth. "Undefining creative activism: From praxis and participation to poiesis and presage." In E. Tilley (Ed.) *Creative Activism: Research, Pedagogy and Practice*, pp. 3–32. Newcastle Upon Tyne: Cambridge Scholars/EBSCO, 2022.

Tong, Rosemarie, and Nancy Williams, "Feminist Ethics." *The Stanford Encyclopaedia of Philosophy* (Spring 2019 Edition), Edward N. Zalta (ed.). https://plato.stanford.edu/archives/spr2019/entries/feminism-ethics/.

Torres-Marín, Jorge, Ginés Navarro-Carrillo, and Hugo Carretero-Dios. "Is the use of humor associated with anger management? The assessment of individual differences in humor styles in Spain." *Personality and Individual Differences*, 120, p. 193, 2018. DOI: 10.1016/j.paid.2017.08.040

Warren, Caleb, Adam Barsky, and A. Peter McGraw. "What Makes Things Funny? An Integrative Review of the Antecedents of Laughter and Amusement." *Personality and Social Psychology Review*, 25(1), pp. 41–65, 2021.

Willett, Cynthia, and Julie Willett. *Uproarious: How Feminists and Other Subversive Comics Speak Truth*. Minneapolis: University of Minnesota Press, 2019.

Zillman, Dolf. "Humor and comedy". In Dolf Zillmann and Peter Vorderer (Eds.), *Media entertainment: The psychology of its appeal*, pp. 37–57. Mahwah, NJ: Erlbaum, 2000.

12 Writing for Change

Guiding Activist Playwrights in Classrooms and Communities

Dana Edell

Introduction

As the world faces global and local interlocking crises that have erupted from systemic racism and sexism, the Covid pandemic and its tragic mismanagement, and climate change, playwrights and theatre makers often feel driven to make new work that addresses the intersecting injustices infecting our communities. They want to use their pens (or keyboards) not just for entertainment or education, but for social change. While training often focuses on content, story, character, and/or form, novice playwrights and playwriting educators need resources that guide them to use their creativity and innovative language chops to create activist texts that clearly articulate calls to action for their audiences.

Plays that address social justice issues may assume that if characters are empathetic enough and stories unforgettable, then audience members will change their minds about these issues once they learn more or connect emotionally with characters or performers who share the impact on their lives and wellbeing. But what if playwrights and performing artists devise and craft new plays that go beyond this cultivation of empathy to include calls to action? Recent critically and commercially successful plays such as Jackie Sibblies Drury's *Fairview* and Aleshea Harris's *What to Send Up When It Goes Down* include provocative moments of direct audience engagement and interaction. These plays, written by Black women, go beyond addressing racism within their content and themes to demand that audience members literally leave their seats in order to experience the full impact. As audiences emerge from Covid-to-blame performances online and the dizzying bingeing of endless hours of digitally streamed shows, it is urgent that our return to the physical theatre also includes a reimagining and reigniting of the unique and powerful relationship between audience and performers together in a live space. Traditionally, the director has been the collaborating artist who made decisions about audience engagement, but it is time to train and support playwrights to explore not just the relationships between their characters, but also the direct relationship between audience and performers/performance.

In this chapter, I share a few tried-and-tested activities, developed over my more than twenty years devising and directing original, collaborative, antiracist, activist plays with teenage girls and nonbinary youth.[1,2] Community-engaged theatre directors or playwriting teachers can use these exercises as they guide novice writers to explore direct audience engagement and calls to action in their texts. This annotated sequence of writing and performance activities borrows from critical pedagogy[3] personal writing, improvisation, Theatre of the Oppressed[4] techniques, and power-mapping to generate collaborative scripts that ignite audiences to make changes in their own lives and/or communities. Though my model has always been to collectively generate, write, and produce theatre, the following writing/devising curriculum can be adapted for individual students or a classroom community.

Story Circles

Every culture across time and region has used a storytelling practice to foster connections, educate children, and establish the cultural narratives that define them. During the civil rights movement, organizer and theatremaker John O'Neal,[5] in collaboration with other Black leaders, codified the practice by articulating the simple structure of the "Story Circle," where we sit together, sharing and listening to personal stories. Community engagement scholar Lizzy Cooper Davis writes, "[Story circles] teach us that it is through listening to our stories, rather than arguing our points, that we discover who we are."[6] For educators and directors interested in generating collaboratively devised, activist plays, I invite you to start with personal stories.

Roses, Thorns, and Buds

We merge the organizing practice of story circles with the popular community-building activity, **Roses, Thorns, and Buds**. All that's needed is a circle of chairs or seats on the floor and approximately five to forty-five minutes depending on the group size and comfort level/interest in detailed personal sharing.

Objectives

- Build trust through sharing personal stories
- Recognize the narrative power of specific stories
- Explore embodied practices of personal storytelling

Directions

1 Individual story-sharing: the artists, along with the staff or teacher, sit in a circle and one-by-one share personal stories that resonate with them that day, including a "Rose" (a positive, uplifting event or situation); "Thorn" (a challenge, struggle, or stressful event that might be prickling that day); and a "Bud" (a hope for the future). As we pass a real rose around the circle, everyone smells the sweet pungency and feels the velvety bud and prick of the thorn. Like Proust's madeleine cookie, the sensual, olfactory, and tactile engagement with the flower instills the experience more forcefully into our memories. We discuss how every rose includes both the beauty of the flower and the sharpness of the thorn, both necessary for survival.
2 Group discussion: following the individual sharings, the group engages in "crosstalk," and reflects upon the connections and similarities between stories, and analyzes how the situations in their lives are often filled with both roses and thorns, and how these experiences help them articulate a dream for the future.

Integral to our playwriting process, this daily ritual builds trust and connection among the group. Meaningful collaboration begins by first understanding others' unique struggles, strengths, celebrations, and desires. Through listening to each other and hearing echoes of their own stories and stresses, writing team members begin to recognize patterns in the cultural stereotypes, social narratives, and systemic injustices that influence the shared content of their experiences. An additional creative opportunity is to rename this exercise to something unique to each group. For example, in a Jewish, feminist activist project, the teens renamed it: "RBGs (positives, as inspired by Ruth Bader Ginsburg); Trumps (challenges, as exemplified by Donald Trump); and AOCs (hopes, as imagined by Alexandria Ocasio-Cortez)."

To expand our creative toolbox, we sometimes invite everyone to share their Rose/Thorn/Bud in different formats, with prompts such as:

- Make a physical shape or five-second gesture that shows either a literal or emotional representation of the experience.
- Tell each story in just six words.
- Tell each story in just one word.
- Tell the story to a partner, then share each other's stories with the group.

Rant and Rave

This embodied, performance-based activity guides performer/writers to tap into their feelings of rage and injustice, as well as identify what keeps them going, providing a potential microcosm of an activist playwriting process. The following script can be spoken and adapted by educators or directors. Each part flows uninterrupted into the next. All that is needed is an open studio space for movement. This activity can take approximately forty-five to sixty minutes.

Objectives

- Harness students' rage and anger at the injustices in their lives and communities.
- Identify how we manifest our own strategies for joy, healing, and gratitude.
- Inspire students to use these powerful emotions and energies to create an original monologue.

Directions

Speak the following text (or adapt it into your own words and voice).

Part One: Rant Walk

- (Introduction) We are going to be engaging in an activity that invites you to consider events, people, policies that ignite anger or rage in you. Please be mindful of scavenging for memories that might bring you unprocessed pain. Take care of your emotional wellbeing and if you choose to focus on past pain or trauma, focus on "*scars*, not *wounds*."

- Walk around the studio, moving through spaces between people so you don't get dizzy by moving in a circle.
- Breathe.
- Think about how your body moves through the space. Pay attention to your pace, your natural rhythms. How you move your arms. What part of your body you lead with. Where you hold strength. Where you hold tension.
- As you move, think about something that fills you with rage.
- Breathe in those feelings of anger. Imagine the color you are inhaling.
- Consider an event, an experience, a vision that fuels anger. Where do you see injustice? It could be an argument with your mother, a simmering frustration with your roommate, rage at a politician or boss. Imagine policies, practices, people that drive you to clench your teeth or squeeze your fists.
- Breathe these feelings in and let them affect the way you move.
- Notice what parts of your body you are leading with, where you are tightening, how your face feels, your pace and rhythm.
- Stop wherever you are.
- Face a wall so you can't see anyone else, and make a gesture with your body that encapsulates these feelings.
- Exaggerate the gesture, make it bigger, bolder.
- Inhale and hold your breath for three seconds.
- Release your breath, move *through* the gesture, and start walking again.

Part Two: Rant Circle

- Holding onto this energy of rage, form a circle in the space, and stand shoulder-to-shoulder.
- I'm going to point to a speck on the floor in the center of the circle, count down from five, and invite you all, at the same time, to shout all your feelings of rage at the speck on the floor for ten seconds. Can we rant for ten straight seconds together? Since we will all be talking at the same time, you won't hear each other's specific words. Ready?
- 5-4-3-2-1, RANT! (*Everyone rants for ten seconds.*)
- STOP! (*Or offer a visual signal to stop such as a wide-armed clap.*)
- Take a breath.

Part Three: Free Write and Monologue Rant

- Get a pen/paper/laptop and start a three-minute free-write with the prompt: *It really makes me mad...* Let all the stories, images, feelings from the past five minutes flow onto your page. It can be a list, a rant, a story, or any other fluid form. Try to not let your hand stop writing. Don't overthink it.
- (*After three to five minutes.*) Stop wherever you are in your ranting.
- Read through what you just wrote. Consider a specific character (or yourself) who is feeling angry about one of the issues you ranted about. Imagine a person in their life who most ignites their rage (it could be a friend, teacher, sibling, celebrity, politician, or even a stranger you just interacted with).
- You have fifteen minutes to write a monologue (a speech spoken to another person with a specific intention) spoken to this other character. Imagine that something has just happened related to the issue you are so enraged about. The monologue begins with the prompt, "You make me so angry! I need you to know..."
- Include in the monologue both one specific story related to the issue you are enraged about and a strategy or need expressed about what you wish the other person would do to improve the situation.

Part Four: Rave Walk

- Come back to the circle.
- Scoop up an armful of rage-filled air from the center of the circle and throw it behind you. Exhale. Shake it off.
- Walk around the space again.
- Think about everything that keeps you going. Despite/because of the rage and anger, how do you still wake up in the morning? Consider what you are grateful for. Visualize the beauty in the world, the love in your life, the joy. What makes you smile? What makes you laugh? Who cheers you up when you are down? What or who inspires you? What gives you hope for the future?
- Breathe these feelings and images in and notice how your body changes. What color are you imagining as you inhale positive energies? Where is your center of gravity? What part of you is meeting the world first? Notice your pace or rhythm.
- Stop. Turn out and face a wall. Shape your body into a gesture of love/joy/gratitude. Exaggerate it. Stretch it wider, bigger. Inhale and hold three seconds.

- Exhale and walk through the gesture until you find your spot in the circle.
- Stand shoulder-to-shoulder. Focus all your energy on the same tiny speck that still reels from our previous rage. On the count of five, we are going to shower love and joy on that little speck for ten seconds. You can speak words, sing, make any sounds of gratitude and bliss. Ready?
- 5-4-3-2-1, RAVE! (*Everyone raves for ten seconds.*)
- STOP!
- Now let's each grab an armful of the air in the center of our circle, spread it over our bodies. Drink it up, breathe it in.

Part Five: Free Write and Monologue, Rave

- Get a pen/paper/laptop and start a three to five minute free write with the prompt: *What keeps me going?*
- Reflect on everything that makes you happy, that brings you joy, all you are grateful for, the people and creatures that you love, the places where you feel safe and whole.
- Let your writing flow in any form, without lifting your hand from writing.
- (*After three to five minutes.*) Gently finish your current thought. Read back what you just wrote.
- Imagine one of the characters (either the speaker or the person they were speaking to) from your previous "Rant" monologue encountering one of the stories, phrases, places, people you just wrote about. How might this encounter change or transform them? Choose a person/animal/place they are speaking to.
- Take fifteen minutes to write a second monologue with the prompt: *If you only knew how much you changed me...*

Part Six: Share and Discuss

- Invite writers to share at least two sentences from each monologue, either with a partner or in front of the whole group.
- Discuss: What was this process like for you? Why did we start with rage?
- Discuss: Why might it be useful for activist theatre to include both anger and hope?

Of course, facilitators must be mindful and transparent about the potentially uncomfortable or triggering content related to marginalized people tapping into past experiences or stories related to trauma or violence. Before leading the **Rant and Rave** activity, I suggest adding the following script, or any variation that feels right to you:

> I am going to invite you to think about past experiences and stories that have filled you with rage. For some of you, this might bring up stories related to trauma or violence or uncomfortable experiences. I encourage you to take care of yourself. Choose a memory or story that feels safe for you to explore here, today. Our goal is to recognize where injustice and anger shows up for us, not to delve into trauma. If you are feeling vulnerable, choose a moment closer to the surface of your feelings, something unfair, frustrating, or irritating. This will mean something different to each of us. Take care of yourself.

Human Barometer

A generative and popular activity, part community-building/part content-generation is the **Human Barometer**, sometimes also called **Take a Stand**.

Objectives

- To discover how we differ or find solidarity on core social or political issues.
- To articulate why we feel the way we feel, and how we can use text and story to try to change others' minds and hearts.

Part One: Where Do I Stand?

- Designate one corner of the room as "YES! I totally agree!" and the opposite diagonal corner as "NO WAY! I absolutely do NOT agree!"
- When a statement is read, each artist stands along the "barometer" according to how much they do or don't agree with the statement. Note: if anyone (for whatever reason) does not want to publicly show where they stand or if they do not know enough about the statement to have a strong opinion, they can opt to stand or sit further off the line.

Barometer statements should reflect issues where there might be multiple points of view and opinions. Possible Human Barometer statements might include:

1 TV does a good job of portraying teenage girls in healthy and positive ways.
2 Fast food and soda should be banned in schools.
3 Politicians care about the interests of teenagers.
4 Standardized tests (like the SAT and Regents) don't really show how much you know.
5 Parents need to trust that teenagers know what's best for us.
6 Police officers in the street make our communities safer.
7 All students should get comprehensive sex education in schools.
8 I would rather be beautiful than smart.
9 It is harder to be a girl than a boy.
10 Social media is a safe and positive space for teens.

After each statement is read and the artists settle themselves on the line, invite them to discuss with someone standing next to them how they feel about the statement, why they chose their barometer location, and a possible personal story related to the issue.

Part Two: Using Text as Persuasion

- Select two to three of the statements that felt the most divisive, that best engaged the artists, that had many artists at both ends of the room or clustered in the middle.
- Read the statement again, but this time randomly assign half the group to one corner and the other half to the other corner.
- Invite the groups to discuss with each other in their group why someone might be standing on this extreme side of the issue. What circumstances, relationships, or life experiences might influence these specific beliefs?
- After approximately five to ten minutes of discussion, propose the following writing task: consider the core topics and ideas from your recent discussion and collectively write a "persuasive pitch statement" attempting to persuade the people on the opposing side to agree with your thoughts and opinions. This succinct single sentence should encapsulate the

core beliefs of your group. A possible prompt might include, "We need you to understand that…"

Part Three: Sharing of Statements

- The people in each of the two groups collectively read (designating one reader, dividing the text into sections, or reading in unison) their persuasive statements to each other, in an attempt to change the hearts and minds of the other side.
- Following the sharing of the statements, engage in a discussion about the different sides of the issue, how effective the pitch statements were and why. Individuals share what it might take to change their minds or if their stance on certain issues is non-negotiable and completely fixed. Discuss how our personal stories, racial and cultural backgrounds, family histories, and other unique identities contribute to how we feel about different issues and the ways they impact our own lives and the lives of people we love.

Part Four: Scenework

- Invite students to imagine two distinct characters who represent each side of this issue.
- Brainstorm how the two characters might know each other (e.g.: sisters, romantic partners, teacher/student, neighbors, etc.).
- Decide on a scenario where an event has just occurred related to this issue that both characters have stakes in.
- Write dialogue between the two characters, incorporating the persuasive texts and content from the previous discussions where they attempt to convince each other of their points of view.
- Include the following as "ingredients" in the scene:
  - A secret;
  - A betrayal;
  - A misunderstanding;
  - A story from the past;
  - A dream for the future;
  - An unexpected resolution.

Call to Action

Following decades of attending plays where the content riled me up about an issue, I began to see the limitations of assuming that just learning about an issue will lead to change. So, we began to embed "Calls to Action" into the scripts themselves where the artists identified key moments that would demand audience members *do* something—or collectively *strategize* what they might do—before they left the theatre. Theatre educator Jonathan P. Jones's research connects to Martin Luther King, Jr.'s work inspiring people to *act*. He writes:

> While it is true that good art makes us think, thinking is not a form of direct action because it fails to dramatize the issue, as called for in Dr. King's letter[7] ... The direct action that I am calling for ... is the employment of the call to action in theatrical performances.[8]

These Calls to Action are directly connected to discussions about *who* has the power to make change and *how* we might reach them. In this section, I invite you to engage with artist-students to strategize how to embed moments into their scripts where the characters either break the fourth wall of the theatre and the actors, as themselves, engage directly with the audience, or where the characters directly interact with the audience. These moments should connect directly to the social justice theme raised in the moments before the break. Though a seemingly simple pivot away from the narrative within the script, moments that directly confront audience members to think and speak out about how to specifically make changes in their lives can begin to normalize discussions about issues people might rarely discuss publicly such as white privilege, ableism, or transphobia.

For example, in one production, the teen artists had articulated that the people with the power to make change related to racism in their schools were teachers, administrators, and other students, so we specifically marketed the performances to these groups to ensure they would be represented in the audience. After a specific scene that illuminated an instance of racism at school, the actors broke character and invited the audience to discuss what they might do to address that situation. Some audience members cowered lower in their seats, terrified of being "called on" or "called out." They were not either! Over the course of the performances, many audience members spoke up and offered ideas, personal stories, and strategies that shifted the onus of making change away from the teenage performers. Whether they spoke up or not, they were confronted about what they needed to do, as well as given some ideas of what they *could* do, after they left the theatre.

Not every Call to Action is an engaged discussion. In the same show, a performer demanded that people get involved in local politics, vote in every election, and connect with elected officials. In this example, she directed the audience to write letters to elected officials, and then provided templates for the letters along with addressed and stamped envelopes which were collected and mailed following the performance.

We've also had shows where the performers divided the audience into small groups to discuss the show's issues, create their own response through art, poetry, or monologues, and then share with their group—or with the full theatre. Another strategy is Brazilian theatre activist Augusto Boal's Forum Theatre,[9] where the characters first present a crisis, then perform again and invite anyone in the audience to stop the action of their play at any moment prior to the crisis and actually come up onto the stage, "replace" the protagonist, and improvise a new strategy for preventing or solving the impending crisis.

Call to Action

Objective

- Embed an interactive moment into the script that invites the audience to participate in strategizing and/or implementing a solution to an issue in the play.
- Power map the social or political justice issue to ensure that the production is marketed to potential audience members who could be potential changemakers.

Directions

Part One: Power Mapping

- Once the core issues of the play have been identified, brainstorm a list of all the people who might have power to enact change.
- Draw a literal map tracking who has the most power and include all the different kinds of people who might have influence over the person/people with the most power. E.g., if the play is addressing an issue in a public school, the map of power might include teachers, the principal, the superintendent, and eventually the mayor, governor, or other elected officials. People who might influence those in power might include parents, students, and journalists.

Part Two: Audience Casting

- Include a marketing strategy for ensuring the people who have the power or influence to make change attend the production.
- Write a "show pitch" that summarizes the key narrative and activist goals of the production and a "hook" to engage potential audience members.

Part Three: Crafting the Call

- After recognizing who might be in the audience, this step invites the playwright to conceptualize a moment or moments in the script where the audience might most effectively interact with the performance in order to move the story or the play forward.
- Write into the script specific instructions for the performers and director for the goals of these moments and offer possibilities for how to stage them.

Preparing for Calls to Action

Though Calls to Action are effective *because* we never know what exactly might happen with audience interactions, we need additional, highly-structured rehearsals to best prepare the performers. We need to anticipate the various ways audiences can derail or disrupt these parts of the performance, and build safeguards into the script. We rehearse with ensemble members pretending to be disruptive or resistant or apathetic audience members. The performers improvise and strategize how to make these moments work if the audience resists. Then we return to the script and add new text, questions, or guided pivots so that everyone feels prepared for whatever might erupt in the live theatre.

The goal of these Calls to Action is to model how theatre can be a form of community organizing. We can shift the balance of power and the burden of change away from the singular vision of the writer and into a collective vision for the community. We can use the space of the theatre to actually practice what dialogue across difference might look and feel like. The script is the launching point, but the real change happens in the interactions between performers and audience *and*, in this model, among audience members together. When these Calls to

Action are embedded in the script, they become a normalized part of making theatre, and our audiences start to expect this direct, meaningful engagement.

Notes

1 I have co-founded and co-directed several community-based, activist theatre organizations within which I co-created and co-directed more than seventy-five productions, all written and performed by teenage girls and nonbinary youth. The organizations include Inside/Out Performing Arts (1998–2000, with Katie Eastburn), a playmaking project with systems-involved teenage girls in the San Francisco Bay Area; viBe Theatre Experience (2002–2020, with chandra thomas through 2012, Toya Lillard through 2020), a [viBe mission]; SPARK Movement (co-founded by Lyn Mikel Brown and Deborah L. Tolman), an intergenerational, antiracist girl-driven, feminist activist organization where I produced annual theatre productions in New York City; and The Teen Activist Theatre Project at the JCC (2021–present, with Andrea Jacobs through 2021) in Wilmington, Delaware.
2 Edell, *Girls, Performance, and Activism: Demanding to Be Heard*; Edell, 'Say It How It Is': Urban Teenage Girls Challenge and Perpetuate Stereotypes Through Writing and Performing Theatre," pp. 51–62.
3 Freire; hooks.
4 Boal.
5 Yuen, O'Neal, and Holden.
6 Davis, p. 128.
7 King.
8 Jones, pp. 52–60.
9 Boal.

References

Boal, Augusto. *Theatre of the Oppressed*. Trans. C.A. McBride. Theatre Communications Group, 1979.
Davis, Lizzy Cooper. *Creating Space for Democracy: A Primer on Dialogue and Deliberation in Higher Education*. Shaffer, TJ and Longo, NV; Eds. Stylus Publishing, LLC. (2019, p. 128).
Edell, Dana. *Girls, Performance, and Activism: Demanding to Be Heard*. 1st ed., Routledge, 2022.
Edell, Dana. "'Say It How It Is': Urban Teenage Girls Challenge and Perpetuate Stereotypes Through Writing and Performing Theatre." *Youth Theatre Journal*, 27(1), 2013, pp. 51–62. *Crossref*, https://doi.org/10.1080/08929092.2012.722903.
Freire, Paolo. *Pedagogy of the Oppressed*. Trans. Myra Bergman Ross. Bloomsbury, 1970.
hooks, bell. *Teaching to Transgress: Education as the Practice of Freedom*. Routledge, 1994.

Jones, Jonathan P. "Call to Action: Elevating Activism in Performance." *Teaching Artist Journal*, 16(1–2), pp. 52–60, 2018. https://doi.org/10.1080/15411796.2018.1470390.

King, Martin Luther, Jr. "Letter from a Birmingham jail." The Martin Luther King, Jr. Research and Education Institute, Stanford University, 1963, April 16. Retrieved 1 January 2022 from: https://kinginstitute.stanford.edu/encyclopedia/letter-birmingham-jail

Yuen, Cheryl, John O'Neal, and Theresa Holden. "Junebug Productions: *Color Line Project*." In *Animating Democracy*. Washington, DC: Americans for the Arts, 2002. Retrieved 1 January 2022 from: http://animatingdemocracy.org/sites/default/files/documents/labs/color_line_project_case_study.pdf.

13 Community-Based Play Creation

Hope McIntyre

Introduction

During twenty-two years as Artistic Director of Sarasvàti Productions, an independent theatre company with a mission to transform society, I facilitated dozens of projects that focused on a collaborative community approach. This approach came from a desire to create work that is more reflective of our whole community. I've adapted the lessons learned during that time to engage students in new ways of writing that encourage a wider range of stories.

In this chapter, I outline the steps for a non-traditional community-based collaborative approach to play creation. I have used this process to work with various community groups, including criminalized women and youth in foster care. This method is also useful for collaborative writing in playwriting classes, as well as for performance, devised theatre, and theatre for social change courses.

The How

For a truly collaborative process, relationships are key. Working with existing community organizations has been a huge benefit and honor. I have at times started with an idea for a project and then approached aligned community organizations; I have also had groups contact me requesting a joint project. As a playwright myself, I leave my own ideas at the door and instead facilitate the process to allow for the creation of the theatrical work desired by the entire group of collaborators.

Working collaboratively is terrain that requires great mindfulness. Considerations include accessibility, creating a safe space, and making sure the work is completely consent-based. Large questions about how to avoid appropriation or the possibility of exploitation come up regularly so talking them through as you embark on a community-based process is important. Expectations have to be made clear at the outset, as recruitment of participants occurs on the first day of work with an existing group. Everything has to be planned based on who the collaborators are. What is their experience of theatre? Are they from a community group that might have particular hesitations or barriers? How can you make sure the set-up is the best fit for those who will be creating together in the space? It is important to note that the process always shifts to meet the unique needs of each collaborative group. Every project I had the honor of working on led to further refinement, new considerations, and greater reflection on how the work can be done responsibly.

The timeframe for this process has also varied a great deal in order to align with what works best for each group. I have done it with weekly three-hour sessions over three months, twice a week for two hours over two months, and weekly for an hour and a half over six months. When working with criminalized women I had to adapt to do three full days back to back for the story gathering then return months later to do the workshopping. In an ideal scenario, having some processing time between sessions is useful, and I prefer two sessions a week for regular contact time. Basically, you have to adjust scope and scale to the time you have with participants.

Step By Step

Community Agreement

At the first session, a Community Agreement is created jointly. I like to begin by asking what each person requires to feel safe, creative, and welcome in the space. With a large group, I split them into smaller groups with flipcharts to discuss and come back with their needs captured on paper. Then all groups share, and the results are compiled. Everyone agrees to respect what is outlined, and the Community Agreement is posted in the space each time we work together.

Opening/Closing

Every session is framed with an opening and closing circle. We often get caught up in the need to get work done, so these short check-ins allow us to acknowledge each other as humans and share when we need or pass when we don't.

To begin myself or another facilitator will lead the opening and closing, but when working over several sessions with a group it is great to get to a point where a participant can choose to step up and ask the opening questions.

Opening Circle

- How is everyone today?
- Anything you care to share as we begin working together?
- Or anything we need to know that might affect our work together today?

Closing Circle

- What excited you about today's session?
- Is there anything you want to focus on more in future sessions?
- Anything you have concerns about?
- Anything you need to leave in the space or feel a need to express before we part ways for the day?

I usually plan one minute for each group member attending, so if there are ten participants I will plan ten minutes for the opening and ten minutes for the closing. Some will only offer a few words and others want to talk longer, so it tends to balance out.

Next, leading a basic warm-up with light stretches and vocal work encourages everyone to be physically, vocally, and mentally present. For non-theatre community groups, it is also a chance to share ways to prepare for the work.

Warming Into Writing with Theatre Games

Starting with fun games to break the ice and create a shared experience has been crucial to the process. Laughing together, letting go, and just engaging in play are things community groups don't often have an opportunity to do. I transition into this work as part of the first session.

I use a lot of old standbys that I also use in my introductory performance classes. Keeping them easy, fun, and accessible to all is important. Favorites include "Name Toss," "Pass the Clap," and "Pass the Sound." (See the resource list at the end for finding similar games and exercises.) All of these are done in a circle standing (or modified to sitting if needed), and require a space large enough to spread out. I vary the order depending on the energy of the group and how keen they are to move right away, rather than ease into it. The warm-up games help those who feel uncomfortable with the notion of just allowing something to happen, preparing the group for improvisational work in the creation process.

This Isn't a Pen

There are many games out there asking participants to transform objects. I remember as a kid being asked at drama camp to take a chair and play a scene where it became many other things. I've adapted this concept so that it is less performative in nature and more imaginative. Viola Spolin's *Improvisation for the Theatre* describes a similar activity called *Transformation of Objects*, but there it is designed without a real object being used.

Objective

This is great for imaginative thinking and demonstrating that in theatre you can suspend disbelief and make believe. I let participants know that as long as you believe it and are consistent, an audience in theatre will accept almost anything.

What We Need

A pen and a bag of other objects. I've used a bowl, clothes hanger, ball of yarn, and a feather boa. Almost anything that can provide a variety of options would work. It is best to keep them hidden in a bag until they are revealed one at a time.

How We Get There

- Take an object, usually a pen is the best way to start as an example. The person starting will say "This isn't a pen, it is a…" They then make it into anything but a pen and use it in this way. For example, it is a moustache and they hold it against their upper lip.
- The pen is then passed to the next person in the circle and they make it something else. For example, they say "This isn't a pen, it is a magic wand" and they twirl it as a fairy might.
- Once an object goes around the circle a new object is introduced.

Tips: Always allow folks to pass if they are stuck - in this way there is no anxiety if someone can't come up with something, although it is also good to keep reminding the group that it can be anything and there are no wrong offers.

This exercise has often helped to see who in the group is openly creative and imaginative, versus those who might need more support to think outside of the box.

Following the encouragement of play in the warm-up activities, I move to the next phase that allows for both validation of personhood and exploration of what each person brings into the space. It is one long exercise that has several possible steps. I developed it when it became clear that a more creative avenue for self-expression was needed before moving into the actual collaborative work. This usually takes place during the second session with a group.

The Story of Me

Objective

To allow members of the group to openly share.

What We Need

One big sheet of paper for each collaborator. I often use flipchart paper. A large selection of colored markers or pencil crayons. The full activity can be done effectively in ninety minutes, but can also last two hours depending on the needs of the group.

How We Get There

Step One:

- Ask each collaborator to write their first name on the page in whatever way they feel communicates their personality.
- Provide examples: use multiple colors, block letters or cursive, bubble letter with polka dots, fill the whole page, or keep it simple if that reflects who you are.

Step Two:

- Surrounding their name, have them note responses to a list of questions.
- They can write responses in words or draw images.
- Start with general questions about their favorites. For example:
  - Favorite food?
  - Favorite colour?

- Favorite song?
- Someone you admire?
- I hate when people…
- I love when people…
- Happy place?
- If I had a million dollars I would…
- I'm scared of…

Step Three:

- Segue to questions associated with the project.
- Specific questions based on project topics could include:
  - What does home mean to you?
  - What does family mean to you?
  - What would be needed to address (whatever issue the play topic covers)?

Step Four:

- Ask collaborators to share their work.
- The papers can be laid out on the floor or taped on the walls, so that folks can wander around and view like a gallery. This can be done in ten minutes. Or, if you have more time, collaborators can take a couple of minutes each to present their work. This generally requires three to five minutes per participant.

Even with adults, this is a very popular exercise, and some participants will spend more than an hour on just their name if they love drawing. Giving a clear sense of the time frame from the beginning, as well as reminders of remaining time will help them gauge how detailed they want to be. I do write the questions on a whiteboard or flipchart so self-pacing is supported. This exercise allows me to get to know who is in the room and is a non-threatening way for the group to share.

Collective Brainstorming

Now we move on to focus on the actual theatrical piece that will be created. By this point, we have usually established a strong sense of community and a good level of trust. This is usually a separate session from previous work, so part of the third encounter.

Brainstorming can be done in many ways depending on the group dynamic. The goals are to decide what the topic or focus of the project will be and to start to narrow down content. The traditional way is to explore with an open flow of ideas without limits. I focus on capturing everything on a whiteboard or flipchart.

If the group has gathered without a set topic to explore, then the brainstorm will be broader; the goal is to discover what they care about. When I worked with a girls' youth group, I asked them what they were most passionate about sharing with an audience, what made them excited, angry, frustrated, what they felt people did not understand about them. We ended up with about a dozen themes hanging all over the walls of the gym. After they each indicated top choices, we narrowed it down. When working with a group that needs more active direction, I've led word association activities on a theme, going back to ideas in "The Story of Me," or asked them to draw images they want to see on stage.

Free Writes

The writing stage now begins! Not every collaborator will want to sit down and write. I always encourage the group to doodle, as well as write words, poems, and descriptions of visuals. Sometimes, when the group is really new to creative work, I use haikus to introduce how language can create images. Collaborators can write individually or in small groups to spur each other on. Allow for contributions of content in all forms. I don't worry about script format or whether what is being written is even feasible on stage. This phase can segue from the brainstorming as part of the same session if time allows, or begin the fourth session.

Prompts are based on the chosen theme or earlier brainstorming. For example:

- Write about an incident related to the topic. It could have happened to you or be something you heard about.
- Explore a memory or story you want to share about the topic.
- Examples of specific prompts I've used:
  - What do you wish you could tell your younger self?
  - What do you want people to know about the prison system?
  - What advice would you want from an elder?
  - What story would you most want to tell an adult to help them understand your life?

At the end of a writing session, anyone can share, but it is never mandatory at this stage.

Improvisational Story Gathering

Once material has been generated through free writing, I like to get participants back up on their feet and working collectively through improvisation to flesh out ideas. If the group seems restless, you can jump in to some of this straight from the free writes, or if folks are content to keep writing then make improvisation the focus of the next session.

For a non-theatre group, basic exercises set up the language and guidelines for improvisation. The goal is working together, accepting ideas, and building a story or a visual as a group. Below is an example of this kind of exercise, ***Postcards***, which was inspired by Augusto Boal's work on statues, as well as my colleague Cairn Moore's offer for non-verbal storytelling. I combined the two to create an activity that introduces embodied storytelling in a collective model. See resources at the end of the chapter for similar games, such as "Tell Me About" and "I Am a Tree." If you are working with experienced theatre folks or students who have done introductory theatre courses, you can jump right in to the improvisational story gathering without introductory improv exercises.

Postcards

Directions

- Have everyone walk around the space with intention and energy, like they are heading for an empty spot in the room but once they get there they need to find a new empty spot to inhabit.

Round One:

- Let them know that you will call out the title of a postcard and as a group, without speaking, they must create a frozen picture that represents the postcard. For example, Paris, Disneyland, the beach...
- Yell out the title and count to ten then call *freeze*.
- Assess if they all have worked together to create one unified image. Sometimes a beach scene has a disconnect over where the water is, so provide feedback to encourage working together.
- Have them go back to walking and call out another postcard title.
- You can do several until they get the hang of it.

Round Two:

- Direct them to create a postcard of their choosing without speaking.
- Again, they walk until you yell *postcard* and then count to ten as they try to see what poses others are offering and create a unified picture.

Round Three:

- Invite one person to start an image that they have in their head.
- Others join one by one building on what they believe to be the image.
- Once all have joined the postcard, check where they believe they are to see if they ended up in the same picture.

Round Four:

- Split collaborators into two groups.
- Each group decides on a postcard without revealing it to the other group.
- The other group has to guess what it is.

Round Five:

- Move into thematic postcards related to the topic of the show you are creating.
- You can work in small groups assigning each a theme to embody in a postcard.
- Give an example: What would "revenge" look like as a story in one image?
- Each group takes a few minutes to prepare.
- As each postcard is shared, discuss what made the theme clear.

This really gets the group thinking visually about storytelling. Sometimes later in the process, I come back to this and create images using characters or settings that have been discussed for the play.

Story Improvisations

Objective

To flesh out story material in an embodied manner.

What We Need

Space to work.

How We Get There

- Take an idea previously shared or a piece of writing created through a free write that is offered by a participant.
- Talk through the basics of the story, the main ideas, and what the intent would be in sharing it (i.e., desired audience effect).
- Ask for volunteers to act out the story and make sure they are comfortable with the roles they are asked to embody.
- Allow them to improvise the incident, story, or idea.
- Encourage them to just go with the framework and see what happens.
- Discuss as a group what stood out, what those watching felt, and how it aligned with the original idea or written story.
- Ask for offers from the group of additions, ideas, or aspects to explore through further improvisation. Or ask the initial contributor of the story to provide feedback.
- Depending on time you can redo one story idea multiple times with new suggestions or just discuss and move on to another seed for a new improvisation.

Tips: It is important to focus any feedback and reflections on the story in a constructive way. Be careful if comments become about the acting or the actors. Prompts like whether something is missing in the story can help keep things focused.

After witnessing the improvisations, collaborators can choose how to proceed with the content. Each member of the group might simply take time to write out their own pieces based on what was learned from the improvs. In this case, the facilitator circulates and offers support. Written drafts can be shared either in pairs or with the full group. Each piece receives some constructive feedback and is revised. Other times improvised versions of ideas will be transcribed and then read back to allow for polishing.

Getting It on Paper

Objective

To capture the full story.

What We Need

A means to record, either video or audio. Time to transcribe the recordings. Print or digital copies of scripts in progress for reading.

How We Get There

- Once you have a solid sense of the story, scene, or idea, do it with the improvisers a final time to record. Be clear that recording is only for transcription and will never be shared outside the group.
- The recording is then transcribed. There are options for this process. If there is time in the session to assign groups to playback and transcribe the various pieces, then it can be done in the moment. You can also have volunteers do it between sessions as long as you are sure the privacy of the recording will be maintained. I have often done the transcribing myself.
- Printed versions of each piece are then brought in.
- Ask for volunteers from the group to read. It can be helpful to have new readers rather than those who improvised the piece initially.
- Feedback is provided by the group and the originator of the ideas.
- Consensus and consent are crucial in this phase, so work through any concerns until everyone accepts the revised piece.
- Work through every story, scene, or idea until they are all accepted by the group.

Once there is something to work with on paper, everything is explored on its feet to see how it works and in order to generate staging ideas. I've often found that some ideas are not text-based and workshopping on your feet is needed to explore how a non-verbal or movement-based idea can be captured. This has also been hugely popular with collaborators for whom writing words on paper may be a challenge. It can take a couple of sessions to work through all the material in this way.

Workshopping the Writing on Your Feet

Goal

Finalize the text and staging ideas, including work that is visual and not text-based, in a script format so it is ready to be used in rehearsal.

Facilitation

- Everyone is divided into groups. I usually begin with the person who generated the story idea and then ask others who are interested in that piece to join them.
- The groups are scheduled to switch at a set time so that working through all the possible scenes is possible. I usually schedule twenty minutes for each if they are short pieces.
- The person who was involved with generating a particular idea can then direct others in the scene, exploring fully how to bring their vision to life.
- If they are not comfortable taking on this directorial role, the facilitator will work as the outside eye and allow the collaborators to explore the scene with offers for staging.
- With a large group I will often bring in additional facilitators if it is clear they need this support.
- Instruct everyone to keep this stage of the process as further idea generation. It's not just about the words on paper, but how it can be presented theatrically.

For non-verbal scenes, it is a great process to talk through how to capture these on the written page so the intent is clear. It can be a great learning tool to discuss how a playwright has to do this, knowing others will interpret their work. The excitement of hearing "actors" speak the text or physicalize an idea is palpable and really re-invigorates the process at this stage.

Compiling

All the work to date is pulled into a script format. The facilitator, with group assistance, will capture revisions from the workshopping and transcribe descriptions for any movement or non-verbal work. To explore the running order, I've often taped index cards for each story/

scene on a whiteboard so they can be moved around. We discuss what the arc of the show might be, how we want to welcome the audience at the start, and what we want to leave them with at the end. It allows us to think intentionally about the relationship with the audience and creating a piece that works as a whole.

Final Script Reading and Agreement

Based on the constant feedback loop, the script is put together in the agreed-upon order. The group then reads it through from start to finish, depending on time this might occur in the same session as compiling or have to wait for the following session. Discussion of any concerns, ideas, or thoughts occurs. Then the script is read a second time, but anyone can stop any time they feel something needs to be addressed. Changes can be proposed to the group for discussion. The goal is consensus. On rare occasions, a vote might be needed if consensus can't be reached. However, I only go to a vote if all agree that they will be able to live with the decision regardless of how the vote goes. The hope is to never go forward with something any collaborator strongly opposes, so that everyone can stand behind the entire show.

Now you have a script!

Pitfalls

Reflecting back on dozens of projects and feedback received, I can share the following lessons learned that motivate me to adapt and improve the process each time.

- Don't be too rigid. Starting on time, regular attendance, and other "professional" expectations may not work in some settings. When working in community, flexibility is required. There are many barriers to participation, and finding ways to reduce these is crucial.
- Consultation is a benefit, not an extra burden. There are experts in every topic your planned play might explore. Work with them, remunerate them, and allow them to be an integral part of the process.
- I cannot overstate the need for transparent and clear communication around issues such as future plans for the writing, ownership, anonymity, control, and future contact. This should be outlined fully from the start.
- All stages of the process must be consent-based. Every participant has the right to decide what they want included in the final script

based on what they feel comfortable sharing publicly. They also choose whether to have their name listed or to be an anonymous contributor.
- Everyone should benefit. Students are learning and getting credit. In community work, payment for participation is crucial.
- Creating a safe space is easier said than done. If you work with students, this is easier as there are parameters that already exist in the classroom. If you are working outside a classroom structure, it will depend on who the collaborators are and what they need.
- Conflict will occur. Mediating early is crucial. Go back to the Community Agreement when needed to resolve issues.
- You will make mistakes as a facilitator. Own up to it. Discuss a way forward.
- This is not about your ego. The process here is often more important than the product. Put the collaborators first, both in terms of mental health and in terms of their learning.
- Do not come in with preconceived notions of what the piece will look like. We sometimes subconsciously guide a process in a direction we want to go because we think the product will be better. Try to let this go and embrace the joy of discovery, the trepidation of not knowing what it will look like, and the beauty of creating something through a shared experience.

Conclusion

This process is a way to develop writing skills and storytelling ability among those who may not feel capable of writing a play. It also produces some of the most original, raw, and genuine moments I've ever seen on stage.

For me there is nothing like being in a space with a diverse group of people who are creating together!

It feels right to end with a response from a past collaborator and from a past community partner.

> It was a memorable experience. Through the development of the piece, we got to sit together and share our experiences with racism. With the help of our facilitators, there was a sense of equality and safety in the room - young or adult, different backgrounds and histories, it was all the same. In a room of new faces, we all seemed to feel safe enough to voice our experiences and begin an eye-opening process of creation. As I listened to the stories of others, I was astounded by the pervasiveness of racism, the costs of it, the different

ways it manifests, and I came to the realization that this is something the public needs to be aware of.

Ashley Chartrand, actor/collaborator (*No Offense...*, 2009)

Voices: Manitoba's Youth in Care Network worked in partnership with Sarasvàti Productions to undertake a unique theatrical community collaboration over a two-year period. The project culminated in the production and tour of *Giving Voice*. Voices worked closely with Sarasvàti, including having representatives at performances in schools where we witnessed the effect of this play on the close to 5,000 youth who saw it. The collaborative creation method that Sarasvàti Productions uses truly gives voice to the community they work with and as part of that process many youth were empowered by sharing their stories and having the unique opportunity to learn theatre skills.

Marie Christian, Program Director (*Giving Voice*, 2014)

References

Many of the exercises I use have been passed on by my teachers, collaborators, and colleagues over the last three decades. I honor their contribution and with their blessing regularly adapt their offerings. As a result, tracing the origin is a challenge. In my early work I drew a great deal on Spolin and Boal. Below are some resources for additional games, exercises, and improvisation activities for those who need to build up their repertoire.

Barker, Clive. *Theatre Games: A New Approach to Drama Training*. Methuen, 1982.
Boal, Augusto. *Games for Actors and Non-Actors*. Routledge, Taylor & Francis Group, 2022.
Spolin, Viola. *Improvisation for the Theatre (Third Edition)*. Northwestern University Press, 1999.
Spolin, Viola. *Theatre Games for the Classroom: A Teacher's Handbook*. Northwestern University Press, 1986.
Swale, Jessica. *Drama Games for Rehearsals*. Nick Hern Books, 2016.
Trefor-Jones, Glyn. *Drama Menu at a Distance: 80 Socially Distanced or Online Theatre Games*. Nick Hern Books, 2020.
Unsworth, Thomasina. *Drama Games for Actors*. Nick Hern Books, 2017.

14 Writing Climate Justice

Personal Storytelling and Source Material Devising as Embodied Methodology

Joan Lipkin and Kasey Lynch

Introduction

Climate change is arguably the largest and most significant challenge facing our world. Writing dramatic material serves as a particularly viable approach to explore issues of huge scale. The pursuit of climate justice encompasses topics such as water systems, vegetation, air quality, human systems, racial equity, labor, immigration, food scarcity, and many more. Philosopher Timothy Morton refers to climate change as an example of a "hyperobject," which he defines as "things that are massively distributed in time and space relative to humans."[1] How do we enter discussions about the hyperobject of climate change, a concept so massive that it can often defy human comprehension?

Thinking about this question in terms of our own relationship to climate change, we find inspiration in this Adrienne Maree Brown quote: "How do we create and proliferate a compelling vision of economies and ecologies that center humans and the natural world over the accumulation of material? / We embody. We learn. We release the idea of failure, because it's all data. / But first we imagine."[2] In this chapter, we propose that embodied exercises create entry points into exploration of the enormity of the climate crisis, unlocking new potential for writing meaningful dramatic work. While there are many approaches, we offer two strategies here, personal storytelling and devising from source material. Both have shown particular success in academic classroom settings but may be applied by anyone interested in writing dramatic text foregrounding the climate crisis. This crisis is urgent,[3] and these methodologies allow us to both center, and decenter, humanity in pursuit of fostering greater understanding, empathy, resilience, and desire to act to repair our relationship with the earth while imagining radical futures.

Embodied methods of writing dramatic text recognize the ways the human body provides, as D. Soyini Madison describes, "the very resources and residues that not only structure our identities, but are inseparable elements of every performance we make and that makes us."[4] Embodied techniques are important to apply to issues of climate change because dramatic texts created from such explorations can not only affect the learning and emotional journeys of writers, actors, and spectators, but can also affect public policy. Theatre can serve as a form of science communication, clarifying dense scientific material for audiences and policymakers. Writing about climate change using the methods we explore in this essay builds on theories of embodied learning put forth by Paulo Freire. For Freire, "knowledge emerges only through invention and reinvention, through the restless, impatient, continuing, hopeful inquiry human beings pursue in the world, with the world, and with each other."[5] The students who utilize the cooperative embodied exercises of devising theatrical material outlined below draw from both personal experience and from source material. They not only find entry points into talking about climate change, but become active agents in creating curriculum, increasing their confidence and investment in exploring their relationship to climate justice.

Personal to Global Storytelling

Breaking down a hyperobject like climate change into comprehensible material can sometimes most optimally begin at the personal level. Climate activist and former President of Ireland Mary Robinson admits that "when faced with the enormity of the climate change problem, it is easy to throw our hands up in the air and admit defeat. But individual empowerment leads to confidence."[6] One way to empower considerations of climate change stems from personal storytelling. The history of storytelling spans thousands of years from early cave drawings to practices of oral tradition. People of all cultures tell stories.

In a world of rapidly accumulating data, one might easily ask what is so powerful about the act of storytelling? In her book *Story Proof: The Science Behind the Startling Power of Story*, Kendall Haven outlines the ways stories have started feuds, forged alliances, changed cultural attitudes, reorganized value systems, swayed public opinion and political debate, and have "changed and continue to change the world—to define our world."[7] Devising climate change work starting from one's own personal, emotional, and physical location provides not only a way to locate issues in the body, but the tools to expand the work on a global scale. The following exercise provides a model for how oral storytelling, an embodied technique, might generate meaningful dramatic text on the topic of climate justice. In this example, students are asked to consider their personal relationship to climate change, and then more specifically, to water. Starting with personal connections to a topic provides students the foundation to creatively employ the storytelling attributes of characters, setting, plot, and conflict. It is crucial to note that the exercises we outline in this chapter can be modified to fit multiple contexts, depending on available resources like time and space. For example, in a classroom setting, the instructor or facilitator might choose to dedicate anywhere from a few days to an entire semester to this work.[8] The exercises can also be tailored to both in-person and virtual settings. We aim to make these exercises easily accessible and adaptable for those interested in entering the conversation on climate change through embodied performance techniques. We encourage modifications to the work over not doing the work at all as the issue of climate justice is imminent. Skipping steps or condensing the exercise is appropriate when needed.

Personal Storytelling: Water

Part One

1. In a few words, write how you feel about climate change.
    a. What emotions does the topic evoke for you?
    b. How did you feel about exploring this theme creatively?
2. Paired sharing: share your response with partner or small group.
3. Group generation: develop a collective story or theme that speaks to your responses.

Part Two

4. Share your most memorable relationship to a body of water while growing up or in recent years. Provide context for your memory.[9]
5. Put the personal memory into a wider context.
    a. Why is water important to the self?[10] Beyond the self? In the U.S.?[11] Globally?[12]
    b. Consider non-human points of view.[13]
6. Using this material, create a story to share with the class. Remember stories generally:
    a. Have a beginning, middle, and end.
    b. Include characters, setting, plot, and conflict.

7 Share your story with the class using any of the following methods:[14]
   a Tell the story out loud.
   b Write the story down.
   c Show the story with pictures and/or sounds.
   d Enact the story through improvisation, movement, and/or dance.
8 Paired sharing: in pairs, reflect on the process of creating this story.
   a Did you have any new insights?
   b How did you feel your creativity was stimulated by specific techniques?

Devising from Source Material

Another embodied technique to approach writing dramatic material that centers issues of climate change begins with source material. In the following two examples, students are given the ability to choose topics that interest them, and then utilize source material such as articles, podcasts, interviews, and videos as fuel for devising dramatic material. Through a series of discussion prompts, students are encouraged to not only unpack the existing scientific and sociopolitical work surrounding their topic of choice, but to explore their emotional and physical reactions to the material.

Sample Topics

1. Meat & dairy consumption
2. Environmental racism
3. Water
4. Environmentally-linked illness
5. Global warming
6. Covid-19
7. Plant and animal extinction
8. Toxic pollution
9. Economic investment and disinvestment
10. Fossil fuel subsidies

Boalian devising techniques provide helpful framing to think about the way both mental and physical exercises can help students and practitioners destabilize their own preconceived notions and habits to explore alternative ways to write about and move through the world. Devising using source material pulls from tenets of Augusto Boal's newspaper theatre methodology. For Boal, newspaper theatre serves multiple objectives. The primary objective is to "devolve theatre to the people;" a secondary objective is to attempt "to demystify the pretended 'objectivity' of most journalism;" and the third goal is "to demonstrate that theatre can be practiced by anyone."[15] (With these objectives in mind and given the rise of disinformation, especially in a U.S. context, another topic to consider might be the ways the climate crisis is covered in the media.)[16] Devising allows us to deconstruct our own ways of knowing and provides space to question objectivity. Approaching source material about climate change with these tenets in mind creates the potential to explore hyperobjects in embodied ways that can lead to meaningful dramatic text.

One important consideration in the source material exercises that we wish to highlight is the value of thinking about points of view not only beyond our own, but those that are non-human as well. Social science scholars Petra Tschakert et al. discuss the idea of "multispecies justice" and the ways that humans must be in communion with the ecological systems with which we interact. Their multispecies justice lens encourages us to embrace the "obligation to decolonize the Anthropocene, de-homogenize 'the human' to fathom different violences, and hold accountable actors and structures that continue to dehumanize."[17] In the following exercise we offer ways of exploring different points of view on the topic of meat and dairy consumption that can be tailored to explore a number of climate-related topics.

Devising from Source Material: Meat and Dairy Consumption

1 Ice breaker exercise.[18]
2 Read source material: "Interactive: What is the climate impact of eating meat and dairy?" by Daisy Dunne.[19]
3 Provide discussion prompts.
   a What might be the experience of animals on their way to slaughter?

    b   What is the environmental effect of cows raised by grain produced in the Amazon?
    c   How does farmers using nitrogen fertilizer to stimulate plant growth affect animal grazing?
    d   What could habitable land be used for if 50% of it was no longer used for food production?
    e   Which meat should be the first eliminated and what will the impact be?
    f   Does eating meat also directly affect vegetation?
    g   What would the world look like if everyone stopped eating meat or cut back 50% on consumption?
    h   Where does your daily cup of coffee come from and how might it contribute to your carbon footprint?

4. Creation/brainstorming time as a group:
    a   Write a monologue/scene/song using these prompts.[20]
        i   Explore circumstances.[21]
        ii Explore points of view.
           1   Are you an animal on its way to be slaughtered?
           2   Are you an animal living in a crowded space?
           3   Are you a cow being raised on grain produced in the Amazon?
           4   Are you the daily cup of coffee or chocolate bar being ingested?
           5   Are you a vegan, vegetarian, pescatarian, or flexitarian?
           6   Are you a person who is trying to not eat meat in a family that has different eating habits?
5. Perform the piece for the class.
6. Reflect as a class and discuss next steps and everyday applications.

In pursuit of climate justice, echoing Tschakert et al., we have much to learn from Indigenous methodologies and belief systems that have celebrated the interconnectedness of humans and the earth for generations. One of the unfortunate byproducts of colonization is a prevailing value of domination not only over other humans, but over the Earth's natural wonders. The fight for environmental justice has much to gain from understanding Indigenous traditions and the spirituality with which many tribes approach their environment. From Indigenous storywork to concepts of relationality, Indigenous scholars and peoples provide integral voices to issues like climate action.[22] Indigenous environmental organizations like Honor the Earth, Indigenous Climate Action, Indigenous Environmental Network, Kuaʻāina Ulu 'Auamo (KUA), Native Conservancy, Seeding Sovereignty, and more have advocated for the preservation of land and contain ecological knowledges deeply rooted in their cultural practices.[23] Theatre practitioners have the unique opportunity to learn from Indigenous relationships to the Earth and create stories oriented toward multispecies justice. In exploring our own bodily stakes in the process, we can begin to decenter ourselves in favor of telling stories that contribute to the larger picture of climate justice.

Devising from Source Material: Environmental Racism

1 Ice breaker exercise.
2 Read source material: Hazel M. Johnson and the Environmental Justice Movement.[24]
3 Provide discussion prompts:
   a What percentage of low-income communities of color are living in hazardous conditions?
      i Where are they located and what are the consequences of this?
      ii Why are these conditions more common in low-income communities of color?
   b Historically, what are some housing units that have been built on dumping sites? Which companies and local legislation enable this?
   c How do companies contribute to environmentally hazardous conditions via dumping to landfills and waste lagoons?
   d What warning signals about public health can we see coming out of the environmentally hazardous areas?
   e What are the racial disparities regarding illness and life expectancy in relation to environment?
   f What do you think constitutes environmental justice and what organizations are doing that work?
   g What has been the relationship of various Indigenous tribes to nature, and how do different perspectives compare/contrast with Anglo perspectives?

4   Creation/brainstorming time as a group.
    a   Write a monologue/scene/song using these prompts:
        i   Explore circumstances.
        ii Explore points of view.
            1   Are you an apartment complex built on a dumping site?
            2   Are you the hazardous condition itself?
            3   Are you a resident who has become ill?
            4   Do you have a family member that has fallen ill?
            5   How old are you?
            6   Are you the cancer itself?
            7   Are you asthma?
            8   Are you the company dumping toxic materials?
            9   Are you an activist speaking out about these conditions and the bias that creates them?
            10 Are you the department in the local government that has supported or is trying to regulate them?
5   Perform the pieces for the class.
6   Reflect as a class and discuss next steps and everyday applications.

Value of Embodied Writing Oriented Toward Climate Justice

The sample exercises and discussion questions provided in this chapter have been successful in a number of ways in the classroom. In one particularly memorable class session, a group of students chose to devise a piece from source material about environmental racism. As a group, they staged a scene set in a support-group meeting. The students chose to explore the points of view of cities facing pollution, so each character portrayed a different city. The actors sat in a semi-circle and expressed the ways climate change specifically affected their city. One character, played by a woman of color, spoke about how bad things had gotten in her city, specifically talking about the asthma rates of her citizens, many of them people of color. After sharing, the character got up, said with disgust "I'm just done," and walked out of the meeting, leaving the other cities to stack the chairs. This was a powerful experience for the actors and the spectators in the class. From the source material provided, these students crafted a compelling scene that not only addressed the enormous and daunting ideas of climate change, racism, and environmental justice, but provided an entry point for their classmates to also better understand and discuss the topics.

In feedback sessions, students have shared the ways these embodied methodologies helped them connect to, invest in, and begin writing about the hyperobject of climate change. The value of point of view exercises was a recurring theme in student reflections, with students citing how imagining themselves as a cup of coffee, a factory employee, or a city facing pollution opened their eyes to new ways of thinking about the climate crisis. Students noted their creative capacity was strengthened, specifically lauding the collective nature of the exercises. Employing active visualization, physicalizing, and group-sharing tactics helps playwrights creatively access and craft dramatic text about a hyperobject like climate change.

Conclusion

It can sometimes feel daunting to find an entry point into writing plays or other dramatic literature about a topic as expansive as the climate crisis. But doing this kind of dramatic writing is imperative to advocacy, education, and action related to such an urgent issue. Creating theatre that specifically explores climate justice is important because as playwright and environmental activist Chantal Bilodeau notes, "in politics, narratives determine policy," and the stories we tell shape our beliefs, values, and actions.[25] Public health scholar Lise Saffran also argues for the importance of narrative in public health policymaking, revealing how "for policymakers, well-told stories can provide an 'anchor for statistical evidence'. For community members, they can help the individual find herself within larger social phenomena to great personal and political effect."[26] The strategies explored throughout this chapter provide ways not only for participants to locate themselves in the phenomena of climate change, but also to embody many perspectives in pursuit of radical new ways of imagining climate justice. While these methodologies can be applied in any group setting, they have been particularly helpful in the classroom. Students have been able to use personal storytelling and source material devising as ways to find confidence in writing about climate change. When students engage in embodied learning, they become invested in the process and, importantly, become agents in advancing climate change curriculum and climate justice.

What could climate justice look like? Feminist performance scholar Jill Dolan reminds us of the ways performance renders topics like climate change simultaneously more real, "in that we grasp them more fully through their embodiment and ours at the theatre," but also less real in the way the theatre "makes glorious, hopeful spectacles of the possibilities of everyday social life."[27] Writing and devising with hope in mind can provide radical insight into considerations of a future where humans live in right relationship with the environment. While writing and producing dramatic text about the climate crisis cannot singlehandedly right the wrongs that we as humans have committed against our environment and each other, it can help us enter the conversation as civically engaged and well-informed advocates. We hope this chapter provides entry points for writing dramatic text about climate change for anyone who wishes to join this vital conversation.

Notes

1. Morton, p. 1.
2. Brown, p. 18.
3. At the time of writing this article, the U.S Supreme Court began overturning a number of environmental protections including West Virginia v. the EPA. Overturning this decision revoked the EPA's ability to regulate the emissions of power plants.
4. Madison, p. 26.
5. Freire, p. 72.
6. Robinson, p. 106.
7. Haven, p. 8.
8. Here is one way to approach a personal storytelling unit in a college classroom setting. Note that this example can also be applied to any topic and to the devising with source material exercises. Spend one class session reading an article or two, or assign reading as homework. In the next class session, spend anywhere from twenty minutes to a full class session discussing the reading with specific discussion prompts. In the third class session, begin the story generation process through creative brainstorming. In the next class session, or over multiple class sessions, dedicate time to exploring ideas not only through discussion, but utilizing embodied techniques like movement, improvisation, and devising. Another class session, or series of class sessions, could then be dedicated to choosing ideas and developing a script.
9. Some questions to prompt context include: Where were you? How old were you? Were you with anyone? How did you feel about this water or experience? What did you do? What came up for you emotionally when you visited and wrote about that memory? How did it make you feel? Did you have any questions about that experience?
10. For example, consider the following: according to the United States Geological Survey, most of the human body is made up of water, on average 60%. The amount of water in the body changes slightly with age, sex, and hydration levels. Organs with high amounts of water include the brain and heart (73%), the lungs (83%), the skin (64%), the muscles and kidneys (79%) and the bones (31%). In our body, water brings nutrients to all the

cells and oxygen to our brain. Water enables nutrients, proteins, amino acids, glucose, and other compounds to be consumed and assimilated by the body.

11 For example, consider the following: in the United States, the West has experienced less rain over the past fifty years, as well as increases in the severity and length of droughts; this has been especially of concern in the Southwest. During California's second-driest year on record, districts' water allocation went from 10% in December 2020 down to 5% by March 2021. The only other time since 1996 that districts have been granted so little was in January 2014, during the last drought. According to data from the American Community Survey, as of 2014, 1.6 million people in the United States reported that they lacked access to one of the following: a toilet, a tub or shower, or running water.

12 For example, consider the following: many industries require large quantities of water for processing, cooling, and diluting products. Examples of industries that consume large quantities of water include the paper industry, the food industry, and the chemical industry. Women are disproportionately affected by the water crisis, as they are often responsible for collecting water. This takes time away from work, school, and their family time. The lack of water and sanitation locks women in a cycle of poverty. As the resource is becoming scarce, tensions among different users may intensify, both at the national and international level.

13 For example, consider you are a body of water, a town that is flooded or suffering from drought, a hungry plant, an animal, etc.

14 While we acknowledge the value and primacy of written text, we want to emphasize that spoken and written text are not the only types. For example, movement and visual text are also valuable to storytelling.

15 Boal, p. 192.

16 For example, consider the following: To what extent do we know about certain environmental issues? Who are the stakeholders in certain issues? Certain news stations? What aspects affect news coverage? Who funds journalism sites? How might people utilize, or not utilize, fact-checking systems like snopes.com?

17 Tschakert et al., p. 2.

18 Choose ice breakers that work for your class or community. Ice breakers are meant to disrupt certain socially proscribed behaviors and foster connection and playfulness with others. Begin with consent, especially if leading an exercise that involves touch. Ice breakers that explore the body can be useful. Some exercises we use include having participants walk around the room in different directions, temporalities, speeds, etc. We also have participants say hello to the person closest to them with a typically under-used body part like the feet, hips, neck, etc.

19 Dunne.

20 The length of the pieces can vary based on time constraints and form. A monologue might be anywhere between two and fifteen minutes. A scene or a short sketch might be between three and eight minutes. If you are wanting to make a larger group project, you could stitch together multiple elements to make a piece that is an hour long. Again, these are adaptable guidelines.

21 Some questions to prompt circumstances include: Where are you/they? Why are they there? What has happened? Where does it leave off for this moment/end? Will this story help us understand things differently?
22 Windchief and Pedro, eds.
23 "Diversify Your Feed: 6 Indigenous Environmental Organizations You Should Follow."
24 Hutcherson.
25 Bilodeau, p. 15.
26 Saffran, p. 107.
27 Dolan, p. 165.

References

Bilodeau, Chantal. "Introduction." In *Lighting the Way: An Anthology of Short Plays About the Climate Crisis*, edited by Chantal Bilodeau and Thomas Peterson, p. 15. Los Angeles: Centre for Sustainable Practice in the Arts and The Arctic Cycle, 2020.

Boal, Augusto. *Legislative Theatre: Using Performance to Make Politics*. Translated by Adrian Jackson. New York: Routledge, 1998.

Brown, Adrienne Maree. *Emergent Strategy: Shaping Change, Changing Worlds*. Edinburgh: AK Press, 2017.

"Diversify Your Feed: 6 Indigenous Environmental Organizations You Should Follow," *Native Americans in Philanthropy*, last modified April 22, 2021. https://nativephilanthropy.org/2021/04/22/diversify-your-feed-6-indigenous-environmental-organizations-you-should-follow/.

Dolan, Jill. *Utopia in Performance: Finding Hope at the Theatre*. Ann Arbor: University of Michigan Press, 2005.

Dunne, Daisy. "Interactive: What Is the Climate Impact of Eating Meat and Dairy." *CarbonBrief*, last modified September 14, 2020. https://interactive.carbonbrief.org/what-is-the-climate-impact-of-eating-meat-and-dairy/.

Freire, Paulo. *Pedagogy of the Oppressed*. 30th anniversary ed. New York: Continuum, 2000.

Haven, Kendall. *Story Proof: The Science Behind the Startling Power of Story*. Westport: Libraries Unlimited, 2017.

Hutcherson, Lori Lakin. "BHM: Good Black News Celebrates Hazel M. Johnson, the 'Mother of Environmental Justice'." *Good Black News*, last modified February 20, 2021. https://goodblacknews.org/2021/02/20/bhm-good-black-news-celebrates-hazel-m-johnson-the-mother-of-environmental-justice/.

Madison, D. Soyini. *Performed Ethnography & Communication: Improvisation and Embodied Experience*. New York: Routledge, 2018.

Morton, Timothy. *Hyperobjects: Philosophy and Ecology after the End of the World*. Minneapolis: University of Minnesota Press, 2013.

Robinson, Mary. *Climate Justice: Hope, Resilience, and the Fight for a Sustainable Future*. New York: Bloomsbury Publishing, 2018.

Saffran, Lise. "'Only Connect': The case for Public Health Humanities." *Medical Humanities*, 40(2), pp. 105–110, 2014.

"Storytelling," *National Geographic*, accessed 9 July 2022. https://education.nationalgeographic.org/resource/storytelling.

Tschakert, Petra, David Schlosberg, Danielle Celermajer, Lauren Rickards, Christine Winter, Mathias Thaler, Makere Stewart-Harawira, and Blanche Verlie. "Multispecies Justice: Climate-just Futures With, For and Beyond Humans." *WIREs Climate Change*, 12(2), pp. 1–10, 2020.

Windchief, Sweeny and Timothy San Pedro, eds. *Applying Indigenous Research Methods: Storying with Peoples and Communities*. New York: Routledge, 2019.

Part V
Curated Exercises

15 Embodied Playwriting Exercises for Classroom, Workshop, and Studio

Skill-Building and Content Generation

Hillary Haft Bucs and Charissa Menefee

Introduction

We have curated a series of embodied writing exercises that can be implemented in the playwriting classroom, workshop space, or devising studio. These exercises range from warm-ups to storytelling techniques to rasa work. Many of the exercises can be used for both introductory skill-building and/or as experiences to generate content. As in previous chapters, the authors of these exercises have included step-by-step instructions, reflection and discussion questions, side-coaching tips, and ideas for next steps in the writing journey.

The Ceiling Fan Speaks!

Alexis Lygoumenos and Gabrielle Sinclair Compton

Rationale for the Exercise

The Ceiling Fan Speaks! is a writing warm-up for playwrights of all ages and experience levels that allows you to quickly generate grounded, surprising characters with their own unique perspectives and emotional lives using both performance and playwriting techniques with minimal effort. Fold this into your daily practice. Five minutes per step works well.

Origins

This playwriting exercise builds on a poetry prompt by Kate Kehoe, which was inspired by the works of Sandra Beasley.

Goals/Objectives

Key elements of this exercise call on the writer to use both writing and acting skills, as you pivot back and forth between your own perspective as a playwright and your perspective as the character. This exercise wards off writer's block as it begins with a simple, non-creative description from a point in space, which stimulates imagination and flow. Characters and scenes generated can serve as starting points for new projects or can be kept in your arsenal to bring in when inspiration runs dry.

What We Need

The exercise follows two steps and can be practiced anywhere (at home, on public transit, in a classroom (both virtual or in person), in a coffee shop, etc.), and the level of movement on the part of the playwright can be as minimal or as involved as you feel comfortable with, making it an accessible and straightforward practice, primed for repetition.

How We Get There

This exercise has two steps:
Step 1: Locate an object in the room and write from its specific perspective (five minutes)
  Look around, taking in your surroundings, checking in with your senses. What stands out to you? Any particular colors or textures? If possible, make physical contact with something in your periphery. Close your eyes, breathe, then open your eyes and look to the room you're in or enter another room (such as, say, the kitchen). Let your eyes settle on ONE OBJECT anywhere in the room (such as a ceiling fan, an electrical outlet, a doorknob, etc.). Compose a monologue from the object's perspective, writing in first person as the object. Begin with a spatial description from your perspective. Where are you? What do you see? What's above or below you? Describe your shape, color, age. Be as specific as possible.
  As your object, state your distance from other things and your experience of the room. What can you see from where you are? Do you move? Are you moved? (For the more experienced performer—might a psychological gesture in the vein of Michael Chekhov come to mind?) Do you make sounds?

After a couple minutes of this spatial inventory, a feeling or a want will emerge. What is your attitude about what and where you are? *Be specific.* Connect your perspective to how you feel until time runs out.

Example: a student selects the ceiling fan in the room. In the center of the page, this student writes CEILING FAN, and begins their monologue from the ceiling fan's point of view. This could begin something like, "I am eight feet up from the floor, at the center of the ceiling. I can spin slow and fast. I'm wooden and white. I'm old and wise. I see everything from up here. I control the air. I feel powerful. No one can stop me!"

Step 2: Write from a second object's point of view about the first object (five minutes)

Close your eyes again and take a few deep breaths in through your nose and out through your mouth as you relax further into a brief moment of stillness. Flutter your eyes open and look around your current space once more. Re-engage your senses and see what else stands out to you. Your eyes will land on a second object in the room. Again, write a monologue, but now from your new object's perspective. This time, as the second object, focus entirely on the first object, beginning spatially. How do you as this new entity feel about the first object? Where is that first object in relation to you? Below you? Far away? Touching? How do you compare in size, movement, power? An opinion of the first object will emerge. Let any emotions or feelings bubble up to the surface as you write, continuing to write in first person as you go.

Example: a student selects an outlet in the room. In the center of the page, this student writes OUTLET, and begins their second monologue from the outlet's point of view describing the ceiling fan (as established by the first monologue). This could begin with something like, "I'm just above the carpet, by the door, and I watch this guy spinning above me, so smug. That guy is so frickin' old and rickety. Me? I'm new, updated, and safe. I wish he would talk to me, though, but he's in his own world up there."

Side Coaching Tips

Optional Meditation/Relaxation Opener: students and instructors may benefit from commencing with a guided meditation, particularly in the early stages of a new class to stimulate further connection. Encourage tranquility by using a calm tone of voice. While substitutions and additions can be made, a rudimentary practice can be achieved by reciting the following:

> After getting yourself into a comfortable position (ideally lying down on your back or sitting upright, yet relaxed) uncross your arms and legs, unclench your jaw, and gently flutter your eyes closed. Take a deep breath in through your nose, and exhale slowly out through your mouth. Beginning with the very top of your head, 'check in' with each part of your body and alignment, making adjustments as you see fit. Next, clench or tense and then release sections of your body as you continue along. Take another deep breath in through the nose and out through the mouth. Now lightly flutter your eyes open, maintaining a gentle gaze. Eyes open, wide awake.

Now you may begin the rest of the exercise. Students may hit a wall while writing before the time is up. Encourage them to check in with their senses. When does their object experience touch? What do they hear? How do they feel about where they are physically right now? Where do they want to be? Return to the basics: color, shape, speed, levels (high or low), etc.

Reflection/Follow Up Questions

Before sharing, give students space to share their initial reactions to the exercise. What was that like? What images were conjured? Was there a moment your object stopped being an object and started becoming a person? What brought this character to life for you and how so?

What Comes Next

If in a classroom setting, have them read aloud their first monologue either seated or up on their feet. Offer side coaching as needed before jumping into the second step. Students may then share their second character monologue on their feet with a partner standing in place of the first object.

Students have now organically created two-character monologues in relationship. To take the next steps in developing a scene: write out a description of your *stage picture* (that is, what the audience sees), describing where your two new characters are in space in regards to each other. This will help "set the stage" for their relationship, dynamic, and tension. Finally, pull a line from each monologue to write the first and second lines and begin your scene. If time allows, read the scene aloud to share with the class.

Letters to Self: An Improvisational Exercise for Playwriting and Personal Writing

Ramón Esquivel

Rationale

Generations of playwrights have been writing themselves into the theatrical landscape even if they have rarely, if ever, seen themselves reflected on stage. How does a student or emerging playwright begin to write about, and from, aspects of their own identities, cultures, and experiences? ***Letters to Self*** is an improvisational exercise for beginning this process.

Objective

Actor-playwrights will create two-voice dialogues by tapping their own voices and the languages, memories, culture, and values of their youth.

Time

45 minutes

What We Need

Paper and pencils or pens; audio recording devices (preferred but optional)

How We Get There

Instructions below are also suggested language for the instructor-facilitator to use when addressing the actor-playwrights.

Part I: Letter to Younger Self

1 **Imagination as Preparation (two minutes)**
   Find some space for yourself. Close your eyes. Picture your Younger Self as a child or adolescent or younger adult. Who are the people that are significant to your Younger Self at this time? What does your Younger Self care about most? With all the life that you, as Older Self, have lived since then, what will you say to your Younger Self?

2 **Speak a Letter to Younger Self (five minutes)**
   Keeping your eyes closed, speak a letter to your Younger Self. Address them with a special name. Use language that Younger Self speaks or hears in places that are safe and welcoming. Keeping in mind the age of your Younger Self, share your words. What will you offer? Encouragement? Wisdom? A memory? Ask your Younger Self about people they care about. Maybe you offer to listen. Is there a person who you appreciate even more years after childhood? Perhaps there is a conflict that you wish you had resolved differently. Be specific and personal here. Help your Younger Self understand why this letter is important.

3 **Record or Write the Letter to Your Younger Self (six minutes)**
   If using audio recording devices, which is preferred but optional: speak your Letter to your Younger Self again, but this time, record your voice, and your voice only. It may help to close your eyes again as you are speaking. Trust that you will recall and include what is most important. When you have finished recording the letter, put the device down.

   If using paper and pencils or pens: write down the letter you just spoke to your Younger Self, as best as you can remember. Trust that you will recall and include what is most important. When you have finished writing down the letter, fold the paper in half.

Part II: Letter to Older Self

1 **Imagination as Preparation (two minutes)**
   Find a new space for yourself. Now imagine that you are your Younger Self. Imagine looking into a mirror. What do you look like? What is happening in your life? Who are the

people that are significant to you? What do you care about most? Be your Younger Self for the next few minutes.

2   **Read or Listen to Letter from Your Older Self (four minutes)**
    Listen to the audio recording of your Older Self's letter, or you can read what they have written. You may wish to do this privately or listen through earphones. The letter is for you.

3   **Speak a Letter to Your Older Self (five minutes)**
    Staying in the mind and voice of your Younger Self, speak a letter in response to your Older Self's letter. How does your Older Self's letter make you feel? Maybe you feel mixed emotions? What does your Older Self remember and understand, or maybe misunderstand and misremember? Ask your Older Self at least one question. Ask several, if that's what your Younger Self would do. Use language that is comfortable for your Younger Self.

4   **Record or Write the Letter to Your Older Self (six minutes)**
    If using audio recording devices, which is preferred but optional: speak your Letter to Your Older Self again, but this time, record your voice, and your voice only. It may help to close your eyes again as you are speaking. Trust that you will recall and include what is most important. When you have finished recording the letter, put the device down.

    If using paper and pencils or pens: write down the letter you just spoke to your Older Self, as best as you can remember. Trust that you will recall and include what is most important. When you have finished writing down the letter, fold the paper in half.

Part III: Scripting a Dialogue: When Your Younger Self and Older Self Meet (ten minutes)

Write a dialogue between your Older Self and Younger Self. Begin the dialogue with one of your Younger Self's questions. Consider using names that distinguish between the two at different ages. Though your Younger Self and Older Self are based on you, the actor-playwright, allow them to grow, develop, and flourish into their own characters, characters that are not you. Aim to guide your Younger Self or your Older Self, or both, to a new understanding of each other and the world.

Time permitting, share the dialogues that you created between your Younger Self and Older Self. It is powerful for a writer to speak their own words. Read each in the voice of your Younger Self or Older Self, or listen as another actor or two actors read the letters. When other actors are reading your words, listen to their interpretation. Ask others listening to tell you the story between these two characters. There can be electricity when a writer hears their words read by other actors. The choice is yours.

Variations on Part III

1. Write dialogue between your Older Self and Younger Self as a text message conversation.
2. Rename characters for the dialogue.
3. Change the relationship between the two characters to become parent-child, teacher-student, mentor-mentee, player-coach, etc.

Reflection (five minutes)

One of the greatest challenges that both playwrights and actors face is creating unique character voices, even though the different characters are springing from the same mind. Look first at the dialogue you wrote, and then revisit both letters. What distinguishes the two voices? Is it vocabulary or word choices? The sophistication or informality or variety of the language? Tone? Pace? The person's knowledge?

Variation on the Exercise

Reverse the order. The actor-playwright is currently your Younger Self. Write a letter to your Older Self that does not exist yet. Then your Older Self writes back.

What Comes Next: Enrichment

Add a third character into the dialogue. Base this character on your "Self" that you could have been, had you made different choices in your childhood, young adulthood, or recently. Aim to change, shift, or complicate the dynamic between your Older Self and Younger Self by introducing elements like doubt, aspiration, regret, bitterness, and satisfaction into the dialogue.

So much of writing is about exploring possibilities. While most playwrights have to rely on imagination to explore the possibilities in character dialogue, exercises like this allow the playwright and actors to collaborate in that exploration. The playwright can literally hear those possibilities, turning a rehearsal into a kind of laboratory. While this exercise focuses on one scene, the principles can be applied to longer pieces too. What one character says or does is going to influence what the other character says and does, so see how far your actors' improvisations can take the work. Enjoy your exploration!

Find the Event in the Tale of the Inanimate Object

Jeanne Leep

Rationale

Students who want to write new works may have a lot to say, but may not know where to begin; students who want to do improvisation may be eager to begin, but may not know what to say.

This exercise aims to explore the very beginning of the creation process for both playwrights and improvisers working towards a written and performance-worthy final product. Taking a step back to find the event explores two things: finding something worth saying and understanding how to say that by clarifying the climax of a scene. This introductory exercise sets the stage for better writing and the creation of scenes that actually go somewhere. They are grounded in Michael Chekhov and Stanislavski, but are infused with more contemporary improvisational techniques.

Origins of the Exercise

Based on elements of Michael Chekhov and Stanislavski's work as used at the Moscow Art Theatre in 2008, and Michael Schurtleff's guidepost work from *Audition*.

Goals

This exercise…

- provides students with the chance to explore the climax of a scene by creating an event in a short etude or mini-scene;
- explores the power of stage directions and physical actions on stage without dialogue as part of storytelling in a playwriting context;
- sets the stage for more in-depth work on inciting incident, point of attack, and other well-made play terminology for playwriting students;
- gives students the experience of visual storytelling by acting a scene with strong physical choices and then putting those choices into a script format.

What We Need

- Students willing to act (or perhaps read) their pieces, a small space to perform such as the front of a typical classroom, and writing materials.
- If reading only, moving seats to a circle can be useful.

How We Get There

Students create a brief scenario designed to find the event within the scene—the challenge is to *find* the event, which doesn't have to be epic. Using this little schematic, I ask students to show the following in a two-minutes-or-less scene.

1. *Normality*: existence as usual.
2. *Something happens of import*, a new element is introduced, or there is a change in the world of the main character.
3. Major turning point, climax: *the event*.
4. *Conclusion*: new results, good or bad or just new; the aftermath.

This *can* be with a human character; however, I recommend you begin with an inanimate object. An inanimate object to start opens the imagination to storytelling and more clearly layers emotions onto objects not typically associated with feelings. The class can also be assigned the same object and explore all the adventures that object can "feel" depending on what direction the student takes it. Later, we add other inanimate characters—two or three, then big groups. Adding new characters means more roles for students to explore, but it could be components of the same object, for example strings on the same guitar. All of it is done without words, just action, giving students the chance to explore the power of writing stage action as storytelling, not just dialogue. Later, we add lines, but lines are less important than the story. It's storyboard kind of work, but with a writer/actor as the living storyboard.

For example: the tale of the tea bag.

1. *Normality*: Normal existence is in a dark tea box. Is this boring, comfortable, filled with anticipation, or dormant? The options here are endless.
2. *Something happens of import*: when the tea bag is chosen to be used. Its wrapper is removed (thrilling, shocking?), it swings in the air (fun, terrifying?), and...
3. *The event*: it lands in hot water. We "see" the character landing in the hot water, which here is quite instantaneously tied to the conclusion.
4. *The conclusion* could be relaxation, complete fulfillment, horrible burning, or a slow death—any of those things could work depending on the choice of the playwright.

Directions

- When beginning, ask them to look around where they live and imagine the "life" of the everyday things they see. What is normal existence for an object? What could or does change for those objects?
- Students imagine a very simple event in the "life" of an inanimate object. The event should be simple enough to be clearly communicated without words from the actor.
- Students write out their wordless scenario with a tight word limit of fifty to three hundred words.
  - With a tight word count, they can create playable stage directions that read as actionable, as opposed to novel like stage directions. Depending on the genre of the piece, it could be comic, tragic, horror, mystery-solving, dramatic, or a host of other things as chosen by the playwright.
- Once students have their ideas, each acts their silent scenario for the other students, and the students watching guess what

the object and the scenario is. This doesn't have to be an acting class exercise where performance is important, but rather a chance for students to see if their idea makes sense when on its feet.
- For the one object exercise, the scenes are played by one actor and can be no longer than the two minutes. Here, the playwright can act their own scene and come to class ready to perform.
- For non-actors: if acting the scenarios out is too daunting for the playwriting students, assign partners, each student acting for the other's script. Give them a few minutes to work in class on this before showing the work. If the emphasis of the class is not at all acting, then simply reading the scripts (and skipping the guessing) is an option, with an opportunity to perform them afterwards with willing students.
- Students give each other feedback after each short performance, telling the playwright/performer what they thought the object and the event were. It should be clear what the object is and what the event is. If there is not a clear event, discuss why. Was it lack of clarity in the script? Too complicated of a scenario? Are the elements of the object unclear and therefore difficult to guess?
- At this point, students can perform again, keeping the same actor, and use specific input from that actor to clarify the script. Alternatively, actors could be rotated so a new classmate performs the newly revised script. If they performed it themselves, then give it to another partner in class. If they already had someone else performing, give the revised script to someone new. In either case—same actor or new actor—the focus here is, can an actor make sense of what you are asking and (try to) do it? If time is short, they could simply read their new versions to the class. It depends on how much time one wants to spend on the exercise.

If Time Allows:

Once students understand the exercise, they can create scenes and short scenarios more freely, and start to add dialogue to help tell the story. As good storytelling has many events, they can start to distinguish between minor events in the scene of a story and the major event of a story, while using action, not just words, to clarify those moments. They can start to glue those short scenes together to create longer pieces.

Side Coaching Tips

- Rotating scripts so more than one classmate can act a playwright's idea for each re-write here is useful. A frank discussion throughout the class about acting levels impacting the work, and imagining the ideal (ideal actor from the professional world, for example) can help with this as well.
- Asking other students what was clear and what was not as clear in the scenario nets results: how the event could be heightened or the storytelling made clearer. Most importantly, when someone acts out their work, the playwrights have an opportunity to see what made sense and what did not in their script. When they act it themselves, the feedback from the audience as they guess the scenario becomes important. It is also important to discuss the idea of acting and physicality in the idea of moving something from the page to performance. There is opportunity to discuss casting and who their ideal professional actor type would be for this scene. Following that, the students have time to edit their script, and perhaps increase the word count, clarifying points that a performer would need to show for the scene to make sense.
- If acting these etudes out is daunting, it can be useful to start the exercise by creating some ideas on paper, maybe using a half-sheet of paper for each student. Have students write two or three little ideas for their object exercises, maybe pass them round and see which idea resonates with the group—which is good practice for "the pitch" of an idea. Have them, perhaps, look in their backpacks and imagine the journeys of the types of objects they carry with them: the lost earbud, the tangled charger cord, the water bottle with the broken cap. Other students can put a mark by the stories that sound interesting, even in just a few words. Getting students to give each other notes even in that very kernel of an idea phase is another way to increase involvement.

Reflection

Starting with inanimate objects take some pressure off creating HUGE drama. The small trials of everyday life, the truth of shared experiences, can have a great deal of power in playwriting.

The ***Find the Event in the Tale of the Inanimate Object*** exercise helps new playwriting students understand that they need to put events (objective and conflict) into a piece so actors can find it—otherwise actors will (and should) invent their own events and feelings about those events.

What Comes Next

Giving students the assignment before class to bring to their next class gives more performance polish to the assignment, but doing this in the class without any preparation can also be useful, as an impromptu exercise. If there is time left after completing the inanimate object "find the event" exercise, give students the assignment for the next class to do the same, but for a human with an everyday "event." Write short and clear stage directions that tell an actor how to perform what they need to accomplish.

Once students have done work with inanimate objects, the exercise can be recycled to be written for a person, duos, and finally groups. Eventually dialogue can be added. But so often the work of a playwriting class is focused on dialogue to tell the story when stage action can be equally or more engaging than words: finding ways for playwrights to explore some of these more physical exercises, even if not executed with great expertise, can awaken the power of specific stage directions.

Many Characters, Many Objects

Wesley Broulik

Rationale

I use this exercise in my Improvisation and Ensemble courses as well as other courses as both a devising and playwriting exercise. It's one of those wonderful ensemble games that inspire the students to create scenes and scenarios by the utilization of objects in imagined environments. The **Many Characters, Many Objects** exercise is a playful way to explore the creation of scenes with multiple characters, distinct voices, and different points of view. I generally introduce this after we have written a few two-character scenes or short works.

Origins

This exercise is an adaptation of Viola Spolin's **Emerging Where** exercise.[1]

Goals

- To explore one's environment to jumpstart a collaborative writing process that involves multiple characters.
- To facilitate embodied editing and drafting of new work.

What We Need

- The coach/facilitator needs a front desk bell to ring to cue the players to explore a new object. (I switched to using bells for clarity. It's easier for the players to hear the "ding" rather than straining to hear if I'm side coaching or inviting them to find a new object to explore.)
- Chairs for the players if they would like to use them.
- No props, as it's all "space objects."
- Peers to record improvisations on their personal devices. Keith Johnstone records students' work to be used as a teaching aide.[2] We discuss when it is appropriate to record work, such as when it's a part of an exercise and serves as a learning tool, versus posting to social media. This delineation is also unpacked on our syllabi.

How We Get There

Step One

- Divide the participants into small groups.
- Have them decide on a WHO/WHAT/WHERE.

- Invite students to keep relationships on a personal level, rather than transactional. One example could be co-workers at a pizza joint cleaning up the restaurant at close.

Step Two: Silent Exploration (Where)

- This step establishes the physical world (WHERE) so they are free to play and explore.
- Ask each participant to enter and exit their playing space one person at a time.
- Use a timer and give each participant a couple of minutes for this portion of the exercise.
- Each participant is to discover a different object in the space.
- They are to remain nonverbal, but are invited to make sounds.
- Invite each participant to explore their environment through the objects in the environment.
- Have each participant establish the space through the use of one object.
- Invite them to explore using their chosen object.
- Invite them to heighten how they are using the object.
- When they are finished exploring, have them put the object back into the space and exit.
- Here are a few examples based on the example of a pizza joint: mopping the floor, eating a slice of pizza, tossing pizza dough in the air and making one last pizza of the night, counting cash from the cash register, wiping down tables, or washing dishes.
- Don't forget to have one of the participants record the exercise.

Step Three: Verbal Exploration (Who)

In the next step of the sequence, the participants enter the same predetermined space again, but this time they are invited to speak and explore relationships (WHO). Invite participants to enter the space one at a time, and remain in the space as others join them.

- Have them begin to use the objects they created in the previous exercise.
- Time this step to five minutes.
- Encourage participants to speak to each other.

- Invite them to keep the relationships (WHO) personal instead of transactional.
- Some suggestions for exploring relationships can include status changes (raising or lowering your own or your fellow player's status) or even something really fun such as revealing a secret to the group about a fellow player. Anything that accepts and builds upon their relationships is encouraged.
- Don't forget to document or record the exploration.

Step Four: Changes

For this next stage, the facilitator will periodically ring the desk bell.

- Invite participants to explore or use a different object in the space they have not used yet each time they hear the bell. Participants are to explore objects created by the other players. (This encourages listening and observing.)
- Encourage them to continue to explore relationships.
- Make sure someone records their work.

Goal

- The changing of objects teaches them to justify and create choices they might otherwise not have come up with on their own.

Step Five: Slow Motion

Have them talk-back through the series of events describing exactly what happened and in what order: who entered where, when, what did each person do, what was revealed, who were they to each other, etc. This is to help them objectively replay what happened. As a facilitator, keep the conversation away from interpretation; stick to the facts of the scene.

- Have the participants re-play the scene they have just created, in the exact same series of events, but this time they are to work in slow motion, with no dinging of the bell.
- The players are in charge now, with the only rule being slow motion at all times.

- Let them know they are free to explore, heighten, and let things evolve and change.
- Invite them to see in slow motion, think in slow motion.
- Keep the timing of this portion to five minutes. They won't get all the way through, and that's okay.
- Remember to record.

Side Coaching

- As a facilitator, if something interesting begins to happen, invite them to explore and heighten or accept and build upon what's happening.
- Keep reminding them to stay committed to the slow motion.

Step Six: Super Speed

As soon as they finish the slow-motion step, have them restart the scene from the top. Refrain from talking about what happened, have them reset and jump back in with super speed.

- Each time they do the scene, it will roughly be the "same" scene, but it will evolve and grow with each playing.
- Don't forget to have someone record the exercise.

Side Coaching

- Everything is up for grabs, so remind them to keep pace and not to take their foot off the gas.
- Keep reminding them they are free to explore, heighten, and let things evolve and change.

Step Seven: Greatest Hits

Have them play the scene one last time. Think of this exercise as the "greatest hits" of the entire sequence.

Goal

Participants will apply what they have discovered from the previous versions of the scene.

- Invite them to think of each step as a draft of a scene. They can take their favorite parts from the previous "drafts" and put them all together into one scene.
- Definitely don't forget to have someone record the scene.

Side Coaching

- Offer up the invitation that if there is something they would like to explore or haven't tried yet, this is their opportunity to test it out.

Overall Side Coaching Tips

- Invite them to show, not tell.
- Keep the focus on the discovering and using new objects.
- What does how you deal with an object reveal about your character?
- Invite them to stay in the space with each other.
- Invite them to explore how they feel about each other and how they feel about what's going on.
- Keep the coaching focused on the physical, i.e., show us how you feel about someone with your shoulders, explore how you feel about what's going on with your feet or hands.
- Invite them to take their time. There's no rush. (Except for the super speed step.)

Reflections/Follow Up Questions:

For the audience/fellow classmates:

- Was the WHO/WHAT/WHERE clear to the audience? Ask them for examples from the "drafts" of the scene where the WHO/WHAT/WHERE become clearer and more established.
- What are some things that changed or evolved from one step to the next?
- Ask for specifics about what changed.
- Were there any surprises regarding what they observed?
- Were there any choices that occurred that they wanted to happen?

- Were there any choices that occurred that they did not see coming?

For the players:

- Was their perception of things similar to what their classmates observed?
- What did they enjoy from one step to the next?
- What did they particularly have fun playing with? Why? What was fun about it?
- If something was fun for them, was it fun for the audience?
- What stood out to them about the exercise, either in their own work or their colleagues' work, as cool, fun, or special?
- If they were to do the exercise again, what would they do differently? Why? What did they edit or explore from one version to the next?

For everyone:

- Would they have come up with stories like these on their own?
- What made each character different?
- Did each character have a different "voice" or perspective?
- How might they incorporate strong characterization in their own writing?
- How did creating characters and perspectives with their colleagues together in a group push creativity, as opposed to writing alone?
- Did each step of the exercise feel like a new "draft" of the scene?
- Do they see how there are pros, cons, and discoveries in each draft?
- If each step is viewed as a draft of the scene, what can they take away and apply to their own process of rewriting?

What Comes Next: The Writing Begins

- Instruct each group to sit down and review the videos of each step. (Yes, the groups must watch their own work.)

- By committee, as a group, the participants can pull from any of the steps in the exercise to put together a version of their scene that they are most happy with in Modern Play Format (or whatever play format you have them write in).
- One person from each group will type it up with input from their group.
- Instruct the participants to use the dialogue from their exercise verbatim. (There's a lot to be learned from how people speak, and how one person alone would never have come up with a scene like this, with this many different characters and points of view.)

The Rewrite

Encourage collaboration and the rewriting process.

- Have each group create a rewrite order. This is to aid them in learning to write collaboratively (such as writing for television).
- This step also allows them to express themselves without the pressure of the group or one member of the group dominating the process.
- Through email, they are each to have the opportunity to perform a rewrite of their group's scene, alone.
- They are not obligated to change anything.
- No one should take more than twenty-four hours to rewrite.
- If they like it as written, they can simply write PASS on an email and send along the draft to the next person in the order.

The Reading

- This occurs after they have all had the opportunity to do a rewrite/pass on the scene.
- Each group should, as a staged reading, read the final draft of their scene for their classmates. (Remember while plays can be read alone, they are best consumed as a piece of theatre either with a staged reading or a production.)

Collaborative Drafting

Rachel Lynett

Rationale

Often, I find that many playwrights, whether they're emerging or established, can forget that a play is a living, breathing document that is meant to change. Plays are meant to be constantly evolving. Instead of thinking of playwrights like architects, we should be thinking about playwrights as editors in motion. We get so caught up in the idea or the premise that we can often miss a critical error in our storytelling. I have found that the more collaborative the process is from the beginning, the easier it is to collaborate in the workshop process.

Goals and Objectives

The main objective is for new writers to be able to claim ownership of their work while also embracing a collaborative approach to playwriting.

- To experiment with the idea before it gets to the page.
- With new playwrights, once something is on the page, it becomes precious and hard to talk about, so the purpose of this exercise is to experiment with the idea before it gets to the page.

What We Need

- At least four students, or students in groups of four
- A recorder
- A timer
- Something to write with (laptop, paper and pen, etc.)

How We Get There

- For this exercise, you need four students. One of the students is "the playwright." Two of the students are "the actors," and the fourth student is "the improviser."

- The playwright comes up with the basic premise (key elements) of the idea:
  1 Who are these people and what is their relationship to each other?
  2 Where are they?
  3 What is the core problem, and how long will it take for the problem to be solved and/or addressed? (For the sake of scene work, I say limit students to five minutes max.)
- The playwright gives this information to the actors. The actors then name and age themselves. While the playwright can be part of the conversation, the final decision is up to the actors. This will be challenging but it helps the playwright see the actors as collaborators.
- Once the playwright has given the information outlined above to the actors and the actors have decided on their names and ages, we're ready to begin.
- The "improviser" sets the clock and begins recording as the actors improvise the scene, uninterrupted. No matter where they are, when the timer goes off, they stop the scene even if they didn't finish it. For example, the playwright can decide the two actors are cousins (how they know each other); that they're stranded in the desert (where they are); and that they need to call for help but their phones are dead (the problem). From there, the actors decide their names and age. Once they're all in agreement, the improviser starts the clock. The actors are free to say whatever dialogue comes to them and the playwright cannot stop them.
- The "improviser" stops the recording and then gives notes on what they noticed, what felt slow, what could be improved. The improviser can change one key element that the playwright established but cannot change the core problem. For example, the "improviser" can change their relationship to each other or where they are. The improviser can even pick the first and last line of dialogue. The only thing the improviser cannot change is the core problem, such as being stranded as in the example above.
- The actors then attempt the scene again. The improviser records the scene again and times it. Again, once the timer goes off, no matter where the actors are, the recording stops.

- For the third and final time, the playwright can give the actors two lines each that the actors can choose to say any time during the scene, but they must find a way to say it before the timer goes off. The improviser can also provide notes again before the third and final attempt but this time can't change anything.
- Finally, once at home or in quiet study, the playwright transcribes the third recording into play format, word for word. Call this scene A. The playwright, using the elements of scene A, can edit the scene however they choose, while promising to keep two elements from the direct recording. This is now scene B and most likely the scene the playwright will keep.

Reflection

While this exercise takes time and depends on a lot of trust, it also helps to focus that our art form should be a collaborative work in progress. Even in the rehearsal room, I have found myself incredibly open to suggestions and line notes from actors. While the playwrights may have written the play, the actors translate it to the audience, so we should all be on the same page about the message that gets sent out.

What Comes Next

Playwrights can either continue to write the remaining scenes in their play with this exercise or use this exercise as a jumping off point to help guide the rest of the play. Happy writing!

Activating a Character

Dennis Schebetta

Rationale

Any time a writer adapts source material, no matter how factual, the mere act of dramatization creates a fictional reality. This exercise allows students to give each other permission to find the dramatic in their own experiences. At the heart of the exercise is creating a monologue that connects a character to their objective and actions. The challenge of writing a monologue, though, is that students can fall into the trap of having the character tell a story (making the character passive or taking the focus out of the present moment). While sometimes necessary as a way of revealing character, it doesn't always connect to what the character wants from the other person in that moment. The monologue can become a device for the writer to deliver exposition or backstory to an audience and not necessarily move the story forward. Another trap of writing a monologue is creating a text that reads more like a confession or therapy session. This exercise counteracts both of those traps by adapting the story into the present moment, activating the character to achieve something from another person and examining how their actions and language relate to that objective.

Origins of the Exercise

I developed this exercise as part of a theatre-lab class that used playwriting, physical theatre, and devising techniques as a way of developing original text. As with all creation, sometimes the best source for material can be someone sitting right next to you, and one need only adapt and maybe embellish the details to make it your own. The exercise can also be used to further develop a character's objective from previously written material by solidifying their actions and use of language.

Goals

- To write a one to two minute monologue freely adapted from a story shared from a fellow student.
- This exercise can be used as a place of creating a character and building a story idea or can be used to build or further explore a character that has already been drafted in other scenes.
- This exercise can be particularly helpful if your characters in the play are all starting to sound similar or have similar actions and objectives.

Monologues Should Contain

- *Main Character/Protagonist* (Who are they?)
- *Opposing Character/Antagonist* (Who are they talking to? What's the relationship?)
- *Objective* (What do they want? What do they need from this person?)
- *Obstacle* (What's in their way?)
- *Action* (How do they get what they want? What tactics do they use?)

What We Need

The instructor should ensure that all students understand the definition and concepts of those five main ideas listed above, particularly action, objective, and obstacle.

Students will need paper and writing utensils for notes and for writing the monologue. Have the students break into pairs and let them know they will be telling each other about an event from their life. This should be personal, but not too intimate or revealing. Remind the students about boundaries and consent and that the material will be used for dramatic purposes (and also may be modified). Any story told should be one they're willing to share with the whole class.

Give these prompt questions as a way to find an event:

- Have you ever argued with your parents about something you wanted?"
- "Have you asked someone out on a date but been afraid they'd say no?"
- "Have you ever told someone you loved them when you were unsure if they felt the same?"
- "Have you ever tried to convince your friend not to do something stupid (like drive drunk, get back together with an ex, or drop out of school)?"
- "Did you ever do or say something you felt bad about and tried to get forgiveness?"

Have students take a few minutes to write any specific thoughts or details about their event.

How We Get There

Explain that they will be creating a monologue for themselves to perform by listening to their partner's story, focusing on the five elements previously established (main character, opposing character, objective, obstacle, action). This monologue could be the launching point of a scene or inserted into a previously written scene, or could be an exercise to discover and enhance a character, focusing on actions and objective. As the story is told, have them write down notes of any details that seem important in the story, but also to pay attention to any words or phrases that may seem useful.

Have each student take five minutes each to tell their story to each other, without any pressure of having to perform or be dramatic, as if talking to a friend. Students can also ask clarifying questions. The short time span is to ensure that students don't get too much information that may not be needed for the building of the monologue.

After the students have both told their stories, have them take ten minutes to each write a one to two-minute monologue based on what they heard, focusing on the character pursuing one specific goal. This monologue only needs to be inspired by the event—any details can be changed and modified (location, time, place, relationship, etc.).

Next, have the students find their own space to move around in as they speak their text. Coach the students to revise and cut as needed, especially if they need to fit the one to two-minute requirement. Encourage the use of chairs for levels. This "rehearsal" may take an additional five to ten minutes.

When finished, present the monologues to class and discuss whether it's clear who the character is talking to and the actions used to achieve the objective/obstacle.

Side Coaching Tips

As the students share their stories, make sure they take detailed notes and/or ask questions about the event. Most importantly, reiterate the objective and the actions of the character—what do they want and how are they trying to get it? Encourage the students to write as if the characters are in that present moment pursuing that objective (not telling the story but acting it out in the present moment).

Remind students that this exercise is about looking for raw material to inspire and prompt a character or circumstances. If the story feels like it can be embellished, feel free to revise it and make it more dramatic (by changing the relationship or raising the stakes). If the student is working with previously written pages and an established character already, encourage them to adapt the story freely, keeping the details they feel are important. Ask follow up questions about what they want and how they get it, such as "how can the stakes be raised?" How would changing the location or relationship change the story?

Reflection/Follow Up Questions

Students may be surprised by how their story gets adapted and modified, so explore the adaptation process (also giving a reminder to share only what feels comfortable).

In terms of the objective of the exercise, here are some questions to lead discussion after each presentation:

- Is your character's objective clear? How will we know when they get what they want?
- What is the relationship between the characters? Are there ways their behavior or the text could make it clearer?
- What is the conflict? How can that conflict be elevated or clarified?
- What is at stake for this character? What happens if they don't get what they want?

What Comes Next

If using this exercise for original content creation, the next step would be to take one of the monologues and expand it into a scene, using that character and their circumstances as a starting point.

- What would the opposing character say in response to this monologue? Does the protagonist get what they want at the end or not? Why or why not? What is the antagonist's reason for opposing them? Working with that conflict, build a scene.

If the students have already drafted scenes or part of their play prior to this exercise, the next step may be one of these options:

- Incorporate the monologue into a previously written scene or create a whole new scene focused around this character (see above).
- Review the monologue you wrote and pay particular attention to the actions, the language, and rhythm. You should hear a distinct voice. Do a character pass on your script where you only look at that character's lines and see if you can rewrite to match those actions and that manner of speaking.

Sharing the Story: A Playwriting Train

Steve Kaliski

Rationale

I am used to writing plays that can responsibly remain within the boundaries of my own invention. Sometimes, however, I encounter a moment in which my caffeinated imagination is not enough to tell the story, and I need help. Other playwrights are likely familiar with this block, and depending on the genre and style of the play itself, the solution may necessitate immersing ourselves deeper in our research, conducting interviews for transcription or adaptation, or presenting the moment to our ensemble in the rehearsal room for devised theatre-making.

I developed this exercise as a variation on the devising approach, but instead of creating the moment in the room, I turn my actors into playwrights and facilitate a remote group drafting process that can unfold over days or weeks. Teachers are also welcome to adapt this exercise for classroom use.

Origins

This is an original exercise. Though I crafted the basic framework in 2019, I have found it to be an especially accessible tool in remote creative settings normalized by the COVID-19 pandemic.

Goals

This exercise invites members of the cast of a new play to share authorship of a moment that the primary playwright cannot write alone.

In doing this exercise, you will:

- Generate a text that can fit within the larger play.
- Empower your actors to genuinely shape the storytelling of the whole.
- Use acting technique to inform the playwriting process.

What We Need

This exercise can happen largely over email, with an option for a few moments of embodied exploration if circumstances allow. It works like assembling a train set, with one actor writing a little bit, sending that along to the next actor, who will add a little bit more, pass it on again, and so on, with the piece growing in length on each turn.

How We Get There

1. Determine both the intended duration of the devised sequence and how many members of the cast you'd like to participate. Perhaps you are hoping to generate a five-minute monologue, and you want each participant to contribute one minute of text. In that case, you should recruit five actors. You might make your decisions based on which actors have the most obvious investment in this section of the play.
2. Roll dice or pull names out of a hat to determine the order of writers. The randomness here is an important element in surrendering some of your control.
3. Create a writing schedule. For collaborators who primarily identify as actors, you might suggest that each writer has one day to complete their section. This strikes a balance between the pressure of improvisational writing and perfectionist impulses that can accompany too much time.
4. Share the writing schedule along with instructions for how each participant should email the next writer on the train. You might want files named a certain way, and you should be

Embodied Playwriting Exercises for Classroom, Workshop, and Studio 235

cc'ed on every email. Do not read anything while the exercise is in progress, but it's good to stay in the loop to make sure everyone is finishing on time.

5 You are now ready to begin the exercise. Send a prompt to all participants with a reminder of the schedule and, more importantly, your "rules" and "ingredients" for the exercise:

   a "Rules" are any constraints you'd like to place on the technical aspects of writing. You might define a word count per minute (I suggest that a minute without pauses is 160–180 words) and how many words equate to a pause or silence. You might allow sections to end mid-sentence so that writers feel no pressure to conclude a beat. Include any other elements of style you'd like. The constraints here will help with creativity.

   b "Ingredients" are storytelling parameters that safeguard your general goals for the sequence while still allowing considerable freedom. Think in actor terms, and have fun here. If creating a monologue, you might define the character's objective. You might provide the first and last lines. You might suggest certain phrases that appear in certain minutes, or you might request that late in minute four, there's a reference to "my childhood home." Include at least one targeted ingredient per section (i.e., "Minute two should include a lyric to a popular song."). It's okay—and maybe even preferable—for you as the primary playwright to not have an intention behind an ingredient. As with the "rules," these devising checkboxes simply help kickstart the creative impulses of artists who might feel daunted by an open-ended playwriting prompt.

6 Let the actors write. They should not edit previous sections as they draft; they should only add.

7 The last actor in the train should send you a complete draft of the sequence.

8 Now is the time to gather in person if you are able, or if not, schedule a group Zoom meeting. As a teacher or playwright, have your actors read and embody the text as many ways as possible. To start, have everyone read the section they wrote.

Then, have them read their sections while the other actors create tableaux inspired by the language. Mix up who reads what. If you use Viewpoints in your practice, have your actors play with such components as spatial relationship, shape, tempo, and gesture as they move to the text. Encourage vocal variety (or Vocal Viewpoints) for those reading the text.

9 Jot down notes as you listen. Afterwards, bold any words, phrases, or passages from this first draft that you absolutely love. Overall, you shouldn't bold more than twenty-five percent of the total text.

10 Send a new, short prompt to your actors letting them know they may each have an additional pass at the text. They may not change anything in bold. Reverse the order of the train, or re-roll the dice. You might have writers only work on one section each (i.e., "Writer One, you may make any changes to minute five of this. Just don't change anything in bold."). Let them know how much time they have.

11 At the end of this step, read the text again. You can consider the exercise complete, or you can repeat steps eight to ten as many times as you'd like.

Side Coaching Tips

If any participants struggle while writing, feel free to add ingredients. You might put these in actor terms. For example, "Add one external and two internal obstacles for the character here," or "Have the character switch tactics three times total during your section."

Reflection/Follow Up Questions

As the teacher or the playwright, ask the following questions to your actors:
1 How do you feel like your acting training informed the process of playwriting?
2 Does the sequence feel coherent/unified? How or how not?
3 What are the pros and cons of group writing vs. writing as an individual?
4 How did embodied exploration help the writing process?

What Comes Next

When you're happy with the text, add it to your script and workshop it as you would any other piece of your play. It's still allowed to change, and you can take more control now. The important part is that you've offered that initial creative spark to your ensemble, and they've generated something in a voice not your own.

Word Choice: Working in Space

Meredith Melville

Rationale

Composition and improvisation go hand and hand. Composition of the space in directing, and as it relates to playwriting, is also invaluable. We often times forget about the space or image as it relates to playwriting.

Origins

Whilst working on composition ("Composition is the practice of selecting and arranging the separate components of theatrical language into a cohesive work of art for the stage")[3] and various workshops on composition, I tailored this exercise to get the actor or playwright to start thinking of not just the mental connections between the stage and the piece, but the visceral connections between the words and the actors. It is not based on any one exercise or improvisational game, but rather an innovative way to approach the work rooted in improvisation and composition.

Goals

- To get the playwright or actors to connect the compositional work of blocking to the text.
- To bring the emotional life to stage visually.

What We Need

Either a text or words to explore are necessary to get started. You can use loosely related words you are exploring for a text (either devised or from a playwright), or you can use a piece or selection from a larger text for the playwrights or actors to expand or start with.

With Actors Devising

This exercise focuses on gesture and composition within constraints to create a word exploration. It can be very informative for the playwright, director, and actors.

How We Get There

- Start with an emotion or theme (taken from your text or list of words) and create a gesture.
  - A gesture is any simple motion linked to an emotion or symbol.
  - Examples of emotional gestures include covering one's face while crying, a shrug, or reaching for someone.
  - Other gestures may include a thumbs up, pointing, or giving someone the "finger."
  - They can overlap, and themes could include a small movement when you think of something sad, or a small movement when you think of something funny.
- From that gesture, ask each actor in your ensemble to create their own gesture.
  - Ask them to present their gesture for the group.
- Then, put them together in a tableau.
  - One person at a time steps forward and presents their gesture again, but this time bring them together into one tableau.
  - They should connect and fill the space. They can fill negative space or connect to each other. Either way is fine, as long as they create one picture or tableau.
- Ask the participants the following questions:
  - What discoveries might occur as you look at that image as a whole, as well as its smallest component? Emotional

gestures (i.e., hands over face for sadness, or rubbing one's eyes, etc.) can convey a whole world without a single word.
- If you are limited in words, which word would you use? Maybe it is a sound. Now add it to the other words you are exploring. This could be a movement piece, or a word symphony. Sometimes a little goes a long way.
- How much can you say with so little? Now the importance of word choice is actualized.
- Change the word by heightening it. Example: sadness to sorrow, or angry to furious, or hungry to ravenous. How does that intensify or change the relationship of the gesture and the word?
- When we interact with the others in our group what happens when we are brought to a point of conflict or resolution? If they must exist in this world together, what happens as they explore the space?

With Playwrights Devising

This exercise is a good way to explore and intensify moments without a lot of re-writes.

How We Get There

- Start with the words they are exploring, or the emotional state they are trying to convey in the excerpt they are sharing.
- Have the playwright read the excerpt out loud.
- After listening to the work, ask the other playwrights/students/participants which words they would use to describe that entire selection.
- Next, ask the participant to take that piece and read it with one of those words in mind.
- After they have done that, take the idea and ask them to generate a gesture (it can be emotional or something communicative, like a thumbs up) and try to embody that feeling with that gesture.
- Next, ask another participant if there is anything they would add. Then, ask them to add it to the gesture already created. The participants will build this in the same way as with the

actors, but the participants do not have to get up unless they are willing to do so. Once the participants have three to five gestures created, put them all together. Look at the picture that has been created.
- Finally, read the piece over the gestural sculpture.
- Example: I read part of a poem. When I am finished, another participant chooses one word to describe it: morose. I then read the poem with that word as the primary description of the piece in mind. After I finish, I create a gesture with that feeling in mind. Finally, everyone in the group or room will also create a gesture based on that word (or feeling). Then, we put them all together. We would then take them all and show them whilst thinking of the word morose, and then hold that position while reading the excerpt over the gestural picture or tableau.

Reflection/Follow Up Questions

- What discoveries have you made about the piece?
- Is there something you could add or take away that would make it more powerful?

Side-Coaching Tips

Encourage the students not to judge the first thing they think of—often it is the best thing, however simple. It does not have to be complex to be useful. Additionally, there are many types of gestures, everything from a thumbs up to full-body breath. Encourage them to really explore and heighten as they create their gestures. These gestures can really expound on where you are headed and create new things—embrace them. This can also be used to develop new work. If you or a student have an idea, but are not sure how to stage it, ask them to create the simplest version of the idea, and then explore in that space. Again, encourage them to really get on their feet (as we engage our movement and our mind we make new discoveries, and use different parts of our brain). It is an exercise that will free them to really explore, if they are open to it.

Reflection/Follow Up Questions

What worked? What didn't work? Sometimes it is just as important to discover what does not work as it is to make a discovery that does work. Be sure to give the group exploring enough time. Repeating these exercises or taking a piece of discovery and expanding on it can be just as valuable as starting again. Encourage the students to not be afraid to heighten and amplify something small, and it turn allow it to become something altogether different.

What Comes Next

In the playwriting room, **Word Choice** leads to three-dimensional thought and how to block moments for the stage. It allows playwrights to not just rely on their words, but on the power that they convey. Additionally, linking the physical with the mental allows us to visualize the work better. The work takes on a quality of life that is often missing as we work alone in front of a computer. The exercise also gets actors out of their heads and into their bodies. This is especially helpful if you are looking at deconstructions or pieces, or if you are looking to explore certain moments without the full text. In the end, this exercise should allow the playwright to expand into the physical and emotional with a quick guide that heightens and strengthens emotional moments.

Uncovering Character through Mask Exploration

Elizabeth Hess

Rationale

Masks from around the world evoke archetypal and numinous expressions of the human condition through embodied storytelling. They reveal the spirit and inner life of a character through a symbolic manifestation. My growing engagement with predominantly non-Western performativity has led me to investigate mask work as a powerful conduit for generating original text that is inclusive, expansive, and inherently theatrical. Global practices can transform magic, metaphor, and myth into individual and collective catharsis. Protecting the identity of the performer also allows them to incorporate shadow contents without self-censorship. When we don a mask as a playwright, we are equally free to uncover complex layers of a character in an unself-conscious and embodied way.

Goals/Objectives

- To increase the awareness and integration of non-Western modes of storytelling.
- To create character narratives and story threads based on embodied exploration.
- To enhance collaborative skills through collective exploration and interweaving of original texts.
- To plant seeds for further script development.

Preliminary Research

Ideally, individually assigned research reports on international mask work would proceed the exploration and the findings shared with fellow playwrights. In a thorough online search, the reports investigate the diverse history/origin, mission/vision, process, and performance practice of selected mask work from around the world. For further illumination, the reports may be augmented by photos, videos and/or the participants' own experience in observing or embodying their assigned practice. The reports are intended to expand the participants' understanding and awareness of global mask performativity while also stimulating their imaginations in the creation of their own original masks.

The findings are condensed into a two-page report written in single-space, bullet format, which is used for reference during the presentations, which can be approximately ten minutes each or longer, depending on the size of the group and length of the session. Allowing time for questions and observations following each report enhances the exchange of cross-cultural points of view amongst the participants.

Reports might include, but not be limited to, some of the following practices/rituals and practitioners: Asaro Mudmen, Nick

Cave, Peking Opera, Egungun Masquerades, Haida Potlatch, Noh Theatre, Dia de los Muertos, Saraikela Chhau, Candomblé, and MahMeri.

Creation of Original Mask

Participants generate their own masks prior to the exploration. They may draw inspiration from their findings in the research reports. The persona of the mask may emerge organically as it is being assembled. It may be human, animal, spirit, or abstract. It can be an expression of "otherness"—something that feels quite different from one's own sense of self. It serves as an outer expression of an inner state of being. There is no prototype for the mask—encouraging the revelation of diverse aesthetics and identities among the participants.

The masks can be created using materials such as a paper plate, cardboard, cloth, clay, and papier-mâché. They can be decorated with paints, colored markers, buttons, fabric, magazine images, photos, collages, found objects, etc. The mask needs to be wearable by attaching elastic, string, or ribbons to the sides so that the playwright can move freely through the space. In addition to face masks, participants might don a paper bag with eye holes, decorate a ski mask with leaves, wrap gauze around their head leaving

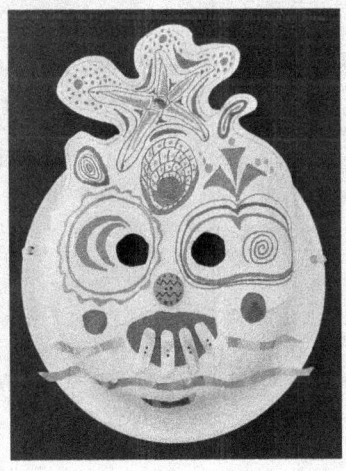

Sample mask.

Sample mask.

slits for the eyes, etc. Participants may reference resources online for mask-making, but I encourage experimentation that expands our understanding of what constitutes a mask.

Mask Exploration

1 Begin the session with five to ten minutes of physical and vocal warm-up to facilitate openness and ease.
2 Ask the participants to put on their masks in silence, listening to their breath inside its "skin" as it reveals its inner life. You may also don a mask at any point during the exploration to show, rather than tell, how to engage one's whole being in the work.
3 Have participants move through the playing space over the next twenty to thirty minutes. The exploration unfolds in four fluid steps which can take five to ten minutes each. The character behind the mask emerges and story threads are revealed through worlds of play in which *essences*, *behaviors*, *relationships*, and *archetypal energies* are initiated, evolve, and deepen.

Step One:
Ask participants to activate their individual *essences*—their intrinsic nature—through dynamic exchange whereby interaction is instinctive and immediate. Let them "test the waters" with others by introducing themselves through physical gestures and movement. Encourage them to respond to each other's inborn dispositions by engaging their impulses organically. Prompts might include: What is your essence? How do you embody it? Are you an animal? A human? A spirit? Who intrigues you? Are they a kindred soul? An alien spirit? How do you approach them? Do you feel welcome? Vulnerable? Challenged? Enlivened?

Step Two:
Encourage participants to engage *behavior* through more sustained partnering that activates their sense of belonging or otherness, of connection or estrangement. By mirroring each other they may uncover complimentary energy. Conversely, by projecting onto the other they may find competing energy. Prompts might include: How do you express your attraction or aversion? Your curiosity or confusion? Your openness or opposition? How are you received? How do you respond? Adjust? Encourage? Confront?

Step Three:
Let body language lead to pre-verbal utterances as *relationships* reveal their character's status in the group's hierarchy of wants and needs. They discover a sense of inclusion or alienation, of acceptance or ostracization, of assertiveness or acquiescence. Actions, objectives, and obstacles are further clarified through vocalization as well as physicality. These vocalizations can include unsculpted sounds, gibberish, or invented language. Prompts might include: How does your tone of voice convey your wants? Your needs? How does the "dialogue" build to an understanding or a confrontation? Are you bombastic? Compliant? Intimidating? Seductive?

Step Four:
Have participants tap into *archetypal energy* by engaging a pattern of behavior that reinforces their character's role in relation to others. Encourage them to explore communal interaction that may meld or divide their worlds of play and lead to rites, rituals, or reckonings

that emerge organically. Archetypes might include such personas as the warrior, the devotee, the trickster, the ghost, etc. Prompts might include: How do you create alliances? Establish boundaries? Loyalties? Who do you trust? Who do you question? Are you part of a tribe? A gathering? Do you create a ritual? A reckoning?

Gently bring the exploration to a close. Instruct participants to remove their masks and study them for a moment in silence as they consider their journey from original concept to embodied experience.

Journaling

Journaling takes ten to fifteen minutes and immediately follows the mask exploration.

1 Ask participants to set their masks aside and feel free to refer to them throughout their journaling.
2 Instructions for journal entries might include the following:
   a Write from the character's point of view in first person, present tense (I am).
   b Compose original text in any language.
   c Engage in "free writing," whereby thoughts are immediate and unedited.
   d Choose a writing style that is in the character's voice, such as composing sentences, writing in a stream of consciousness, scribbling text fragments, or inventing language.
   e Reveal the character's inner life and world of play by giving voice to their unspoken hopes and fears, desires and dislikes, secrets, and beliefs. Prompts might include: Who are you? What is your greatest desire? Secret? Hope? Fear? Who supports you? Opposes you? What archetype did you tap into? How does it inform your truth? Your sense of self? Your journey? Is there a pivotal moment when something shifted powerfully? How has your voice and vision evolved? Devolved? Transformed?

Solo Impromptus

Impromptus are short, unrehearsed, and improvisational embodied explorations. They take three to five minutes each and the overall timeframe for impromptus will depend on the size of the group. The original text is the entry point for the impromptus and the individual playwrights throw their own words into their bodies, letting the earlier mask exploration inform the embodiment of their character.

1. Have participants select a fragment of their text that "sparks" them. They repeat the fragment aloud to themselves until it is "off the page" and then everyone sets their journals aside.
2. Ask participants to put their masks on and enter the playing space, one at a time, as they incorporate their text with movement.
3. Have the participant remain in the playing space once they have completed their impromptu, so that they become silent, yet active, characters within each other's worlds. For example, another participant might choose to step around them, make eye contact, or dance among the collective as it grows in size during the exercise.
4. There is no side coaching during the impromptus, but you may wish to ask participants to respond to the experience afterwards.

Performance Projects

The original text becomes the basis for partnered mask work. Preparation takes ten to fifteen minutes. Presentations take three to five minutes each. Discussion about the process, critique and feedback takes an additional five to ten minutes. The overall time will depend on the size of the group. The performance projects can also take place during a separate session.

The playwrights interweave their entire original texts in a spontaneous call and response. Rather than discuss their texts beforehand, they allow the meaning to emerge from the material through embodied exchange with their partner that is informed by the earlier mask exploration. They may find that their characters and worlds are strangely sympatico or wildly divergent. Rather than improvise text to create a homogeneous world, the understanding of their individual texts is influenced by their interaction. This keeps the work fresh and surprising, rather than studied and static. For example, one participant might be a ghost who comforts a lost soul. Their partner might be a warrior who wants to rule the world. Their interaction might uncover a deeper understanding of absence and ambition, of loss and longing, of vulnerability and armoring. One character might become the inner voice of the other. Or their conscience. Or their nemesis.

Preparation

1. Ask participants to put on their masks and begin building the piece by starting at the top of their texts. They may carry their journals with them to refer to their words but then lift them off the page and make eye contact with their partner. Everyone works at the same time, scattered throughout the playing space.
2. Have one partner start at the top of their journal entry, take a short section of text, and throw their character into their voice and body as they begin a dialogue with their partner.
3. Have their partner respond by adding their initial section of text as they further the dialogue by likewise throwing their character into their voice and body.
4. Allow the partners to continue to interweave their words and movement as they progress through their texts, embracing each other's worlds of play as they unfold—providing unexpected layers of complexity to their characters' interplay.
5. Encourage their interplay to lead to a pivotal moment that changes the relationship between the characters as their worlds coalesce or collide.
6. Suggest that the pivotal moment leads to a reversal, so that the characters' relationship goes through a story arc by the end of their texts.

Presentation

1. Remind participants that the performance projects are works-in-progress, rather than result-oriented. The interweaving of texts remains the same, but participants do not attempt to replicate the preparatory work but allow it to inform their interaction during the presentation as they continue to explore their character's relationship to self and other. It should be gloriously messy and surprising!
2. You may wish to ask the partners to discuss their process following each presentation.
3. You may choose to offer a critique of the presentation. You may also want to ask what they think might be the next step in development.
4. You may wish to facilitate guided feedback and questions from fellow playwrights.

What Comes Next

The impromptus and performance projects may become the basis for further script development by individual playwrights and/or lead to collaborative creations.

Writing Inside the (Rasa) Box

Tiffany Antone

Rationale

Just as actors need to develop emotional agility, so too do playwrights. Working with Rasaboxes invites playwrights to physically inhabit their characters' worlds and "write on their feet" in an organic physical process.

Origins of the Exercise

This writing exercise utilizes Richard Schechner's Rasaboxes[4] – a physical tool designed to help performers access and communicate emotion:

> Rasaboxes trains participants to physically express eight key emotions first identified in the Natyasastra, a Sanskrit text dealing with theatre, dance, and music. Rasaboxes integrates this ancient theory with contemporary emotion research about the 'brain in the belly' (the enteric nervous system), studies in facial expression of emotion, neuroscience, and performance theory — including Antonin Artaud's provocative assertion that the actor is "an athlete of the emotions.[5]

Objectives

Using Rasaboxes, we will create a grounded action verb playspace that playwrights can literally enter, physically explore (using non-naturalistic and expressive gesture), and write from. Thus, playwrights are able to enter the Rasabox with a story or character idea, and leave with eight pieces of newly written text. This allows playwrights to explore, analyze, and write their characters from within, offering writers intimate access to their character's emotional center.

What We Need

- Open performance space with a smooth floor
- Chalk
- Masking tape (colored or not)
- Playwrights will need writing tools and paper (paper and pen/pencil recommended to avoid damaging computer tech)

How We Get There

1 Rasabox work is highly physical and can, when participants are fully engaged, be vocally demanding as well. It is *highly* recommended you begin with a physical and vocal warm up, as this will help participants get into their bodies, ready to work and explore in a supported physical manner.
2 Invite each playwright to draw their own Rasabox (approximately 6'x6') on the floor space in front of them using chalk or tape. The Rasabox should be large enough for them to move freely in each clearly delineated square.
   - If work space is limited, or if you have a large number of playwrights to account for, you can also choose to create one or two larger Rasaboxes that multiple playwrights can operate in at the same time. In this arrangement, you should establish the entry/exit flow (enter in the top right corner, proceeding in an "S" shape through each square until exiting from the bottom left corner). Working this way, a group Rasabox allows up to nine playwrights to work in each Rasabox at any given time.
   - If you have more than nine playwrights per square, they can queue at the entry point. In this way, participants will each get some observation time as part of their Rasabox exploration.

Table 15.1. Sample Rasabox

Love/Desire	Humor/Laughter	Pity/Grief
Rage	Bliss	Surprise/Wonder
Fear/Shame	Disgust	Energy/Vigor

3   Briefly go over each rasa's definition:
    - The eight rasas—in Sanskrit with rough translations—are: *sringara* (desire, love); *hasya* (humor, laughter); *karuna* (pity, grief); *raudra* (rage); *adbhuta* (surprise, wonder); *bhayanaka* (fear, shame); *bibhatsa* (disgust); *vira* (energy, vigor).
4   Invite each playwright to assign one rasa to each square, leaving the center square blank. This square is left empty for *shanta*, which can be roughly translated as "bliss".
5   The playwrights will now cycle through their Rasaboxes a total of three times, each time with different intentions. To begin, playwrights step inside the first square where they will consider and weigh its assigned rasa, and then, using the chalk, write in their own associations/related feelings/action verbs (or even draw images) in the square. Each playwright will do this for every square. Give them three to four minutes per square.
    - A note on *shanta*: humans are rarely ever truly blissful. It is even rarer still to see a character on stage experiencing true bliss. Thus, the *shanta* box is an interesting space to work from in that it invites a sense of peace our characters may be chasing, but rarely access. *Shanta* should be explored by playwrights with this in mind, knowing that *shanta* is often pursued but rarely actualized.
    - Once completed, each square will have an array of hand-written additions to each box. Rage, for instance, may now feature a frowny face, flames, and text that includes things like "ROAR, to excoriate, explosion, punch, #!*@, stomach pains, betrayal," etc. Each rasa, then, has been contextualized by the playwright(s) to mean more than just the word. Playwrights are then given time to walk around the Rasabox to read over/take in what has been written down. This is particularly important if working with a shared Rasabox, as each box will include a multitude of written contributions.
6   For the second cycle, playwrights put down their chalk and enter the Rasaboxes as a body only. As they move through each square, rather than writing down words, they will explore/create expressive physical gestures and vocalizations which bring the rasa to life for themselves. This is an individual exploration, with interpretations being entirely personal. Give them two to three minutes per square.

- This can be very intimidating for folks who are not usually physically expressive. Encourage your playwrights to remember that no one is watching them work, that they're all engaged in the same (sometimes silly-feeling) work, and that it will only be useful for them if they physically commit to the exercise.

7 Once each playwright has physically/vocally explored each rasa, they are ready to begin the third (and final) cycle. With notebook and pencil handy, playwrights enter each square, recreating their physical/vocal expressions from cycle two. Playwrights should lean into the created gesture, working with repetition until they are fully "primed"—meaning they *feel the rasa in their bodies.*

- If playwrights are working from a particular character perspective, then they should be physicalizing each rasa as the character they want to explore. Once "primed," the playwright uses that energy to write a monologue or a scene for the character in which the character is consumed by the rasic feeling of each square.
- If playwrights are working from a broader story idea, they should be encouraged to imagine when/where/why these rasas might appear in the world of their play. Once physically/vocally "primed," playwrights use that energy to write down any rasic-fueled scenes, character ideas, monologues, stage directions, etc. that come to mind from each rasa.
- This is a free writing exercise, but playwrights should still be given a set amount of time for each square, lest they get carried away in one and miss out on writing in others. Three to five minutes is a good start, but writing allotment per square could certainly stretch longer. Either way, persons leading the exercise should make sure to keep playwrights aware of time and ensure all squares are visited and written from.

Side Coaching Tips

- Rasabox work can be intimidating, especially for people who are not readily demonstrative. You will need to be a cheerleader, and remind students that no one is judging their physical/vocal work. Rather, this is an opportunity to get out

of their heads and into their bodies to create written work drawn from psycho-physical engagement.
- Playing music can sometimes help students feel less "on the spot" and encourage a more relaxed atmosphere, as it helps participants feel less "observed" in their exploration. I suggest instrumental music, tonally mixed so that you don't unintentionally trap the room (and the writers) in one mood.
- Beginning Rasaboxers will sometimes land on the first, easiest/expected physical gesture and stay there. If you see this happening, acknowledge the work while also encouraging students to dig deeper. Sometimes asking them to work in threes can help, which sounds like this: "Great first choice for that rasa! What if I asked you to make a second, different choice to express/explore the same rasa? Awesome. And what if you had to make a third, different choice?" By helping participants push through their initial (easy) choices, they will discover richer, more complex (and specific) choices on the other side of their comfort.

Reflection

- Did any of your characters reveal a secret or truth you hadn't yet known?
- What was it like to physicalize these rasas as your characters/play elements, rather than rely strictly on brain work?
- How has your relationship to your characters/the world of your play grown/changed through this exercise?

What Comes Next

From here playwrights are able to continue their writing process, building from the work drafted during the exercise. Once a full draft is complete, Rasaboxes may be used as a Diagnostic Tool. See "Diagnosing the (Rasa) Box" in the next chapter.

Notes

1 Spolin, pp. 90–91.
2 Johnstone, p. 95.
3 Bogart and Landau, p. 12.
4 Schechner, pp. 27–50.
5 Calzadilla and Minnick.

References

Bogart, Anne, and Tina Landau. *The Viewpoints Book: A Practical Guide to Viewpoints and Composition*. Theatre Communications Group, 2007.

Calzadilla, Fernando, and Michelle Minnick. "What is Rasaboxes?" Facebook, https://www.facebook.com/groups/436306506474754/.

Johnstone, Keith. *Impro: Improvisation and the Theatre*, New York: Routledge, 1981.

Schechner, Richard. (2001). Rasaesthetics. *TDR*, 45(3), 27–50. https://doi.org/10.1162/10542040152587105

Spolin, Viola. *Improvisation for the Theatre*, 3rd Ed. Northwestern University Press, 1963.

16 Embodied Playwriting Exercises for Classroom, Workshop, and Studio

The Revision Process

Hillary Haft Bucs and Charissa Menefee

Introduction

This chapter contains four additional exercises that focus specifically on the revision process, encouraging collaborations between playwrights and actors. Matt Fotis' ***Half-Life as a Tool for Revision*** uses a popular short-form game as a tool to find the essence of a scene. Ramón Esquivel's ***Acting Tactics for Writers*** includes collaboration with actors and the playwright, as writers revise their dialogue around a set tactic chosen by an actor. Sage Tokach's ***Spectator Storyboard*** adapts Boal's Image Theatre techniques and utilizes tableau as a story response, inviting the playwright into the audience's process of comprehension, interpretation, and negotiation of meaning. Tiffany Antone's ***Diagnosing The (Rasa) Box*** is the second part of her ***Writing Inside the (Rasa) Box***, found in the previous chapter; the exercise employs Richard Schechner's Rasaboxes as a revision tool to allow playwrights and actors to explore what has been written in a collaborative psycho-physical format.

Half-Life as a Tool for Revision

Matt Fotis

Rationale

This exercise is part of the revision process and helps a playwright reveal or discover the true essence of an already existing scene to focus or sharpen it. While the exercise may be done with a particularly tricky scene, it can be done with any scene in the play, as we often think a scene is about one thing only to discover later it was actually about something entirely different. It can be helpful to do the exercise for the first time with a crystal-clear scene so the actors understand the mechanics before trying it with a more complicated or messy scene.

Origins of the Exercise

The idea of repetition is fundamental to improvisation and found in many games and exercises. The roots of the **Half-Life** game can be found in Spolin's *Point of Concentration*. When improvisers would stray in a scene or become lost, Spolin would often side-coach players with "timing" calls of "one minute" or "thirty seconds" to help them focus on the scene's *Point of Concentration*. Additionally, the side-coaching was meant to help hone a player's sense of timing, something Spolin argued needed to be taught through experience rather than lecture.

Objective

The main objective is to reveal the essence of the scene—what is this scene *truly* about? Rather than getting there through textual analysis, the objective is to discover the meaning/goal/purpose of the scene through physical play. The exercise forces the actors to continually and rapidly cut the scene again and again until all that is left is the most important bit.

What We Need

- A timer or timing app on your phone.
- An original two to three-minute scene or ten-minute play ready to be revised.
  - A ten-minute play is the longest recommended in order to maintain the effectiveness of the exercise.
  - Finding a two to three-minute scene in itself can be a great exercise for finding the essence of the play.
- Actors to perform the scene/play.
- Any props or set pieces fundamental to the scene should be included in the exercise (to find out if they really are fundamental to the scene).
- The playwright should remain silent during the exercise. They might want to coach the actors or tell them what to do, but it is vital the actors make those choices and the playwright watches the process.

Embodied Playwriting Exercises for Classroom, Workshop, and Studio 257

How We Get There

- Have actors perform the piece as written, holding their scripts.
- After performing the piece as written, instruct the actors to set aside their scripts, and have them perform the same scene but in half the time (e.g. a two-minute scene would become a one-minute scene). *Note:* The first time the scene will be AWFUL—that's because they are 1) perhaps still figuring out the exercise; 2) trying to say their actual lines or getting tripped up trying to stick to memorization; and/or 3) still figuring out what's important to the scene and what's less important. If the issue is the first or second, remind them of the mechanics of the exercise. If the issue is the third, congratulate them because there is no issue—they are doing the exercise!
- The actors then repeat the exercise, again cutting the time in half (one minute becomes thirty seconds). Again, there is no script.
- The actors then cut the scene in half once more (thirty seconds becomes fifteen seconds).
- Side Coaching: this is a good time to remind them the goal of the exercise is to find the essence of the scene. What is most important to this scene? What is most fundamental to your character? What can you physicalize?
- The exercise continues until we are left with only one word.

Variations

One of the great things about improv exercises is that each exercise is itself adaptable to a number of functions; you can use this exercise at least three ways.

1. For new play development
    a. The one-word finale should be "This scene is about _____."
    b. In this case, we're often dealing with a student writer who is probably working on their first play, and if you've ever taught playwriting, you know most new plays need a lot of cutting. It's much more effective for the playwright to see that the first three minutes of their ten-minute play are not necessary rather than for you to keep telling them that.

    c   Important note: *nobody* can change the script other than the playwright. You might make some brilliant edits, but they aren't yours to make or implement.

2 For actors to define playable actions—if an actor(s) is stuck in a scene or seems like they can't quite figure out their objective, wants, etc.

    a   The one-word finale in this case should be "My objective is _____." Or action, or whatever actor vocabulary you're using.

    b   The time compression also does tend to make the actors physicalize more—they realize they don't have time to say all of their lines, so even if the actors "get" the scene, the exercise can help them to physicalize it more effectively. This works similarly for new play development, where the playwright *sees* the scene rather than only *hearing* the scene, which often leads them to "show" more and "tell" less.

3 For script analysis

    a   The one-word finale in this case should again be "This scene is about _____."

    b   As with number two, the exercise can be applied to any play you are working on, not just a new play.

Ideally, everyone will hit on the same one word (outside of the individual actors' objectives, but even then you kind of know when they're "right"). If not, that gives you the opportunity to shape a new discussion about the scene and dig into why each actor made the edits they made with each iteration.

Side Coaching Tips

There is not a lot of side coaching to be done while the actors are playing, especially as the scene progresses and the time gets reduced to almost nothing. Instead, there is ample time between each iteration to remind actors of the goal of the exercise or provide brief feedback/direction.

    One of the most common pitfalls for actors is in the first cut they cut nothing and try to speed through the scene. Remind them the goal is to focus on what they think is most important and to find the root of the scene, not to try and shove the entire scene into an ever-shrinking window.

They can change the focus with each iteration—so they are not locked into anything—each iteration is a fresh start. They certainly can do the same thing or continue refining the same thread, but they don't have to. Often the first cut will be clumsy and actors will realize they've cut out the wrong things or simply want to experiment to deepen their understanding of the scene. The director can also give notes between scenes to shape the direction if they so desire.

Reflection/Follow-Up Questions

The exercise inherently asks the question why? Why did you cut X and not Y? Why did you choose that final word/pose/gesture/movement? If everyone seems to have come to the same conclusion, how did we get there? If not, what is the reason? What parts of the scene or of your character are still confusing or unclear? Often smaller characters might find themselves with nothing to do or say in the last few takes of the exercise: why? Are they necessary to the scene/play?

What Comes Next

If the playwright so chooses, they may revise the script based on the exercise. Again, the cast or director cannot make any changes without the playwright's permission. The goal is not to take a five-minute scene and ultimately reduce it to two minutes in the final script. Instead, the goal is for the playwright to focus their play around what truly matters. While they might cut unnecessary bits, the goal is not simply to reduce the run time of the play or scene. The goal is *to focus* the play or scene.

Acting Tactics for Writers: An Improvisational Exercise for Revising Dialogue

Ramón Esquivel

Rationale

In a conventional theatrical collaboration, especially between artists trained in the Stanislavski system, actors and directors work a playwright's dialogue to ascertain objectives, discover motivations, and examine relationships between characters. Actors apply different tactics to attain their character objectives but they do not deviate from the written text. This exercise flips that convention by asking writers to revise their dialogue around a set tactic chosen by the actor.

Objective

Playwrights will revise dialogue to strengthen actors' choices of tactics and actions for the scene.

Time

Twenty to thirty minutes

What We Need

Script pages of scene or dialogue; paper or index cards for revision; pens or pencils; Dramatic Tactics table (included in lesson).

How We Get There

Instructions below are also suggested language for the instructor-facilitator to use when addressing the actor-playwrights.

Part I: Determine Tactics/Actions of First Draft of Scene

1. *Read First Draft of Scene* (two to four minutes)
   Actors, do a cold read of the first draft of the playwright's scene or dialogue. Playwrights, listen for the dynamic and rapport between characters.
2. *Actors Identify Tactics/Actions of First Draft of Scene* (four to five minutes)
   Actors, how would you describe the dynamic and rapport between characters in this scene? Consider concepts like relationship, status, and styles of communication. Using the Dramatic Tactics table, identify the tactics/actions/verbs you applied in that first read through. Example: "In this scene, my character is persuading a sibling to seek help for feeling depressed."

Part II: New Tactics/Actions

1. *Actors Choose Different Tactics for the First Draft* (three to five minutes)

    Actors, choose a different tactic/action/verb from the Dramatic Tactics table that you think would be interesting or surprising or unexpected. Read through the first draft of the scene again using this different tactic/action/verb. Playwrights, listen to how the dynamics and rapport shift with these new tactics. Time-permitting, actors can choose two or three different tactics.

    Example: "My character is now pressuring a sibling to seek help for feeling depressed."

2. *Possibilities and Opportunities* (two to three minutes)

    Playwrights and actors, discuss the new tactics/actions. What changed in the dynamics, status, and relationship between characters? What new possibilities do these new tactics/actions reveal?

Part III: Revising

1. *Playwrights Revise* (three to five minutes)

    Playwrights, based on the action/tactic that you and the actors found most compelling or promising, revise your dialogue or scene to amplify that tactic. For example, in the example dialogue, you might revise the dialogue to amplify the pressure that one character is putting on their sibling to seek help.

2. *Variations*

    Time-permitting, write two or three different dialogues using the same tactic/action. Which one is most compelling, raises the stakes or tension, or introduces complications or change?

Part IV: Reading Revised Dialogue

Read Revised Draft of Scene (two to three minutes)

Actors, read the revised draft of the playwright's scene or dialogue. Playwrights, listen for the dynamic and rapport between characters.

Reflection (four to five minutes)

How did your understanding of your character(s) deepen as you gave them different actions/tactics to play? What new qualities, dimensions, emotions, or flaws did you discover? How did the character's language evolve throughout this exercise? How can you revise the entire piece with this deeper, more complex understanding of your character(s)?

Dramatic Tactics

This list can give actors options for speaking dialogue using different actions/tactics: admit, agree, amplify, argue, articulate, ask, beg, compliment, confess, contradict, convince, direct, disagree, disclose, implore, inform, inquire.

What Comes Next

Go through this process again, perhaps with an extended dialogue or entire scene.

Actors, try two tactics/actions this time, switching between them at some point during the dialogue. Playwrights, listen for the shift in the dialogue as the actors shift their two tactics/actions. Revise accordingly. Continue with three or more different tactics/actions for the same dialogue or scene, with playwrights continuing to revise and refine their dialogue as new beats reveal themselves.

Spectator Storyboarding

Sage Tokach

Origins of the Exercise

Tableau has been used as a theatrical convention since the Middle Ages[1] and continues to be utilized in performance, rehearsal, and classroom spaces. After reading a story, educators often use tableau as an efficient way to gauge group understanding.[2] Augusto Boal popularized its use to express personal experiences and emotional responses, inviting additional participants to sculpt the image and change the narrative.[3] This exercise adapts Boal's technique and utilizes tableau as a story response, inviting the playwright into the audience's process of comprehension, interpretation, and negotiation of meaning.

Rationale

Tableau offers educators an accessible way to gauge understanding without the use of verbal or written language. This exercise allows students of any age to create tableaux that give educators and playwrights quick, big-picture feedback in a straightforward manner, providing playwrights with valuable information without subjecting them to personal criticism.

Objectives

During the revision process, this exercise provides a method of gauging audience perception through collective, embodied feedback, rather than verbal critiques or individual opinions. By synthesizing the story into a few main points, participants share valuable information about their understanding of the plot, conflict, and characters that may or may not align with the playwright's intention. The audience's storyboard helps the playwright zoom out and refocus on the most important aspects of the story, exposing details that might not serve the plot and highlighting moments that could use further development.

What We Need

- An open performance space
- An editable script that is visible to the entire class (via Google docs, projector, etc.)

How We Get There

1. Read the playwright's draft aloud in class, casting students to play each character.
2. After the reading, invite participants (including the playwright) to silently ponder the most important plot points.

What key moments are essential to the story? If these moments were removed, how would the story change?

3 Divide students into two groups, and ask each group to agree on three to five main story points that compose the plot. For each point, the group should create a tableau to embody the moment.

4 While students are creating tableaux, invite the playwright to ponder their own three to five main story points in their script and then silently observe the groupwork.

5 When students are ready to share, invite one group to embody and title their tableaux for the rest of the class. Before transitioning from each image, invite participants in the audience to share their observations. Ask what they notice about the image's composition. *Which characters are present, and what does their posture, expression, or positioning tell us about them? Are any non-human elements embodied? Can we assume anything about relationships or power dynamics based on the image?*

6 Switch groups and repeat step five.

7 Discuss differences between the groups' series of tableaux. *Did they choose different main story points? Did their selections differ from the playwright's? If they chose the same story point, how was the embodiment different? How did the tableau titles differ? Whose story are we telling? Do the groups agree?*

8 Invite the playwright to share the main story points they had in mind and discuss their experience of watching the tableaux. *Do their original choices still capture the story they want to tell? Do they want to explore different choices after seeing the tableaux?* If the playwright's main story points are different than the groups' choices, assist them in directing their classmates to visualize their final tableau progression.

9 Share one copy of the script in a way that the entire class can see. Ask the playwright to lead the class in locating the main story points and highlighting them. In a one-act or full-length play, a key moment might be a full scene, but encourage students to choose the most essential one to two lines or stage directions.

10 As a class, use a different color to highlight three moments that do not relate to one of the main story points. For a short play, students may read the script aloud and raise their hands when they hear a moment that does not connect to a main story point. For longer plays, the playwright may talk through the plot out loud, summarizing each scene while other students raise their hands to identify these moments.

11 Encourage the playwright to choose one of the moments and explore that section of the script. *What happens to the story if the moment is cut? How might the moment connect to one of the main story points? What purpose does the moment serve (foreshadowing, exposition, obstacle, etc.), and what happens if it serves a new purpose?*
12 Give the playwright time to write and revise.

Side Coaching Tips

- Prompt students with questions while they create tableaux to make their images as clear, specific, and dynamic as possible.
- Remind participants that there are no "right" or "wrong" choices. The moments that seem most important to them might be different for someone else.
- For nonlinear stories, questions may shift from characters and plot to themes, ideas, and their progression.
- For both linear and nonlinear scripts, invite the playwright to consider reordering the tableaux and exploring how the story changes.

Reflection

- How did the process of creating tableaux affect your understanding of the story?
- As the playwright, what was it like to watch the tableaux? What was surprising? How did they affect your understanding of the story?
- What is the value in seeing the audience's perception of a script? How is visual expression different from verbal feedback?
- How did highlighting main story points affect other moments in the script? What happened when these moments were revised?

What Comes Next

When the playwright is finished revising one of the identified moments, the class reads the script or section aloud and discusses the changes and their effect on the story. The playwright may want to revise the moment further, edit one of the other minor story points, or revisit the tableaux exercise to explore a different main point. If the playwright does not know how to continue the story, participants may create additional tableaux that explore possible endings.

Diagnosing the (Rasa) Box

Tiffany Antone

Rationale

Working with Rasaboxes as a diagnostic tool allows playwrights and actors to explore what has been written in a psycho-physical format, through dynamic and organic collaboration.

Origins of the exercise

This writing exercise utilizes Richard Schechner's Rasaboxes[4]—a physical tool designed to help performers access and communicate emotion:

> Rasaboxes trains participants to physically express eight key emotions first identified in the Natyasastra, a Sanskrit text dealing with theatre, dance, and music. Rasaboxes integrates this ancient theory with contemporary emotion research about the 'brain in the belly' (the enteric nervous system), studies in facial expression of emotion, neuroscience, and performance theory—including Antonin Artaud's provocative assertion that the actor is 'an athlete of the emotions.'[5]

Objectives

Using Rasaboxes, we will create a grounded action verb playspace where playwrights will work with actors to physically explore what has been written.

Note: Each play requires its own Rasabox, and therefore this exercise is best undertaken one play at a time.

What We Need

- Open performance space with a smooth floor
- Chalk
- Masking tape (colored or not)
- Printed copies of the play for all participants
- Playwrights will need their preferred notation tools—pens/pencils/highlighters/etc.

How We Get There

1. In preparation for this work, you will need to cast your play. It is best if actors are able to read the play ahead of time, as this will allow them to be of more service to the playwright.
   - This work will be most helpful if done with actors who are already familiar with Rasaboxes, but if working with less experienced performers, be sure to choose those who have a healthy sense of physical and expressive confidence. The work will only be useful to the playwrights if actors are able to really "go there."
2. Rasabox work is highly physical and can, when participants are fully engaged, be vocally demanding as well. It is *highly* recommended actors and playwrights begin with a physical and vocal warm up, as this will help everyone get into their bodies, ready to work and explore in a supported physical manner.
3. The playwright will use chalk or tape to construct a giant Rasabox. Consider the size of your cast—is this a two-person play? You will be able to work with a smaller Rasabox than if your cast calls for ten actors. Make sure you allow for the possibility that multiple bodies may want to be in one box at the same time, and size your Rasabox accordingly.
4. Briefly go over each rasa's definition:
   - The eight rasas—in Sanskrit with rough translations—are: *sringara* (desire, love); *hasya* (humor, laughter); *karuna* (pity, grief); *raudra* (rage); *adbhuta* (surprise, wonder); *bhayanaka* (fear, shame); *bibhatsa* (disgust); and *vira* (energy, vigor).
5. Invite the playwright to assign one rasa to each square, leaving the center square blank. This box is left empty for *shanta*, which can be roughly translated as "bliss".

Table 16.1. Sample Rasabox.

Love/Desire	Humor/Laughter	Pity/Grief
Rage	Bliss	Surprise/Wonder
Fear/Shame	Disgust	Energy/Vigor

6. The playwrights and actors will now cycle through the Rasabox a total of three times, with different intentionalities.
   - First, establish the entry/exit flow (bodies enter in the top right corner, proceeding in an "S" shape through each

square until exiting from the bottom left corner. Once someone exits, they re-enter the Rasabox via the top right corner). Working this way, a group Rasabox allows nine bodies to work in the shared space together.
- If you have more than nine bodies involved, they can queue at the entry point. In this way, participants will each get some observation time as part of their Rasabox exploration.

7 Each participant will choose a square in which to begin. They will then consider and weigh the square's assigned rasa, and then, using the chalk, write their own associations/related feelings/action verbs (or even draw images) in the square. Each person will do this for every square. Give them two to three minutes per square.
- A note on *shanta*: humans are rarely ever truly blissful. It is even rarer still to see a character on stage experiencing true bliss. Thus, the *shanta* box is an interesting space to work from in that it invites a sense of peace our characters may be chasing, but rarely access. *Shanta* should be explored with this in mind, knowing that bliss is often pursued but rarely actualized.
- Once completed, each square will have an array of hand-written additions to each square. Rage, for instance, may now feature a frowny face, flames, and text that includes things like "ROAR, to excoriate, explosion, punch, #!*@, stomach pains, betrayal," etc. Each rasa, then, has been contextualized by the participants to mean more than just the word. Give everyone a few minutes to read over/take in what has been written in each square.

8 For the second cycle, participants put down their chalk and enter the boxes as bodies only. As they move through each box, rather than writing down words, they will explore/create expressive physical gestures and vocalizations which bring the rasa to life for themselves. This is an individual exploration, with interpretations being entirely personal. Give them two to three minutes per square.
- This can be very intimidating for folks who are not usually physically expressive. Encourage participants to remember that no one is watching them work, that they're all engaged in the same (sometimes silly-feeling) work, and that

it will only be useful for them if they physically commit to the exercise.

9. Once everyone has physically/vocally explored each box, they are ready to begin the third (and final) cycle. Once the physical/vocal work has been established, the playwright enters the *shanta* box, bringing the script and writing materials with them.
10. Actors work the text by moving through the rasas they think each character is emotionally working from. Actors should bring their gestural/vocal work from the second cycle into the text. Playwrights should record helpful observations/notes as the actors explore the text around them.
    - Remember: the playwright is the only one who should inhabit *shanta* during the third cycle, and they are there as the omniscient observer. If an actor believes their character is experiencing *shanta* at any point during the play, this is a good opportunity to ask why.
11. At the conclusion of each scene, actors should step out of the Rasabox entirely and the playwright can, from here, ask actors questions about their choices, or request the actors work the scene again, either with text revisions (if they work that fast) or from different rasas, if they feel it will help them see into the scene differently.
    - If a play is not broken into scenes, places for pause should be worked ahead of time in order to allow for these important moments of reflection/rasic revision.
12. Working scene by scene, or section by section, the playwright and actors "map out" the characters' major rasas, and explore what that means in the context of the play's world.
13. Once the play has been fully explored, engage in reflection with both the playwright and the actors.

Side Coaching Tips

- There is no "rule" for how much each rasa should/should not be present in a "good" play, so watch out for anyone thinking they need to revise their play to include more/fewer rasas. Rather, playwrights should be reminded that this is a tool to help them see into the deeper psycho-physical states of their characters.

- This is a highly collaborative process—it's important to remind playwrights that the actors are being invited in to help them see what is being telegraphed through the page. They are working from *shanta* as the omniscient observer. Ego has no place inside *shanta* and will only blur the work if allowed to fester.
- Although helpful in generative Rasaboxing, it is *not* recommended to play music during diagnostic practice unless the play itself incorporates specific musical elements.

Reflection

- Did anything about this process surprise you? What/why? How are these observations useful?
- Which rasas were most heavily trafficked during this process?
- Did you feel any rasas were under or over-utilized?
- What energies did you feel as the actors worked through your script around you?
- How did sitting inside the work space impact your assumptions about the play?
- What questions will you bring into your revisions from here?

What Comes Next

Playwrights bring this experience to the revision process. In addition to their observations from *shanta*, they may wish to stay in contact with their actors, even inviting them to "remount" the exercise with subsequent drafts.

Notes

1 Konstantinakou.
2 Wilson.
3 Boal.
4 Schechner.
5 Calzadilla and Minnick.

References

Boal, Augusto. *The Rainbow of Desire: The Boal Method of Theatre and Therapy.* Taylor & Francis: UK, 2013.

Calzadilla, Fernando, and Michelle Minnick. "What is Rasaboxes?" *Facebook*, https://www.facebook.com/groups/436306506474754/.
Konstantinakou, Panagiota. Early 20th century Greek tableaux vivants: staging and the nation. No. IKEEART-2020–3367. Aristotle University of Thessaloniki, 2017.
Schechner, Richard. (2001). Rasaesthetics. *TDR*, 45(3), pp. 27–50. https://doi.org/10.1162/10542040152587105.
Wilson, Georgia P. "Thinking Through Performance: Children Make Sense of Characters and Social Relationships Through a Gesture-based Theatre Convention (Tableau)", University of New Hampshire, Ann Arbor, 1999. ProQuest, https://www.proquest.com/dissertations-theses/thinking-through-performance-children-make-sense/docview/304514469/se-2?accountid=10003.

Acknowledgments

Our book started with the spark of an idea while we had dinner together in the Westin Hotel lobby at the 2018 Association for Theatre in Higher Education (ATHE) conference in Boston. We had just finished our successful panel entitled *Interactive Pedagogy: Using Acting and Improvisation Techniques in the Playwriting Course,* and we wondered if we should collaborate on a book to explore the topic further. Hillary fell in love with Charissa's character exercise (Chapter One) and has used it in her classroom every semester since that summer. Finally, we knew it was time to create a book that we could use in our own classes and share with others. Our vision was of instructors, playwrights, and devising directors carrying our book, pages dog-eared and marked up, in their bags to classes, rehearsals, and writing sessions.

Thanks to ATHE (and the Acting, Playwriting and Creative Teams, Directing, and Theatre as a Liberal Art focus groups), an inspirational community of educators, practitioners, and scholars that encourages experiments, lifelong learning, and idea sharing. Through the ATHE community and our friends, like Theresa Robbins Dudek of the Global Improvisation Initiative, we were able to bring together a wide range of practitioners from multiple countries to share their embodied playwriting exercises.

Much gratitude to our twenty-eight contributors who worked so hard over the last year and a half to craft their chapters and exercises. Amazing and generous collaborators all! We are so fortunate to partner with you on this project and to learn so much from the experiences and exercises you share in these pages. Editing your work was an honor and a pleasure.

We are very grateful to Stacey Walker, our publisher at Routledge, for her enthusiasm for our project and support in helping us bring it to fruition. We are indebted to Lucia Accorsi, Senior Editorial Assistant for Theatre & Performance, for her patience, guidance, kindness, and support, as we undertook this project during a pandemic.

Charissa would like to thank her incredible co-editor, Hillary, for being such a generous and flexible collaborator as we steadily pursued this project during challenging times; her constant belief in the gift this book would be to other teachers, students, and writers was inspiring. Charissa is so grateful for the never-ending generosity and support of her favorite group of artists and collaborators: Lena, Vivian, Tristan, Carson, and especially, always, K.L.

Hillary is indebted to her co-editor, Charissa, for her detailed and expert editing style, and for her patience during all the highs, lows, and in-between complications that life has to offer. Hillary is grateful to the improv pioneers of Chicago in the 1980s who introduced her to both improv comedy as a means to write sketch comedy, as well as the value of long form improvisation to create plays. These pioneers who shaped her improv education, and the connection improv has to writing, include Michael Gellman, Del Close, Charna Halpern, Noah Gregoropoulous, and Mick Napier. Hillary would like to thank her wonderful students at Western New England University, including her Spring and Fall 2022 Playwriting classes, Fall 2022 Introduction to Theatre class, and *WNE Improv on the Rocks*, who all joyfully indulged her experimentation with exercises from the book. Many thanks to Dr. Doug Battema, Chair of WNE's Department of Communications, Media, and the Arts for his support and leniency in handing in her annual review two months late to finish editing the book. In addition, she would like to thank her fellow Western Massachusetts improv troupes, *The Silver Lining* and the *Happier Valley Comedy* Long Form House Team, for their inspiration and encouragement, and especially her *Happier Valley Comedy* teachers/directors Pam Victor and Scott Braidman for their amazing teaching, direction, and encouragement. Hillary is grateful to her amazing daughters, Chloe and Marissa, and her husband Jeff for their support and well-timed cheerleading. Hillary dedicates this book to the memory of her father, Herbert L. Haft, who passed away in July 2022 and her step-father, Gary Worth, who passed away in June 2022.

Index

absurdism 21
acting tactics exercise 259–262
activating a character exercise 228–233
activist playwriting: calls to action exercise 170–173; human barometer exercise 167–169; rant and rave exercise 163–167; roses, thorns, buds exercise 161–163; story circles 161–169; *see also* diversity; social justice comedy
activity, meanings expressed through 23–24
Anansegoro 132
asides (improv exercise) 17–18
ASL playwriting: character building exercises 83–87; movement, posture, and gesture (MPG) 87–89; visualization exercises 80–82
Atkinson, Brooks 11
Austin, Gary 127
authenticity exercises: decision island 58–59; definitions for 40–41; existential focus 41–46; funeral parlor 43–44; meaning orchestra 45–46; mortality echo 41–43; overview 39–41; past focus 46–49; past metaphors 48–49; polar emotions 55–56; protagonist Hemingway 57–58; psyche spectrum 54–55; psychological focus 53–59; relationship focus 50–53; resistance traps 44–45; tagging the past 47–48; unconditional positive regard 52–53; "you make me feel" confessionals 50–51

Baker, Annie 21
Barthes, Roland 67, 69
Beckett, Samuel 21
Black Improv Alliance 27
blank page (fear of) 9
Blatner, Adam 91
Boal, Augusto 54, 171, 194
body play 148
breathing together exercise 84–85
Brumm, Beverly 124

calls to action exercise 170–173
Camera Lucida 67, 69
Cariani, John 109
Carnicke, Sharon 12
ceiling fan speaks! exercise 205–209
change: once actors involved 10; to something about the character 8–9
character interviews exercise 74–75
Chaskele game: as metaphor 138; overview 133–136; for performance purposes 136–139; setup of 137
Chekhov, Anton 11, 21
Chekhov, Michael 83
Cherry Orchard, The 11
Clark, Leroy 13
climate justice writing: devising from source material 193–197; disinformation and 194; environmental racism exercise 196–197; Indigenous traditions 195–196; meat and dairy consumption

exercise 194–196; overview 190–191; personal to global storytelling 191–193; value of 197–198; water exercise 192–192
Cohen, Robert 122
collaboration: sharing the story (playwriting train) 233–237; *see also* community-based approach; psychodrama
collaborative drafting 226–228
colonization 195
comedy: from disruption 150; humor theory 146; mind humor 149; relief theory 148; spirit humor 150; *see also* social justice comedy
community-based approach: agreement creation 176; collective brainstorming 180–181; getting it on paper 185–187; improvisational story gathering 182–184; opening/closing circles 176–177; overview 175–176; pitfalls 187–188; postcards exercise 182–183; story of me exercise 179–180; this isn't a pen exercise 178–179; warm ups 177–178
counter will 54–55
cultural competency challenge 31, 36, 37–38

Da Doo Ron Ron compliments exercise 149–150
Daly, Timothy 19
Davis, Lizzy Cooper 161
decision island exercise 58–59
Delsarte, François 87
description interjection exercise 33–36
devising 131, 132, 161, 190, 191, 193, 194, 196, 218, 229, 233, 238, 239
disinformation 194
disruption (comedy from) 145, 146, 150
diversity: cultural representation 27; description interjection 33–36; outfit monologues 31; scene three ways 37–38; in social justice comedy 155–156; what you wouldn't guess 32; *see also* activist playwriting

divided double 99–100
Doll's House, A 15–16
doubling roles 98–99
Downs, W. 12, 16
drafting by phone process 82
"dramatic irony" 15
Dunne, Will 14

emotional subtext 14–15
"endowment" 14
entrances and exits exercise 117–118
environmental police exercise 138–139
environmental racism exercise 196–197
ethics 154–156

failure-as-success 148
folkgames 131–134; *see also* Chaskele game
Fornes, Maria Irene 67
Foucault, Michel 145
funeral parlor exercise 43–44

games: folkgames 131–134; I need you 124–127; six movements 127–129; stay! 122–124
Gellman, Michael J 124
God of Carnage 148
Goods, Moses 109
group playwriting *see* community-based approach; psychodrama

half-life game 255–259
hands on exercise 94
handshape hand-off exercise 85
Hayford, Michelle 129
Hill, Claire 40
hot-seating improv exercise 18–19
human barometer exercise 167–169
humor theory 146; *see also* comedy; social justice comedy

Ibsen, Henrik 15
incongruity 146
Indigenous traditions 195–196
indirect communication 22–24
I need you exercise 124–127
innate blueprint 40, 41, 46, 55–56

Index

interconnectedness 195

Jeffreys, Stephen 24
Johnstone, Keith 146, 149–150
Jones, Jonathan P. 170

Koppett, Kat 21

laughter 146, 148
Lavery, Bryony 16
letters to self exercise 209–213
linear sociogram exercise 94–95
Lucid Body Actor Training 65

McLaughlin, Buzz 20, 24
magical objects exercise 116–117
many characters, many objects exercise 218–225
Margulies, Donald 121
Martin, Jane 121
Meara, Anne 121
mask exploration 241–249
meaning orchestra exercise 45–46
meat and dairy consumption exercise 194–196
meet and greet exercise: coaching 6–9; fear of participating 10; overview 3–4; process 4–6
Meisner approach 124
Meisner, Sanford 85
Misattribution Theory 146–147
missing chair exercise 92–93
monologuist exercise 110–112
Moreno, Jacob 91
Moreno, Zerka 91
mortality echo exercise 41–43
movement, posture, gesture (MPG) 87–89

New York Writers' Bloc 122
non-human characters 97, 194, 205–209, 213–218
non-verbal subtext 19–20
Nottage, Lynn 21
number ping-pong exercise 147–148
numbing (psychic) 146

O'Neal, John 161
one word scenes exercise 20

outfit monologues exercise 31

Parks, Suzan-Lori 21
past metaphors exercise 48–49
pause button exercises 21–22
pauses 20–22
physical cues (to a character) 66
Picture Project, The: character interviews exercise 74–75; origins of 66–67; overview 65–66; performance 75–77; photo selection 67–68, 69–71; physical exploration 71–73; physical preparation for 68; process of 69–76; punctum 67, 69; scene detectives 73–74; writing the monologue 75
Pinter, Harold 21
poetry 9, 30
pointing at things warm-up 146
polar emotions exercise 55–56
postcards exercise 182–183
privilege 155
protagonist Hemingway exercise 57–58
psyche spectrum exercise 54–55
psychodrama: action phase 95–97; divided double 99–100; doubling roles 98–99; hands on exercise 94; linear sociogram 94–95; missing chair 92–93; overview 91–92; role reversal 98; surplus reality 100–101; warm-ups 92–95
psychotherapy (three-step framework of) 40
punctum 67, 69

rant and rave exercise 163–167
Rasabox work 249–253, 266–270
relationship focus 50–53
relief theory 148
resistance traps exercise 44–45
revision process: acting tactics for writers 259–262; half-life game 255–259; spectator storyboarding 262–265
role reversal exercise 98
roses, thorns, and buds exercise 161–163
Russin, R. 12, 16

safe place to play exercise 83–84
scene detectives exercise 73–74
scene three ways exercise 37–38
Schechner, Richard 249, 255, 266
Seagull, The 11
secrets exercise 13
"secret weapon" activity 151–152
shaping spaces exercises 114–116
sharing the story exercise 233–237
silent subtext 15–16, 20–22
Simpson, Fay 66
six movements exercise 127–129
social justice comedy: aims of 144–146; character generation for 152–154; Da Doo Ron Ron compliments exercise 149–150; ethics in 154–156; improv for writing 150–152; number ping-pong 147–148; overview 133–134; pointing at things 146; relief theory 148; status differences and 151–152; warm ups 146–150
sociometry 92
space: shaping 114–116; working in 237–241
spectator storyboarding exercise 262–265
spirit humor 150
spoken word improv exercise 29–30
Spolin, Viola 118, 150, 178, 219
Spoon River exercise 66
Stanislavsky, Konstantin 11–12
status differences 151–152
stay! exercise 122–124
stereotypes 8, 27, 36
Stiller, Jerry 121
story circles 161–169
story gathering 182–184
story of me exercise 179–180
stream of consciousness exercise 84
Strindberg, August 15–16
subtext: adding 16–17; asides (improv exercise) 17–18; communicating 12; emotional 14–15; hot-seating improv exercise 18–19; indirect communication 22–24; inferring 14–15; non-verbal 19–20; pauses 20–22; secrets exercise 13; silent 15–16
surplus reality 100–101
Sweet, Jeffrey 121

tagging the past exercise 47–48
take a stand exercise 167–169
tale of the inanimate object exercise 213–218
this isn't a pen exercise 178–179
three-step framework of psychotherapy 40

unconditional positive regard exercise 52–53

Van Itallie, Jean Claude 20, 23
visualization: what's beyond? 81; what's next? 81–82; where? 80

water exercise 192–192
what's beyond? exercise 81
what's next? exercise 81–82
what you wouldn't guess exercise 32
where? exercise 80
will and counter will 54–55
Williams, Raymond 11
worldbuilding: active worldbuilding 112; brainstorming the world 109; climate change 118–119; definitions 108–109; entrances and exits 117–118; fragility of world 119; magical objects 116–117; monologuist 110–112; power play 113; resources for 108; shaping spaces 114–116
Wright, Michael 127, 129
writer's block 9

you know that thing exercise 28–29
"you make me feel" confessionals 50–51

For Product Safety Concerns and Information please contact our EU representative GPSR@taylorandfrancis.com
Taylor & Francis Verlag GmbH, Kaufingerstraße 24, 80331 München, Germany

www.ingramcontent.com/pod-product-compliance
Lightning Source LLC
Chambersburg PA
CBHW071158300426
44113CB00009B/1240